The Touch of Śakti

The Touch of Śakti

A Study in Non-dualistic Trika Śaivism of Kashmir

Ernst Fürlinger

D.K. Printworld (P) Ltd.
New Delhi

Cataloging in Publication Data — DK
[Courtesy: D.K. Agencies (P) Ltd. <docinfo@dkagencies.com>]
Fürlinger, Ernst, 1962-
Touch of Śakti: A Study in Non-dualistic Trika Śaivism of Kashmir / Ernst Fürlinger.
p. cm.
Study based mainly on Tantrāloka of Abhinavagupta Rājānaka, fl. c. 975–1025 and Śivastotrāvalī of Utpala, fl. 900-950.
Includes bibliographical references (p.)
Includes index.
ISBN 13: 9788124604632
ISBN 10: 8124604630

1. Abhinavagupta, Rājānaka, fl. c. 975-1025. Tantrāloka. 2. Utpala, fl. 900-950. Śivastotrāvalī. 3. Kashmir Śaivism. I. Title.

DDC 294.551 3 22

ISBN 13: 978-81-246-0463-2
ISBN 10: 81-246-0463-0
First published in India in 2009

Front page : Goddess Bhairavī, Himachal Pradesh or Jammu & Kashmir, 10th century (Private Collection)

Published and printed by:
D.K. Printworld (P) Ltd.
Regd. Office: 'Srikunj', F-52, Bali Nagar
Ramesh Nagar Metro Station
New Delhi-110 015
Phones: (011) 2545 3975; 2546 6019; *Fax*: (011) 2546 5926
E-mail: dkprintworld@vsnl.net
Website: www.dkprintworld.com

Dedicated to

Pandit H.N. Chakravarti

Contents

Foreword by André Padoux ix

Preface xvii

Abbreviations xxi

List of Plates xxiii

1. **Introduction**

Trika Śaivism of Kashmir 1

Scriptural Authority 2

Historical Development 4

The Different Meanings of Sparśa in Indian Traditions 19

The Term Sparśa in Early Texts of Non-dualistic Kashmir Śaivism 28

2. **Hermeneutical Reflections**

Is Cit "Consciousness"? 40

Is Vimarśa "Reflective Awareness"? 53

Remarks on Tāntric Language and its Interpretation with the Example of Tantrāloka 57

3. **The Touch of Śakti (Śaktisparśa): Selected Texts of Non-dualistic Śaivism of Kashmir**

Utpaladeva: Śivastotrāvalī With 71

The Commentary (Vivṛtti) By Kṣemarāja 71
Introduction 71
Abhinavagupta : Tantrāloka With Commentary (Viveka) By Jayaratha 133
Introduction 133
The Sensual Touch 139
The Touch of the Mirror 148
The Touch of Anuttara-Saṁvit 154
A Note on Anuttara 156
The "Touch of Ants" (Pipīlikāsparśa) 174
The "Touch of Fullness" (Pūrṇatāsparśa) 191
Sparśa as Consonant 199
"Śakti, of the Nature of Touch" 203
A Note on the Touch of the Sexual Fluids 207
"Uccāra of Oṁ" 215
The Practice of Uccāra according to the Tantrāloka 219
The twelve main stages of the Power 223
Sparśa in the process of manifestation: Svacchandatantra 11 237
'Light,' 'Sound,' 'Touch' as Stages of Nearness 240

4. **Conclusion: The Question of the Liberating and Critical Potential of Trika Śaivism** 247

Bibliography 259

Index 275

Foreword

The Kashmirian Śaiva tradition, especially in its non-dualistic form, is perhaps the richest philosophical one in India. It is among the few that have survived to our days. It has even spread (if in not always very valid versions) to the Western world. A study such as this one, on the particularly interesting subject of *śaktisparśa*, cannot therefore but be welcome.

In his introduction, Dr Fürlinger gives very usefully an overview of the historical development of the Kashmirian Śaiva traditions, and especially of the Trika, the non-dualistic system made famous by the work of its most remarkable exponent, Abhinavagupta. In this overview, he relies to a large extent on the work of Professor Sanderson, the best expert on the subject, who however does not fail to remind us that due to the lack of explicit and datable documents our knowledge of this tradition is far from perfect. One goes on discovering manuscripts of hitherto unknown texts which sometimes open new perspectives: the work is in progress. We however know enough to allow some conclusions, and the well-grounded examination of some particular points — as is precisely the case here.

Dr Fürlinger's study is based mainly on Abhinavagupta's most well-known and in many respects the richest and most fascinating work, the *Tantrāloka*, in which, adding to the Trika elements from the tradition of the Krama, he expounds, on the basis of the *Mālinīvijayottaratantra*, his vision of the nature of ultimate reality together with the means to attain and experiment directly this reality. In this work, an important place is given to ritual, in spite of the fact that for Abhinavagupta (as in non-dualist Śaivism generally), in opposition to the Saiddhāntika's view, it is knowledge (*jñāna*) which liberates, not ritual. Abhinavagupta however knew and said that non-ritual ways toward liberation were not meant for the majority of believers. The way of pure spiritual, mystical, intuition, the way of Śambhu (*śāmbhavopāya*) as he called it, or that of power or knowledge (the *śāktopāya* or *jñānopāya*), are meant only for a few elects. All others, ordinary limited human creatures (*aṇu*), need the help of rites and follow the *naropāya* or *āṇavopāya*, which is also *kriyopāya*, the way of ritual action. But rites are not mere actions. They are not merely visibly acted out, they are also consciously experienced, they are a body-mind experience. The movements of the body in ritual action as performed, felt and lived out both physically and mentally, infused as they are by yogically experienced mental representations, are total experiences identifying the worshipper with the deity he worships. This Abhinavagupta of course knew, and he sometimes alludes to it in the *Tantrāloka* and in the *Parātriṁśikāvivaraṇa*[1]: the very process, and the beauty, of the ritual performance help to bring about the performer's, if not experience of, at least, orientation toward the transcendent. Worth mentioning in this perspective are also the *mudrās* described in chapter 32 of the *Tantrāloka* on the basis of the ancient *Devyayāmalatantra*. These *mudrās* are complex bodily postures associated with mental concentration

1. The point is specially clearly made in the *Parātrīśikālaghuvṛtti*, but one believes now that this work is in all likelihood not by Abhinavagupta.

and visualizations which both identify the performer with the deity he evokes, since the *mudrā* he acts out reproduces the appearance of the deity (which is being mentally visualized by the performer), is its reflection (*pratibimba*), and brings about the presence of the deity, a presence arising from that reflection.

This, I admit, is a very special case, it is however a form among others of the bodily experience of the transcendent power, the *śakti*, of the deity, an experience which is the theme of Dr Fürlinger's study: *śaktisparśa*. The body, in the present case, is not in the forefront. But mystical experience is most often (if not always) to a large extent a bodily experience. This, Abhinavagupta, who was also a Tāntric *yogin*, would not have denied, even if he privileged the spiritual way, a way upheld by Swami Lakshman Joo to whose teaching Dr Fürlinger often refers. The religious ritual aspect of the Trika as a system of Śaiva worship as it was practised in Kashmir in Abhinavagupta's time, had indeed since long — perhaps since the thirteenth century — disappeared. Only the spiritual tradition, the theoretical superstructure, survived to our days, which Swami Lakshman Joo was the last and only one to embody, all the other contemporary (mostly Western) versions of the so-called Kashmir Śaivism having no real traditional validity or textual basis. The other Śaiva tradition, which is sometimes mentioned since its tenets were to a large extent taken over by Abhinavagupta, the Krama, seems also to have disappeared comparatively early from Kashmir as a system of practice, only some of its theoretical, gnostic aspects having survived until recently. Of the ancient Kashmirian Śaiva traditions of the Kula, only the Tripurā or Śrīvidyā cult is still active in India today albeit in a vedantised "de-tāntricised" form, with the Śaṅkarācāryas as spiritual guides.

In his "Hermeneutical Reflexions" (Part II of the volume), Dr Fürlinger cautions us very wisely against the risk of translating Sanskrit terms into English (or into any other language). *Cit* is indeed untranslatable, as well as *saṁvit*, two terms both usually "translated" as consciousness, a word that does not in any way reflect their nuances of meaning nor the scope of their semantic fields, and especially not their "cosmotheandric" dimension, this being especially the case in the *saṁvidadvaya*, "non-duality of consciousness" system, of the Trika. The term *vimarśa*, essential to the understanding of the Trika's conception of consciousness, is also untranslatable (perhaps even more so). But can we abstain from translating, and thus write for those only who know Sanskrit? Dr Fürlinger underlines also very appositely the multidimensionality of the metaphorical language of Abhinavagupta (or of other Śaiva authors) whose concrete-abstract richness is for us both an opening to new vistas and, often, a tantalisingly closed field.

The imbrication or coalescence of the abstract and the concrete, of the spirit and the flesh (if one may use these terms), is continuously to be seen in part III of this study, which deals with its central theme, the touch of Śakti, *śaktisparśa*. This main and fundamental part of the work I shall not attempt to present or discuss here, for one must not simplify a very complex and subtle subject. This part begins very appositely with a survey of Utpaladeva's (and other exegetes') frequent use of terms made on the Sanskrit root *spṛś*, to touch, which they use to describe or evoke the spiritual approach of the absolute. Such terms were indeed sometimes used metaphorically. But not always. And when not, they have concrete connotations. In the works of such authors, one is never in the idealistic realm of "pure" spirit, but in that of spiritual experience. Metaphysical or philosophical, often very subtle, reasoning is never cut off from life and experience. The living body of the devotee is there, which feels sensuously the divine presence he approaches and by which he will be penetrated — possessed. We may remember in this connection that the *samāveśa* — shall we say fusion, absorption? — though conceived of in the Trika as an essentially mystical experience, was heir to the *āveśa*, the bodily possession of a worshipper by a deity, of the older Tāntric Śaiva cults; and that in Trika works *samāveśa* is often a synonym of *āveśa*, implying possession rather than mystical experience. Such is in all likelihood, for instance, the case in the *Mālinīvijayottaratantra* (2.13-24) which mentions 50 forms of *rudraśaktisamāveśa*. This is of course also to be found in several places in the *Tantrāloka*, passages which are sometimes quoted here. We may mention also, looking at ritual, the case, in the *nirvāṇa dīkṣā/sādhakābhiṣeka*, of the initiator who is brought in front of a *maṇḍala* where the *mantras* of deities have been placed and who is immediately possessed by the power of these *mantras* and falls to the ground. The total — bodily and mental — nature of the *śaktisparśa* experience appears in the many instances quoted in this study. The conception of spiritual life as implying the whole person, body and mind, is in fact, I feel, not proper to non-dualist Kashmirian Śaivism but something more general and, I would say, typically Indian. It is to be found almost everywhere in Indian religions. And not only in the course of spiritual or mystical experiences, as we see here, but also in a number of rites.[2] Let us think, for instance, of rites where the ontological status of the performer is transcendentally transformed — divinized or cosmicized — by *mantras* placed on his body by the rite of *nyāsa*. Or the *uccāra*, the uttering of a *mantra* linked to the ascent of *kuṇḍalinī* in the *suṣumnā*, where the *yogin* or

2. Ritual, in a Tāntric context, is never to be neglected: often theoretical developments have a ritual substrate or starting point.

devotee is identified with the deity, thus experiencing in body and mind higher transcendent planes of consciousness. Admittedly, such practices are more imaginary (imagination, of course, in its creative form — as Einbildungskraft) or visionary than really "embodied": they are not physically perceptible. But a number of other bodily signs[3] are however to be found throughout the history of India's religious life: they are sometimes of a surprising intensity — see for instance Caitanya's extraordinary body distortions. But I am perhaps giving now too much importance to bodily reactions to spiritual experience when, on the contrary, precedence should be given to the "participability" of the absolute, to the fact that the absolute lets itself be touched. This study is in fact of cases where the body is not affected or modified but transcended. The body is an intermediate, the base and receptacle of effects, an accessory to the fact of experiencing the supreme, not the main actor. Dr Fürlinger comments here with a fine penetrative understanding the varieties of *sparśa* — the sensual touch, the touch of the mirror, the touch of fullness, the touch of *anuttarasaṁvit*, the touch of ants — noting, as he proceeds, some analogies to be found among Christian mystics. (Concerning the touch of ants — *pipīlikasparśa* — I know this particular experience exists also in at least one Sūfī Indian transmission.). The notion of *vapus* (one more untranslatable term!), too, is a very interesting one since the *vapus* can be understood both as the cosmic body of Śiva and as an essential

3. Several Śaiva Tantras (such as the *Mālinīvijayottara*, the *Kubjikā* or the *Tantrasadbhāva*), and evidently the *Tantrāloka*, mention bodily signs, *cihna*, of the possession (*āveśa*) by Rudra or other deities. See for instance *Tantrāloka* (5.111-112) quoting the *Triśirobhairavatantra*, which connects these signs with different forms of bliss (*ānanda*) appearing each on the level of a *cakra* as the *kuṇḍalinī* rises in the *suṣumnā*.

level of the embodied human creature. On this subject, I have found particularly illuminating his analysis, with reference to Kṣemarāja's commentary of Utpaladeva's *Śivastotrāvalī* of what he calls "the '*cit*-dimension,' or 'deep-dimension' of the physical senses" which permits the human contact with the absolute. Many other points would be worth mentioning here. But a foreword must not be too long. The book is to be read. Much is to be found in this very perceptive study.

Prof. André Padoux

Preface

"See, brother: The highest wisdom is that to know, that in the presented simile the untouchable is touched in a untouching manner."

(*Ecce frater: Summa sapientia est haec, ut scias quomodo in similitudine iam dicta attingitur inattingibile inattingibiliter*)

Nicholas of Cusa: *Idiota de sapientia*
("The Layman on Wisdom", 1450), Liber primus, 7.18[1]

THIS volume contains a study of the theme of touch (Skr. *sparśa*), focusing on the "touch of Śakti" (*śaktisparśa*), that is, in the context of Śaiva Kuṇḍalinī-Yoga. Kuṇḍalinī is here not understood in the modern sense of a mere spiritual phenomenon in the body of the practitioner, but rather according to the traditional understanding of the Tantras as both microcosmic and macrocosmic, immanent and transcendent Divine reality. I study this theme of *sparśa* in selected texts of non-dualistic Trika Śaivism of Kashmir, especially Utpaladeva's *Śivastotrāvalī* (tenth century) and Abhinavagupta's *Tantrāloka* (eleventh century).

The following text is the English translation and revised version of the first chapter of my dissertation which I

1. Nicholas of Cusa (1401-1464): *The Layman on Wisdom*. Trans. Jasper Hopkins, Minneapolis: Arthur J. Banning Press, 1996.

concluded in June 2005. The full text of my Ph.D. thesis is published in German under the title: *Understanding by Touching: Interreligious Hermeneutics — the Example of Non-dualistic Śaivism of Kashmir* (Vienna/Innsbruck: Tyrolia, 2006).

This is the place to thank all who have supported and encouraged my study over the last four years. Above all I must thank, with deep respect, Pandit Hemendra Nath Chakravarty, with whom I studied Sanskrit texts of non-dualistic Kashmir Śaivism from 2002 till 2004 in his house in Bhelopur, Varanasi. It was he who opened the fascinating world of Abhinavagupta's *Tantrāloka* for me, and shared his stupendous insight into the Tantras. Once I compared him with a mountain guide in the Himalayas of this monumental work of Abhinavagupta, and he answered with his dry humour: "At least you have arrived at this mountain." I dedicate this book to him.

I must equally express my gratitude to Dr Bettina Bäumer. She inspired me in 2001 to start with a dissertation on non-dualistic Kashmir Śaivism in the field of Religious Studies at the University of Vienna under her supervision. It was a privilege and joy to study with her some texts of Kṣemarāja and Abhinavagupta in Varanasi. This time with her was a beautiful experience of friendship, sharing, learning, spiritual practice, and diving into the spirit of this ancient holy city.

I was lucky to study in Varanasi with another eminent scholar of non-dualistic Kashmir Śaivism, Dr Mark Dyczkowski. I participated in his study group beginning in November 2003, and afterwards in private lessons on a text of the Krama-school, in his red house at Nārad Ghāṭ. I thank him for infecting me with his passion and enthusiasm for Kashmir Śaivism and Indian philosophy in general, and his support.

I thank Dr Sadananda Das, my first Sanskrit teacher — who introduced me to the "forest of grammar" (*Tantrāloka* 37.58) — for his encouragement and patience, also his family, with whom I could live together in Samneghāṭ, at the bank of the Ganges. I express my gratitude to Professor Dr Johann Figl, head of the Institute for Religious Studies at the University of Vienna, who was extraordinarily supportive during my doctorate studies.

I should not forget to thank my colleague and friend in Varanasi, Borghild Baldauf, who read the whole text carefully and discussed her comments with me, on the stairs of the Ghāṭs. I gratefully acknowledge the financial support of the University of Vienna and the Muktabodha Indological Research Institute.

It is a great honour and joy for me that Professor André Padoux, one of the foremost scholars in the field of non-dualistic Kashmir Śaivism, was ready to write the Foreword. I am glad about his encouragement and his interest in my work.

Last but not least I thank my friend and colleague Michael Ianuzielo (Varanasi/Montreal) for his engaged, repeated language proof-reading and for his encouragement to create an English version, and Mr Susheel K. Mittal, director of D.K. Printworld, for his co-operation in publication of this work.

Vienna, March 2008 **Ernst Fürlinger**

Abbreviations

AbhiBhā	Abhinavagupta: *Abhinava-Bhāratī*
BhG	*Bhagavad-Gītā*
Ca. Sa.	*Caraka Saṁhitā*
CU	*Chāndogya Upaniṣad*
DSp	*Dictionnaire de Spiritualité*
HTSL	Teun Goudriaan/Sanjukta Gupta: *Hindu Tantric and Śākta Literature*
ĪPK	Utpaladeva: *Īśvarapratyabhijñākārikā*
ĪPV	*Abhinavagupta: Īśvarapratyabhijñāsūttravimarśinī*
ĪPVV	*Abhinavagupta: Īśvarapratyabhijñāvivṛttivimarśinī*
JIP	*Journal of Indian Philosophy*
JY	*Jayadrathayāmala*
K	Lilian Silburn: *Kuṇḍalinī: The Energy of the Depths*, Albany, 1983.
KSTS	Kashmir Series of Texts and Studies
KTK	*Kalātattvakośa: A Lexicon of Fundamental Concepts of the Indian Arts*
Lumière	Abhinavagupta: *La Lumière sur les Tantras*. Chapitres 1 à 5 du Tantrāloka. Traduits et commentés par Lilian Silburn et André Padoux, Paris, 1998.
MHP	Rājānaka Shiti Kaṇṭha: *Mahānayaprakāśa*
MHP (A)	Arṇasiṁha: *Mahānayaprakāśa*

MtU	*Maitrāyaṇīya (Maitrī) Upaniṣad*
MVT	*Mālinivijayottara Tantra*
MVV	Abhinavagupta: *Mālinīvijayottaravārttika*
MW	Monier Monier-Williams: *A Sanskrit-English Dictionary*
NŚ	*Nāṭya-Śāstra*
NT	*Netratantra*
PEW	Philosophy East and West
PHṛ	Kṣemarāja: *Pratyabhijñāhṛdayam*
PP	Kṣemarāja: *Parāprāveśikā*
PT	*Parātrīśikā Tantra*
PTlv	*Parātrīśikālaghuvṛttiḥ*
PTV	Abhinavagupta: *Parātrīśikā-Vivaraṇa*
ṚV	*Ṛgveda*
ŚD	Somānanda: *Śivadṛṣṭi*
SpN	*Spanda-Kārikās mit Kṣemarājas Nirṇaya*
SpS	Kṣemarāja: *Spandasaṁdoha*
ŚSĀ	Utpaladeva: *Śivastotrāvalī*
ŚS	*Śivasūtra*
ŚSV	Kṣemarāja: *Śivasūtravimarśinī*
SvT	*Svacchandatantra*
SvT U	Kṣemarāja: *Svacchandratantra Uddyota*
TĀ	Abhinavagupta: *Tantrāloka*
TĀV	Jayaratha: *Tantrālokaviveka*
Vāc	André Padoux: *Vāc: The Concept of the Word in Selected Hindu Tantras*, Albany, 1990.
VBh	*Vijñāna Bhairava*
VS	*Vātūlanāthasūtrāṇi*
YHṛ	*Yoginīhṛdaya*
YS	Patañjali: *Yoga-Sūtra*

List of Plates

Pl. 1 : Śiva-Sadāśivamūrti. Parel, Mumbai (Maharashtra). *Ca.* first half sixth century. Stele. Stone. Height: 348. Courtesy: American Institute of Indian Studies.

Pl. 2 : Durgā Mahiṣāsuramardinī. "Durgā" temple, north wall. Aihoḷe, Bijapur (Karnataka). Late seventh/ early eighth century. Courtesy: American Institute of Indian Studies.

Pl. 3 : Śiva Ardhanārīśvara. Cave 1, west wall. Bādāmī (Karnataka). Sandstone. *Ca.* CE 500-99. Courtesy: American Institute of Indian Studies.

Pl. 4 : Śiva Naṭarāja. Façade of cave 1. Bādāmī (Karnataka). Sandstone. Early Western Cāḷukya Period. *Ca.* CE 575-85. Courtesy: American Institute of Indian Studies.

Pl. 5 : Vīṇādhara Śiva. Malhar, Bilaspur (Madhya Pradesh). Buff sandstone. 101 × 49.5 cm. *Ca.* CE 900-99. Courtesy: American Institute of Indian Studies.

Pl. 6 : Kālī, dancing. Gurgī, Rewā. (Madhya Pradesh). Plum sandstone. 68 × 36.5 cm. *Ca.* CE 1000-99. Courtesy: American Institute of Indian Studies.

Pl. 7 : Kālī. Hemavati, Anantapur (Andhra Pradesh). Black stone. *Ca.* 900-99. Courtesy: American Institute of Indian Studies.

Pl. 8 : Ardhanārīśvara. Śiva cave, south wall. Elephaṇṭā (Maharashtra). Possibly Kalacuri Period. *Ca.* mid-sixth century. Courtesy: American Institute of Indian Studies.

1: Śiva-Sadāśivamūrti. Parel, Mumbai. *Ca.* first half sixth century.

2: Durgā Mahiṣāsuramardinī. "Durgā" temple, Aihoḷe, Bijapur.
Late seventh/early eight century.

3: Śiva Ardhanārīśvara. Cave 1, Bādamī. *Ca.* CE 500-99.

4: Śiva Naṭarāja. Façade of cave 1, Bādamī. *Ca.* CE 575-85.

5: Viṇādhara Śiva. Malhar, Bilaspur. *Ca.* CE 900-99.

6: Kālī, dancing. Gurgī, Rewā. *Ca.* CE 1000-99.

7: Kālī. Hemavati, Anantapur. *Ca.* 900-99.

8: Ardhanārīśvara. Śiva cave, south wall. Elephaṇṭā.
Ca. mid-sixth century.

1

Introduction

When I go from hence let this be my parting word,
that what I have seen is unsurpassable. (. . .)
My whole body and my limbs have thrilled
with his touch who is beyond touch;
and if the end comes here, let it come —
let this be my parting word.
— Rabindranath Tagore: *Gītāñjali*, Nr. 96

Trika Śaivism of Kashmir

NON-DUALISTIC (Advaita) Trika Śaivism of Kashmir[1] is one of the distinct systems within Śaivism, along with the Pāśupatas, Saiddhāntikas, the Vīraśaivas (or Liṅgāyatas), and other Śaiva sects. It flourished in Kashmir and other parts of India from about CE 900 until the thirteenth century. In the tenth century, Śaivism in Kashmir was characterized by the opposition of two schools: a group of non-dualistic (Advaita) traditions, most notably the Trika and Krama, on the left, and the dualistic, conservative (more Veda-congruent) Śaiva-Siddhānta

1. On the following see the important article of Alexis Sanderson, "Śaivism and the Tantric Traditions," in: Stewart Sutherland/ Leslie Houlden/Peter Clarke/Friedhelm Hardy (eds.), *The World's Religions*, New York/London: Routledge, 1988, pp. 660-704. Also entry "Śaivism," in: *EncRel* (Eliade, 1st edn., 1987) 13, pp. 6-20.

on the right. While Śaiva-Siddhānta teaches that salvation can only be attained by rituals, their non-dualistic opponents criticised ritualism and claimed that one can also attain liberation through spiritual insight (*jñāna*), a mystical unfolding of one's true nature as identical with Śiva, be it spontaneous or gradual. According to these schools, liberation can be attained not only at death, but in this life too one can become a *jīvanmukta* ("liberated in life"). The non-dualistic traditions culminate in the works of Abhinavagupta (*c.* CE 975–1025) which represent the definitive formulation of the doctrines of these schools on the left. This stream has been denoted as "Kashmir Śaivism"[2] — an unfortunate term, since it does not take into account that Śaiva-Siddhānta was the dominant Śaiva doctrine in the tenth and eleventh centuries in Kashmir, whereas the principal Śaiva cult in that region was, as it has remained, the worship of Svacchandabhairava and his consort Aghoreśvarī.[3]

SCRIPTURAL AUTHORITY

Trika Śaivism belongs to the Tāntric traditions within the Hindu religion; it is based on the scriptural revelations called Tantras or Āgamaśāstra. The Kashmiri authors distinguish three groups within the Śaiva scriptures:[4]

---

2. See J.C. Chatterji, *Kashmir Shaivism* (1914), Srinagar: Research and Publication Department, 2nd edn., 1962. Reprint, Delhi: Parimal Publications, 1987.

3. Cf. Alexis Sanderson, "Śaivism in Kashmir," in: *EncRel* (Eliade, 1st edn. 1987) 14, pp. 16-17.

4. Cf. Jayaratha, commentary *TĀ* 1.18 (*TĀV*, vol. II, pp. 36ff.); on the classification of the Śaiva scriptures see Hélène Brunner, "On the Threefold Classification of Śaiva Tāntras," in: *Proceedings of the Fifth World Sanskrit Conference*, New Delhi: Rashtriya Sanskrit Sansthan, 1985, pp. 464-74; Sanderson, "Śaivism and the Tantric →

— Śiva-Āgamas: 10 dualistic Tantras
— Rudra-Āgamas: 18 non-dualistic Tantras
— Bhairava-Āgamas: 64 non-dualistic Tantras

The first two groups build the canon of the 28 Tantras of Śaiva-Siddhānta.[5] The third group is less defined and variously listed; it includes several texts which contributed to the elaboration of Abhinavagupta's Trika doctrine. The primary division within this third group of Tantras is between the "seat of the *mantras*" (*mantrapīṭha*) and the "seat of *vidyās*" (*vidyāpīṭha*).[6] The latter group is divided into Yāmala-Tantras (*Picumata-Brahmayāmalatantra,* etc.) and Śakti-Tantras. Within the Śakti-Tantras one can distinguish among the Trika-Tantras (*Siddhayogeśvarīmata, Tantrasadbhāva, Mālinīvijayottaratantra*), the scriptural authority for the system which is later called Trika, and texts dealing with the esoteric cults of the goddess Kālī (*Jayadrathayāmalatantra,* etc.). The authors of non-dualistic Trika

→ Traditions," op. cit., pp. 668ff; André Padoux, *Vāc. The Concept of the Word in Selected Hindu Tantras,* trans. Jacques Gontier, Albany: State University of New York Press, 1990; Delhi: Sri Satguru Publications, 1992, pp. 54ff (Abbr.: *Vāc*); Mark Dyczkowski: *The Canon of the Śaivāgama and the Kubjikā Tantras of the Western Kaula Tradition* (SUNY Series in the Shaiva Traditions of Kashmir) Albany: State University of New York Press, 1988; Delhi: Motilal Banarsidass, 1989.

5. *Kiraṇa, Rauravasūtrasaṁgraha, Svayambhuvasūtrasaṁgraha, Parākhya, Niśvāsatattvasaṁhitā,* etc. On the lists of the canonical 28 Siddhāntas see: *Bhaṭṭa Rāmakaṇṭha's Commentary on the Kiraṇatantra.* Vol. 1: chapters 1-6. Critical edition and annotated translation by Dominic Goodall (Publications du Département d'Indologie; 86.1) Pondichéry: Institut Français de Pondichéry/ École Française d'Extrême-Orient, 1998, intro. (especially pp. lxxi ff) and Appendix III (comparative table of lists of the 28 Siddhāntas).

6. The words *mantra* and *vidyā* denote the sacred sound-formulas.

Śaivism consider the Bhairavaśāstra to be superior to the other Śaiva texts, and within this group of 64 Tantras they view the Tantras of Kālī, followed by the Śakti-Tantras, as the highest revelation.

HISTORICAL DEVELOPMENT

Alexis Sanderson has distinguished three major phases in the development of Trika Śaivism:[7]

(1) In the early period, probably before CE 800, Trika Śaivism is characterized by a cult of supernatural power which is centred on a "triad" (*trika*) of goddesses, Parā, Parāparā and Aparā. They are worshipped alone or with subordinate Bhairavas. Part of this system of ritual is the cult of the eight mother-goddesses[8] and their embodiments in "clans" or "families" (*kula*) of wild female spirits (*yoginī*s), invoked with offerings of blood, flesh, wine, and sexual fluids by the adepts, to share their supernatural power and occult knowledge with them. The most efficacious place for its practice was the cremation ground. The leader of the hordes of *yoginī*s is Śiva in the archaic, four-faced form as Manthana-Rudra or Manthana-Bhairava. The cult of *yoginī*s permeates all levels of the Trika-Tantras.[9]

(2) In the second phase, the cult of the goddess Kālī is incorporated into Trika: Trika assimilates the cult of

---

7. Cf. Sanderson, "Śaivism and the Tantric Traditions," op. cit., p. 696; id.: "Trika Śaivism," in: *EncRel* (Eliade), vol. 13, p. 15.

8. Brāhmī, Māheśvarī, Kaumārī, Vaiṣṇavī, Indrāṇī, Vārāhī, Cāmuṇḍā and Mahālakṣmī.

9. Cf. Sanderson, "Śaivism and the Tantric Traditions," op. cit., pp. 672-74.

Kālī as the "Destroyer of Time" (Kālasaṁkarṣiṇī), whose hundred-plus manifestations are described in the *Jayadrathayāmalatantra*.[10] In this Kālī-based stratum of Trika, Kālasaṁkarṣiṇī transcends the three goddesses of Trika and is worshipped above them (see *Devyayāmalatantra*). This second phase includes texts such as the *Devyayāmala*, the *Trikasadbhāva* and the *Trikahṛdaya*.

(3) In the third phase, Trika Śaivism develops a solid philosophical base which it defends against the Buddhists, Nyāya and Śaiva-Siddhānta. It distances itself from its heterodox ritual origins, and infuses many traditional terms (e.g. cremation ground) with new meanings related to subtle, internal yogic processes within the practitioner. This development was aimed at both respectability among the Śaiva mainstream and a broader base in the Śaiva community, as part of the rivalry with the dominant Śaiva-Siddhānta. This phase is principally represented by the works of Abhinavagupta, based on the advanced and complex philosophy of the Pratyabhijñā school. His later works like the *Tantrāloka* (*TĀ*) and the masterly prose commentary on the *Parātriśikā Tantra*, the *Parātriśikāvivaraṇa* (*PTV*),[11] particularly

10. The *Jayadrathayāmala* comprises four parts, and each part consists of more than six thousand stanzas. Like other scriptures of the Kālīkula, it is only preserved in Nepalese manuscripts.

11. *Parātriṁśikāvivaraṇa of Abhinavagupta*, ed. Madhusudan Kaul (KSTS; 18) Srinagar 1918. — I use in this study the edition and translation by Jaideva Singh (*Abhinavagupta: Parātrīśikā-Vivaraṇa. The Secret of Tantric Mysticism.* English translation with notes and running exposition by Jaideva Singh, ed. Bettina Bäumer, Delhi et al.: Motilal Banarsidass, 1988; reprint 2000).

demonstrate the grand synthesis of the different schools and streams (Pratyabhijñā, Krama, Kaula, Spanda), representing the peak of non-dualistic Tāntric Śaivism of Kashmir. As Abhinavagupta himself states at the end of the *Tantrāloka*, Trika distances itself both from the ritualism of Śaiva-Siddhānta and the fixation on supernatural powers in the "left" traditions,[12] the attainment of which is not viewed as goal in itself by Trika. In this way, the cults of the early Trika which focused on the gain of supernatural power through the manipulation of impurity recede into the background. These rituals (described in the *Tantrāloka* ch. 29) at this point seem to have been reinterpreted within the general framework of the central goal: to attain the liberating insight (*jñāna*), the unfolding of *cit*, of one's own true nature in the unity with the Absolute, the Highest (*anuttara*), especially by means of the sexual ritual (*kulayāga*), the sexual union in the state of deep absorption (*samāveśa*), without any thought (*nirvikalpa*). In this interiorization of the rituals of the early period of Trika, Abhinavagupta is strongly influenced by a variety of Kaulism, a sexual-spiritual

12. "This the supreme Lord declared in *Ratnamālā* (Tantra): the essence of all Tantras, present in the right and left traditions, and which has been unified in the Kaula (is to be discovered) in the Trika. The ritual is overemphasized in the Siddhānta, which moreover is not free from the taint of *māyā*, and other things. The right tradition abounds in awesome rites, whereas in the left one supernatural powers (*siddhis*) are predominant. Keep far away from those disciplinarian texts, which bring little merit and much affliction, which no personal intuition illuminates, and which are lacking in wisdom (*vidyā*) and liberation (*mokṣa*)." (*TĀ* 37.25-28). Translation quoted from *Vāc*, p. 58, fn. 65.

tradition associated with Macchanda (or Matsyendranātha), with the ritual practice of sexual intercourse at its core wherein it is not the production of sexual fluids which is emphasized, but rather orgasm itself as the means to attain the highest state, the divine pervasion (*Śivavyāpti*). The Kaulas rejected the external aspects of the rituals of the cremation grounds and interpreted the Yoginī cult in terms of inner, sensual and spiritual processes.[13]

This third phase begins in the ninth century, with the works *Śivasūtra* (Aphorisms of Śiva), in the light of the tradition expounded by Vasugupta,[14] and *Spandakārikā* (Concise Verses on Vibration), attributed by some to Vasugupta, by others to his pupil Kallaṭa (*c.* 850–900). It unfolds the doctrine of *spanda* ("vibration," in the sense of a "motionless motion") as the essential nature of the deity.[15] The concept of *spanda* is already present in the *Jayadrathayāmala* and other texts of the Kālī cults,[16] which could be the scriptural background of *Spandakārikā*.

The non-dualistic theology was developed, conceptually refined and elaborated in the early tenth century by Somānanda (*c.* 900-50) with his work *Śivadṛṣṭi* (Perception of

13. See Sanderson, "Śaivism and the Tantric Traditions," op. cit., pp. 679f. (The Kaula reformation of the Yoginī Cult).

14. On *Śivasūtra* there are the commentaries of Kṣemarāja, the disciple of Abhinavagupta (*Śivasūtravimarśinī*), and of Bhaṭṭa Bhāskara (*Śivasūtravārttika*).

15. On the Spanda school see Mark S.G. Dyczkowski, *The Doctrine of Vibration: An Analysis of the Doctrines and Practices of Kashmir Śaivism*, Albany: State University of New York Press, 1987; Delhi: Motilal Banarsidass, 1989.

16. Cf. Sanderson, "Śaivism and the Tantric Traditions," op. cit., p. 695.

Śiva)[17] considered to be the first work of the Pratyabhijñā school.[18] At its core it says that Śiva is the only reality; even in the basest object the whole nature of Śiva is present (cf. *Śivadṛṣṭi* 3.18ab). His essence, *cit*, exists equally in all things (cf. *Śivadṛṣṭi* 5.12). The self of all things is also oneself, as well as that of all other subjects: "The jar knows by my own self. I know by its self . . ." (*Śivadṛṣṭi* 5.106ab).[19] All manifested things and subjects are states of Śiva, in which Śiva freely manifests Himself (cf. 4.47). Somānanda's disciple Utpaladeva established the classical form of this Śaiva non-dualism (*c.* 925-75) in his *Īśvarapratyabhijñākārikā* (Concise Verses on the Recognition of the Deity),[20] which formed the philosophical base of Trika Śaivism. Salvation is described as the "recognition" (*pratyabhijñā*) of one's own identity (*ātman*) as Śiva. The Pratyabhijñā school, though founded by Somānanda, got its name from this work. The targets of Utpaladeva's logical argumentation and critique are both Nyāya, one of the classical streams of Indian philosophy, and Buddhism, particularly its logical school[21] — yet at the same time the Pratyabhijñā philosophy is influenced by Buddhist doctrines and

---

17. *Śivadṛṣṭi of Somānanda, with Utpaladeva's Vṛtti* (KSTS; 54) Srinagar 1934. — The text was partly (ch. 1) translated by Gnoli into English: Raniero Gnoli, *Śivadṛṣṭi by Somānanda*: East and West 8, no. 1 (1957) pp. 16-22; and into Italian (ch. 2): *Vāc. Il secondo capitolo della Śivadṛṣṭi di Somānanda*: Rivista degli Studi Orientali 34 (1959).

18. On the following see *The Īśvarapratyabhijñākārikā of Utpaladeva with the Author's Vṛtti*. Critical edition and annotated translation by Raffaele Torella, corrected edition Delhi et al.: Motilal Banarsidass, 2002; introduction by Torella, XIVff. (= *ĪPK*).

19. Quoted from ibid., XVI.

20. See fn. 18.

21. Cf. *ĪPK*, intro., XXI ff.

terminologies.[22] Utpaladeva composed two commentaries on the *Īśvarapratyabhijñākārikā*: a short one (*vṛtti*)[23] and a long one (*vivṛti* or *ṭīkā*), of which only fragments are available.[24] He was not only an author of philosophical treatises, but was also a *yogī*, as is shown by the *Śivastotrāvalī*, a collection of his hymns. Besides the *Tantrāloka* of Abhinavagupta, the latter shall be one of our main texts which we will examine for our topic, together with the commentary by Kṣemarāja.

Without any doubt Abhinavagupta (*c.* CE 975–1025), a disciple of Utpaladeva's disciple Lakṣmaṇagupta, represents the zenith of this evolution of the non-dualistic Tāntric Trika Śaivism of Kashmir, which Torella has described as ". . . an extraordinary series of works and masters that between the ninth and twelfth centuries constituted one of the highest achievements of Indian speculation and spirituality of all time."[25] All the more amazing is the fact that this school is almost completely neglected within the academic study of philosophy in India today.

One of the unique features of Abhinavagupta is that he was more autobiographical than most classical Indian

---

22. See Raffaele Torella, "The Pratyabhijñā and the Logical-Epistemological School of Buddhism," in: Teun Goudriaan (ed.), *Ritual and Speculation in Early Tantrism. Studies in Honor of André Padoux*, Albany: State University of New York Press, 1992; Delhi: Sri Satguru Publications, 1993, pp. 327-45.

23. This commentary is edited and translated by Torella in his edition of *ĪPK* and the *vṛtti* (see fn. 18).

24. Torella, Raffaele, *A Fragment of Utpaladeva's Īśvarapratyabhijñā-vivṛti*: East and West 38 (1988) pp. 137-44.

25. *ĪPK*, intro., p. XIII.

philosophers.[26] From his own descriptions, in the 37th chapter of *Tantrāloka* as well as at the end of the *Parātrīśikāvivaraṇa*, we get a vibrant picture of his personality. He was born in the middle of the tenth century into a brāhmaṇa family. He himself informs us that his family descended from Atrigupta, a brāhmaṇa, who had been brought to Kashmir by King Lalitāditya (*c.* 724-60) after his conquest of Kanauj (cf. *Tantrāloka* 37.37-39). The king gave him a place in his capital Pravarapura (today Srinagar) on the bank of the "Vitastā" (Jhelum) river, facing the Śiva temple of Sitāṁśumaulin (cf. *Tantrāloka* 37.52). Abhinavagupta was conceived during the sexual (Kaula) ritual, that is, by his parents, Narasiṁha and Vimalā, during spiritual absorption (*samādhi*), and therefore was "one born from a *yoginī*" (*yoginībhū*).[27] He lost his mother in early childhood, an event which he views as the beginning of his spiritual quest. Abhinavagupta's father, whose name was Narasiṁha but who was known as Cukhulaka, was a Śaivite (cf. *Tanṭrāloka* 37.54), a learned man, who introduced Abhinavagupta to Sanskrit grammar. Abhinavagupta's brother, Manoratha, became his first disciple (cf. *Tantrāloka* 37.64). He describes himself his intellectual and spiritual development in the following words:

---

26. Cf. Arindam Chakrabarti, "The Heart of Repose, The Repose of the Heart. A Phenomenological Analysis of the Concept of Viśrānti," in: Sadananda Das/Ernst Fürlinger (eds.), *Sāmarasya: Studies in Indian Arts, Philosophy and Interreligious Dialogue — in Honour of Bettina Bäumer*, New Delhi: D.K. Printworld, 2005, pp. 27-36; here: p. 27.

27. Abhinavagupta indicates it in his opening verse of *TĀ*; Jayaratha in his commentary on *TĀ* 1.1 confirms that Abhinavagupta himself was *yoginībhū*. On *yoginībhū* see Lilian Silburn, *Kuṇḍalinī: The Energy of the Depths — A Comprehensive Study Based on the Scriptures of Non-dualistic Kaśmir Śaivism*, trans. Jacques Gontier (SUNY Series in the Shaiva Traditions of Kashmir) Albany: State University of New York Press, 1988, pp. 174f. (= *K*).

> [The author] was introduced into the forest of grammar by his father, had his mind clarified by a few drops of the sea of logic, and, when intent on enjoying the full *rasa*[28] of literature, was seized with an intoxicating devotion to Śiva. Being wholly filled with that, he no longer cared for any worldly pursuit, until, in order to increase his enjoyment of that devotion, he went to serve in the houses of [religious] masters. — *Tantrāloka* 37.58-59[29]

He also mentions his teachers in different fields of studies: among them Bhūtirāja, his *guru* of the Krama (cf. last verses of the *Bhagavadgītārthasaṁgraha*), Udbhaṭa (cf. *Tantrāloka* 37.62) and Lakṣmaṇagupta, his teacher in Pratyabhijñā philosophy. His master Śambhunātha introduced him to the Kaula tradition; Abhinavagupta pays obeisance to him and his *dūtī* (female partner in Kaula ritual), Bhaṭṭārikā, in the beginning of *Tantrāloka* (*TĀ* 1.13-14.16).

Abhinavagupta composed a large number of works. His major works can be divided into four groups, treating the schools of Trika, Krama, Pratyabhijñā as well as aesthetics:[30]

---

28. *Rasa*: literally "essence, juice"; in the field of aesthetics, the aesthetic experience is called the "tasting of *rasa*" (*rasāsvāda*), which is compared to the spiritual experience of the Absolute (*Brahman*). See Bettina Bäumer, "Brahman," in: *Kalātattvakośa. Vol. I: Pervasive Terms - Vyāpti*, ed. Bettina Bäumer, Delhi: Indira Gandhi National Centre for the Arts/Motilal Banarsidass, 1988, revised edition 2001, pp. 1-28; here: pp. 21ff.

29. Quoted from *The Dhvanyāloka of Ānandavardhana with the Locana of Abhinavagupta*. Trans. Daniel H.H. Ingalls, Jeffrey Moussaieff Masson and M. V. Patwardhan, ed. with an introduction by Daniel H.H. Ingalls, Cambridge, Mass./London: Harvard University Press, 1990, p. 32 (intro.).

30. See on the following Alexis Sanderson, "Abhinavagupta," in: *EncRel* (Eliade, 1st edn. 1987), vol. 1, pp. 8-9.

(*a*) ***Trika***

— *Mālinīvijayavārttika* (or *Mālinīślokavārttika*):[31] This text is an exegesis of the beginning of the *Mālinīvijayottara-tantra* or *Pūrvaśāstra* (Primal Teaching),[32] which Abhinavagupta views as the "essence of the Trika scriptures" (*Tantrāloka* 1.18). He elaborates here that Trika represents a "supreme non-dualism" (*paramādvayavāda*) — the Absolute contains both plurality and unity as modes of its self-representation — and from this he derives the claim that Trika transcends the dichotomy of the dualist and non-dualist directions in Śaivism.

— *Tantrāloka* (for the main work of Abhinavagupta, see part III).

— *Tantrasāra*: a summary of the *Tantrāloka*.

— *Parātriśikāvivaraṇa*: focused on the Kaula practices of the Trika.

---

31. *Śrī Mālinīvijaya Vārttikam of Abhinavagupta*, ed. with notes by Madhusudan Kaul Shastri (KSTS; 31), Srinagar, 1921; partially translated by Jürgen Hanneder, *Abhinavagupta's Philosophy of Revelation. An Edition and Annotated Translation of Mālinīślokavārttika I*, pp. 1-399 (Groningen Oriental Studies; 14) Groningen: Egbert Forsten, 1998.

32. *Mālinivijayottaratantram*, ed. Madhusudan Kaul (KSTS; 37) Bombay 1922; partially translated by Vasudeva, Somadeva, *The Yoga of the Mālinīvijayottaratantra*. Chapters 1-4, 7, 11-17. Critical Edition, translation and notes (Collection Indologie Pondichéry; 97) Pondichéry: Institut Français de Pondichéry/École française d'Extrême-Orient, 2005. — On the *MVT* see Alexis Sanderson: "The Doctrine of Mālinīvijayottaratantra," in: Teun Goudriaan (ed.), *Ritual and Speculation in Early Tantrism: Studies in Honor of André Padoux*, Albany: State University of New York Press, 1992; Delhi: Sri Satguru Publications, 1993, pp. 281-312.

(*b*) *Krama* (*Sequence*)

Kramakeli: a commentary on the *Kramastotra* of Eraka which was not preserved. A manuscript of the *Kramakeli* is not available. The text is mentioned by Abhinavagupta himself in his *Parātriśikāvivaraṇa*[33] and quoted by Jayaratha in his commentary on the *Tantrāloka* (*Tantrālokaviveka*)[34] as well as by Kṣemarāja in his commentary on Utpaladeva's *Śivastotrāvalī*. Of Abhinavagupta's works on the Krama tradition only his short *Kramastotra* (Krama Hymn) in 30 verses is known; it is one of the three dated works of Abhinavagupta, according to the concluding verse completed in 991.

(*c*) *Pratyabhijñā*

Abhinavagupta analysed and supported the philosophical position of the Pratyabhijñā doctrine in two masterly commentaries: in his commentary of Utpaladeva's *Īśvarapratyabhijñākārikā* (*Īśvarapratyabhijñāvimarśinī*)[35] and in a much longer commentary on Utpaladeva's *Vivṛtti* (*Īśvarapratyabhijñāvivṛttivimarśinī*).[36] Sanderson summarizes the significance of these philosophical works in the following way: "Through the profound

---

33. Cf. *PTV*, Sanskrit text: p. 84, translation: p. 223.

34. Commentary on *TĀ* 4.173ab; cf. *Tantrāloka*, ed. Dwivedi/Rastogi, op. cit., vol. III, p. 807.

35. *Bhāskarī: A Commentary on the Īśvarapratyabhijñāvimarśinī of Ācārya Abhinavagupta*, ed. K.A. Subramania Iyer/K.C. Pandey, vol. I: Varanasi (1938), 2nd edn. 1998; vol. II (1950): Delhi: Motilal Banarsidass, 2nd edn. 1986. vol. III: An English Translation by K.C. Pandey, Varanasi (1954), 2nd edn. 1998.

36. *Īśvarapratyabhijñāvivṛttivimarśinī by Abhinavagupta*, ed. Madhusudan Kaul Shastri, vols. I-III (KSTS; 60, 62, 66) Bombay 1938-43.

philosophical scholarship of these works the non-dualistic tradition was fully equipped to justify its rejection of the dualism of the Śaiva-Siddhānta, the illusionism of Vedānta, and the lack of the concept of transcendental synthesis in the non-dualistic idealism of the Yogācāra Buddhists, while seeing these positions as approximations to its own."[37]

(*d*) *Aesthetics*

Abhinavagupta is famous in India in the field of aesthetics; he is recognized as an aesthetician with the following works:

— *Locana* (eye):[38] a commentary on the *Dhvanyāloka* of the Kashmiri author Rājānaka Ānandavardhana (ninth century); both represent the most influential works of India on the theory and practice of literary criticism; and

— *Abhinavabhāratī*:[39] a commentary on the *Nāṭya-Śāstra* of Bharata; expounds a subtle theory of the nature of

---

37. Alexis Sanderson, "Abhinavagupta," in: *EncRel* (Eliade, 1st edn. 1987), vol. 1, p. 9.

38. *Dhvanyāloka of Ānandavardhana: With the Locana Commentary of Abhinavagupta, the Bālapriyā Subcommentary of Rāmaśāraka, and the Divyāñjana notes of Pt. Mahādeva Śāstrī*, ed. Pt. Pattābhirāma Śāstrī (Kashi Sanskrit Series 135, Alaṅkāra Section, no. 5) Benares: Chowkhamba Sanskrit Series Office, 1940. — English translation, based on the Kashi edition: *The Dhvanyāloka of Ānandavardhana with the Locana of Abhinavagupta*. Trans. Daniel H. H. Ingalls, Jeffrey Moussaieff Masson and M.V. Patwardhan, ed. with an introduction by Daniel H. H. Ingalls, Cambridge, Mass./London: Harvard University Press, 1990.

39. *Nāṭya-Śāstra of Bharata: With the Abhinavabhāratī of Abhinavagupta*, 4 vols., ed. Manavalli Ramakrishna Kavi (Gaekwad's Oriental Series 36, 68, 124, 145) Baroda: Oriental Institute, vol. 1 (2nd edn.) 1956; vol. 2: 1934; vol. 3: 1954; vol. 4: 1964.

aesthetic experience, dramaturgy, musicology and related disciplines.

The most important disciple of Abhinavagupta is Kṣemarāja (*c.* 1000-50). He wrote a large number of works, in which he on the one hand popularizes the essence of the doctrine of Trika Śaivism in a concise and lucid form, and on the other hand applies the doctrine to the cult of Svacchanda Bhairava and the cults linked with it. The former include shorter texts like *Parāprāveśikā*,[40] *Pratyabhijñāhṛdaya* (Heart of Recognition),[41] his commentary on Utpaladeva's *Śivastotrāvalī*, on the *Śivasūtra*,[42] on the *Vijñāna-Bhairava Tantra*,[43] on the first verse of the *Spandakārikā* (*Spandasaṁdoha*, "The Essence of Spanda"),[44] on the entire text of *Spandakārikā* (*Spandanirṇaya*, "Discernment

---

40. *Parāprāveśikā of* Kṣemarāja, ed. with notes by Paṇḍit Mukunda Rāma Śāstrī (KSTS; 15) Bombay 1918.

41. *Pratyabhijñāhṛdayam by Kṣemarāja* (KSTS; 3) Bombay, 1918. — English tr. *Pratyabhijñāhṛdayam: The Secret of Self-recognition*, trans. Jaideva Singh (1963) Delhi.: Motilal Banarsidass, 4th rev. edn. 1982. Reprint 1998.

42. *Śivasūtra Vṛtti by Kṣemarāja* (KSTS; 4 and 5) Srinagar 1913. — English tr. *Śiva Sūtras: The Yoga of Supreme Identity. Text of the Sūtras and the Commentary Vimarśinī of Kṣemarāja*, trans. Jaideva Singh, Delhi: Motilal Banarsidass, 1979; reprint 2000.

43. *The Vijñāna-Bhairava with Commentary partly by Kṣhemarāja and partly by Śivopādhyāya*, ed. with notes by Pt. Mukunda Rāma Śāstrī (KSTS; 8) Bombay, 1918. — Only Kṣemarāja's commentary on the introductory verses of *VBh* has survived.

44. *Spandasaṁdoha by Kṣemarāja*, ed. M.R. Śāstrī (KSTS; 16) Srinagar, 1917. — English tr. *The Stanzas on Vibration. The Spandakārikā with four Commentaries*. Translated with an Introduction and Exposition by Mark S. G. Dyczkowski, Varanasi: Dilip Kumar Publishers, 1994.

of Spanda")[45] and on Bhaṭṭa-Nārāyaṇa's *Stavacintāmaṇi.*[46] Among the latter are the long commentaries on the *Netra Tantra* or *Mṛtyuñjaya Tantra*[47] and also on the *Svacchanda Tantra,*[48] the principal Tantra and the scriptural base for the cult of the Śaiva majority, the cult of Svacchanda Bhairava. In his commentary, Kṣemarāja countered the traditional, dualistic exegesis of this scripture from the standpoint of the non-dualism of Trika Śaivism.[49]

The non-dualism of Trika was introduced into the Kaula cult of the goddess Tripurasundarī (the Beautiful Goddess of the Three Worlds), or Śrīvidyā, which became popular in the Kashmir valley in the eleventh century.[50] A representative of this Trika-based Śrīvidyā in Kashmir is Rājānaka Jayaratha (thirteenth century), the commentator of Abhinavagupta's

45. *Spandanirṇaya by Kṣemarāja,* ed. Madhusudan Kaul (KSTS; 43), Srinagar 1943. — English tr. *Spanda-Kārikās: The Divine Creative Pulsation. The Kārikās and the Spanda-nirṇaya,* trans. Jaideva Singh, Delhi: Motilal Banarsidass, 1980. Reprint 1994.

46. *The Stava-Cintāmaṇi of Bhaṭṭa Nārāyaṇa with Commentary by Kṣemarāja,* ed. with notes by Mahāmahopādhyāya Paṇḍit Mukunda Rāma Śāstrī (KSTS; 10) Srinagar: The Research Department of Jammu & Kashmir, 1918.

47. *Netratantra with the Commentary Uddyota by Kṣemarāja,* 2 vols. (KSTS; 46 und 61), Bombay 1926-39; New edition by V.V. Dvivedi, *Netratantram (Mṛtyuñjaya Bhaṭṭārakaḥ) with Commentary Udyota by Kṣemarāja,* Delhi: Parimal Publications, 1985.

48. *The Svacchandatantram with Commentary Udyota of Kṣemarāja,* ed. Vraj Vallabh Dvivedi, 2 vols., Delhi: Parimal Publications, 1985.

49. Cf. Sanderson, "Śaivism and the Tantric Traditions," op. cit., p. 700.

50. Cf. Alexis Sanderson, "Śaivism in Kashmir," in: *EncRel* (Eliade, 1st edn. 1987), vol. 13, 16-17; Sanderson, "Śaivism and the Tantric Traditions," op. cit., pp. 688ff.

Tantrāloka, who wrote the *Vāmakeśvarīmatavivaraṇa*,[51] a commentary on the basic scripture of the Kaula cult of Tripurasundarī, the *Vāmakeśvarīmata*, also known as the *Nityāṣoḍaśikārṇava*.[52] Jayaratha was thereby the most important personal link between Śrīvidyā and Trika Śaivism. Another important surviving text of the southern transmission is the *Yoginīhṛdaya*;[53] the first known commentary on *Yoginīhṛdaya* is written by Amṛtānanda (fourteenth century).[54] Later representatives are the Kashmirian Śrīvidyā author Sāhib Kaula in the seventeenth century, who adapted the whole of Kṣemarāja's *Pratyabhijñāhṛdaya* in his *Devīnāmavilāsa*,[55] Śivopādhyāya in the eighteenth century and Harabhaṭṭa (1874–1951).

After Abhinavagupta and Kṣemarāja, the Trika Śaivism of the third phase spread to the Tamil lands by the twelfth century and became the standard reading of the Kaula cults in south

---

51. *The Vāmakeśvarīmatam. With the Commentary of Rājānaka Jayaratha*, ed. Madhusudan Kaul Shastri (KSTS; 66), Srinagar, 1945.

52. *Nityāśoḍaśikārṇava with Two Commentaries*, ed. V.V. Dvivedi (Yoga-Tantra-Granthamālā; 1) Varanasi, 1968.

53. *Yoginīhṛdayam with Dīpikā*, ed. V.V. Dvivedi, Delhi: Motilal Banarsidass, 1988. French translation: André Padoux, *Le Coeur de la Yoginī. Yoginīhṛdaya avec le commentaire Dīpikā d' Amṛtānanda*, Paris: Éditions de Boccard, 1994 (introduction in English).

54. On Amṛtānanda see *Vāc*, pp. 63 and 75.

55. Sāhib Kaul, *The Devīnāmavilāsa*, ed. Madhusudan Kaul Śāstrī (KSTS; 63) Lahore, 1942. — On Sāhib Kaul's adaptation of *Pratyabhijñāhṛdaya* see Jürgen Hanneder: "Sāhib Kaul's Presentation of Pratyabhijñā Philosophy in his *Devīnāmavilāsa*," in: *Le Parole E I Marmi. Studi in onore di Raniero Gnoli nel suo 70º compleanno*. A cura di Raffaele Torella (Serie Orientale Roma; XCII, 2) Roma 2001, pp. 399-418.

India.[56] The Śrīvidyā tradition — originally one of the Kashmiri Kaula cults — has survived till today, especially in south India. It was adopted in a purified form by the Śaṅkarācāryas of Śṛṅgerī and Kāñcīpuram. In this way it has lost most of its Tāntric (Kaula) characteristics; Padoux calls this Vedāntized, puritanical form "a deviant and bowdlerised [. . .] form of the cult of Tripurasundarī."[57]

Let us try to summarize: the goal of the spiritual ways (*upāya*) in Trika Śaivism is found to be in correspondence with the core of Upaniṣadic spirituality, to recognize one's own Self as identical with "that," the Highest (*Brahman*). But the Kaula Tantrism of Abhinavagupta's reveals in the most detailed and systematic way what is only indicated in the Upaniṣads and the Veda, that the sexual act can be one of the most powerful means to open this recognition of one's true nature — the highest state of becoming one with the Highest (Śiva). It is the overwhelming discovery in the midst of a culture of asceticism that the senses, the body, sexuality, aesthetic and sensual experience have not to be condemned and abandoned to reach the spiritual goal, but rather are the principal means to attain it.

---

56. Cf. Sanderson, "Śaivism and the Tantric Traditions," op. cit., p. 690.

57. André Padoux, *Le Coeur de la Yoginī: Yoginīhṛdaya avec le commentaire Dīpikā d'Amṛtānanda*, Paris: Éd. Boccard, 1994, 9 (intro.). See the critique of this position by Annette Wilke, defending the dynamism of a living tradition which undergoes continuous processes of new interpretation and transformation (see Annette Wilke: "A New Theology of Bliss. Vedantization of Tantra and Tantrization of Advaita Vedānta in the Lalitātriśatibhāṣya," in: *Sāmarasya: Studies in Indian Arts, Philosophy and Interreligious Dialogue*, ed. Sadananda Das/Ernst Fürlinger, Delhi: D.K. Printworld, 2005, pp. 149-75, especially pp. 151ff).

The Different Meanings of Sparśa in Indian Traditions

The word *sparśa* belongs to the realm of the senses: the verbal root *spṛś*, from which the substantive is derived, means "to touch, to feel with the hand, to come into contact, or to experience" (cf. MW 1268f.). Like in other languages, the word *sparśa* denotes at the same time the touching, the sensation which is engendered by touching and being touched, the tactile quality of a thing, as well as contact in a general sense. Utpaladeva, the "grand-teacher" of Abhinavagupta, uses the word *sparśa* in his *magnum opus*, the *Īśvarapratyabhijñākārikā* (*ĪPK*), with its usual meaning: in the sense of the sensation of softness, warmth, etc. which a blind person can feel by touch (cf. *ĪPK* I.7.10). He uses it also for the "inner touch" (*āntare vā sparśa*, I.6.4-5 *vṛtti*), for *sparśa* as one of the five "subtle elements" (*tanmātra*, III.1.10-11 *v*) and also in the sense of "contact" with an inner sensation like happiness, etc. (III.2.15 *v*) or with non-being (II.3.14, here: *sa-sparśa*). However, in his *Śivastotrāvalī* (Hymns to Śiva), *sparśa* and its derivations have mainly a spiritual meaning, as we will see.

In the sense of "contact" the word is used in Indian astronomy, especially for the beginning of an eclipse,[58] when the celestial bodies seem to touch each other. Traditionally, *sparśa* is associated with the element "air" (*vāyu*).[59] Therefore, *sparśana* is one of the names for *vāyu*[60] — that invisible element

---

58. Cf. MW 1269.

59. Cf. *Nirukta* XIV.4: "Wind originates from space (*ākāśa*) and possesses two qualities: sound and touch." Quoted after Bettina Bäumer: "Vāyu," in: *Kalātattvakośa*, vol. III: Primal Elements — *Mahābhūta*, ed. Bettina Bäumer, Delhi: Indira Gandhi National Centre for the Arts/Motilal Banarsidass, 1996, pp. 143-87; here: p. 169 (Abbr.: *KTK*). See also *MBh* XII.177.33 and XII.247.6 (ibid., p. 170).

60. Cf. *Halāyudhakośaḥ*, Lucknow (1957), 2nd edn. 1967, verse 75, p. 10.

which becomes sensually perceivable through its touch in the form of wind, and by its sound. Because of the energy of *vāyu* in the body (i.e. in *vāta*), the atoms which comprise our bodies touch each other, as stated in one of India's oldest medical texts, the great medical encyclopaedia by Caraka:

> Minutest units into which all organs of the body (*śarīra*) are divided are known as *paramāṇus* and they cannot be counted because (1) they are extremely numerous, (2) they are extremely subtle, and (3) they are beyond sensory perception. *Vāyu* and the specific nature of the results of the past action associated with these *paramāṇus* are responsible for their union (*saṁyoga*) and disjunction (*vibhāga*).
>
> — *Caraka Saṁhitā, Śarīrasthāna*, 7.17[61]

Sparśa is also the collective name of the 25 consonants of the Sanskrit alphabet (*sparśavarga*, cf. MW 1268), obviously because one has to touch the tongue to the side of the oral cavity to create them.

Belonging to the senses, *sparśa* is an important topic in the Indian philosophical traditions, be it the Hindu, Buddhist, Muslim, Jaina or others.[62] The classical philosophical systems of India (*darśana*), especially Sāṁkhya, discuss *sparśa* in epistemology and in metaphysics (*prameya sāśtra*) as an element of the ontological and epistemological categories and principles

---

61. *Caraka Saṁhitā. Text with English Translation and Critical Exposition based on Cakrapāṇi Datta's Āyūrveda Dīpikā*, vol. II, ed. R.K. Sharma and Bhagwan Dash, Varanasi: Choukhamba Sanskrit Series Office, reprint 2003.

62. See the survey in Kapila Vatsyayan: "Indriya," in: *KTK* IV: *Manifestation of Nature — Sṛṣṭi Vistāra*, ed. by Advaitavadini Kaul/ Sukumar Chattopadhyay, Delhi: Indira Gandhi National Centre for the Arts/Motilal Banarsidass, 1999, pp. 1-68.

of reality (*tattva*).[63] *Sparśa* is one of the five "subtle elements" (*tanmātra*), along with *śabda* (sound), *rūpa* (form), *rasa* (taste), *gandha* (smell) — the properties of the elements which can be perceived by the sense-organs. *Sparśa* is thereby associated with *tvak* (skin), one of the five sense-organs of cognition (*buddhīndriya*), the other organs being *śrota* (ear), *cakṣus* (eye), *rasana* (tongue), and *ghrāṇa* (nose). *Tvak* is the skin, the organ of touch, which is itself called *sparśana*.[64] More important than the physical organ is the non-material aspect, the sense-ability connected with it (*sparśanendriya*) — the energy which operates through the physical organ (*indriyaśakti*, see for example *ĪPK* III.2.16 *v*).[65] J.C. Chatterji therefore translates *tvak* as "the power of feeling-by-touch."[66]

According to the conception of the body within the classical Indian medical system of Āyurveda, all sensations (touch, sound, etc.) are transported through one of the 24

---

63. Abhinavagupta comprehensively deals with *tanmātra* and *indriya* in chapter 9 and 10 of *TĀ*, where he explains the connection of the 36 "principles" (*tattva*) from "Śiva" down to the element "earth."

64. Cf. *Aṣṭāṅgasaṁgraham* — *Sūtrasthāna* 20.3; quoted in: V.V. Subrahmanya Sastri, *Tridosha Theory: A Study on the Fundamental Principles of Ayurveda* (Kottakkal Ayurveda Series; 18) Kottakkal: Arya Vaidya Sala, 1977, 4th rev. edn. 2002, p. 232, fn. 8.

65. The word *indriya* is derived from Indra (cf. K. Vatsyayan, "Indriya," in: *KTK* IV, op. cit., 1). In Vedic mythology he is the lord of the gods in the intermediate realm, who conquers the demons of darkness; he symbolizes strength, power, energy.

66. J.C. Chatterji, *Kashmir Shaivism* (1914), Delhi: Parimal Publications, reprint 1987, p. 118. This characterization of the *indriya*s is adopted by Kanti Chandra Pandey, *Abhinavagupta: A Historical and Philosophical Study* (The Chaukamba Sanskrit Studies; 1) Varanasi: Chaukamba Amarabharati Prakashan, 1963, 3rd edn. 2000, pp. 380f.

channels (*dhamanī*) which start from the navel.[67] More specifically, there are 10 channels which proceed from the navel to the heart and there divide into three groups. Again, among these 30 channels, eight carry the sensual sensations, while others give passage to speech (*bhāṣā*), tears, mother's milk (or semen, in the case of men) and so forth. Four of the 24 *dhamanīs*, which start from the navel, divide into hundreds of thousands of channels whose ends are connected to the hair follicles. Through them the sensations of touch — pleasant or unpleasant — are experienced.

Among the senses *sparśa* is the most important in the view of Āyurveda, since the tactile contact is crucial for every sensation: in the case of seeing, the touch of the retina by direct or reflected light;[68] in the case of hearing, the touch of the eardrum by sound waves; in the case of smelling, the touch of the epithelium by the smelled, etc. In the *CaSa* (*Sūtrasthana*, 1.38) we find the important remark that *sparśa* pervades all the senses.[69] Therefore *sparśanendriya* can be used as a term for any sense whose touch or contact causes happiness or unhappiness (cf. *CaSa* 1.133) — be it an actual physical touch (*sparśanendriya saṁsparśa*) or mental contact (*mānasasparśa*).

Abhinavagupta seems to refer to this tradition which considers the sense of touch as the sole sense when he reflects

---

67. Cf. Dominik Wujastyk, "The Science of Medicine," in: Gavin Flood (ed.), *The Blackwell Companion to Hinduism*, Oxford: Blackwell, 2003, pp. 393-409; here: p. 400.

68. Also the antique Greek physiology understands seeing as the touch by impressions (for this notice I want to thank Dr Ursula Baatz, Vienna).

69. Cf. Subrahmanya Sastri, *Tridosha Theory*, op. cit., p. 17.

upon the "inner touch" (*āntarasparśa*).[70] According to the doctrine of recognition (*pratyabhijñāśāstra*) developed by Utpaladeva, the teacher of his teacher, the all-encompassing Self (*para pramātā*) appears as the limited self (*māyāpramātā*). Its contraction manifests itself on four levels: as the sensationless void (*śūnya*), the inner sensation (*āntara sparśa*), the intellect (*buddhi*) and the body (*deha*, cf. *ĪPK* I. 6.4-5 and *v*; *passim*). What is the meaning of "inner touch"? It is *prāṇa* (life, power of life, breath). Utpaladeva uses *prāṇa* synonymously with *āntara sparśa* (see for example *ĪPK* III. 2.11 *v*). Under the influence of *māyā*, the void, inner touch, intellect and body, which are not the Self (*ātman*), are perceived as true "I" (cf. *ĪPK* III. 1.8). Only a cognition in the form of the "immersion into that" (*tat samāveśa*), into the Self, makes visible the true active dynamics of *cit*, of the Self (*cidātmanaḥ*), and also the dependence of the void, the inner touch, the intellect and the body upon it (cf. *ĪPK* III. 2.12).

Of course, the special status of the sense of touch in Āyurveda has to be seen in the context of the general statements of Indian philosophies on the topic of the senses. According to them, it is usually the eye (*akṣa*) which is placed at the top of the hierarchy of the senses.

Important for our theme is the meaning of *sparśa* as the expression for sexual union (cf. MW 1269), which even now enjoys use in contemporary Hindi. Its past context is evident on examining a related term: a *sparśā* (f.) is — in the discreet style of Sir Monier-Williams in the nineteenth century — an "unchaste woman" (WM, 1269), common in current Hindi for

70. Cf. *ĪPVV*, vol. 2, pp. 295-97. See R. Torella: *ĪPK*, p. 132, fn. 10; Alexis Sanderson, "Maṇḍala and Āgamic Identity in the Trika of Kashmir," in: André Padoux (ed.), *Mantras et Diagrammes Rituelles dans l'Hinduisme*, Paris: CNRS, 1986, pp. 169-207; here: pp. 177f.

a prostitute. Abhinavagupta uses the word *sparśa* for the sexual act many times, especially in his commentary (*Vivaraṇa*) to the *Parātrīśikā-Tantra*. For example, he denotes the sexual organ as the "place of touch" (*sparśa-kṣetra*). Abhinavagupta here observes that even the memory of sexual union (*sparśa*) causes a "reflection" in the "place of touch" and in the "medium channel," belonging to the "natural highest Śakti." This is because even in the absence of the "touch of a *śakti* [a woman]" the mere recollection of the touch of the woman (*śāktasparśa*) stirs up the energy of semen, which rests within "it" [= in the medium channel, *suṣumnā*).[71]

In the same way, the word *sparśa* is used in its sexual meaning by Abhinavagupta in his *TĀ*:

> Sound (*śabda*) is reflected in ether (*nabhasi*), a very pleasant (*sundara*) touch in the region of touch (*sparśadhāmani*).
>
> — *TĀ* 3.36ab

In his commentary Jayaratha clarifies what is meant by a "region of touch" in the body:

> . . . [it is] the place of [sexual] joy (*ānandasthāna*) in the specific regions like the *kanda*,[72] [in the] heart and even in the lower

71. Cf. Abhinavagupta: *Parātrīśikā-Vivaraṇa: The Secret of Tantric Mysticism.* English translation with notes and running exposition by Jaideva Singh, ed. Bettina Bäumer, Delhi: Motilal Banarsidass, 1988, reprint 2000, p. 45; Sanskrit text: p. 17 (quoted: PTV and page number).

72. *Kanda* literally means: "root," synonymous with *mūla* (cf. *Amarakośa* III.6.35). According to yogic physiology it is placed at the base of the sexual organ, "situated five fingers' breadth below the navel and two above the virile member" (*K* 27, fn. 5). It is part of the *mūlādhāra-cakra* at the base of the spine, one of the main "wheels" (*cakra*) within the subtle dimension of the body, which are recognized by Trika (see *K* 25-33). We meet here one of the →

> realm of the palate (*tātutala*) and other [places]. Because of the purity (*nirmalya*) of touch, touch is reflected (*pratisaṁkrāmati*), and the touch which corresponds to the enjoyment (*upabhoga*) of the sexual union (*mithuna*), is reflected [there]. Because of it, the ejaculation of semen and happiness (*sukhādi*) arise. — *TĀ*, vol. II, 317

The (erotic) touch is "beautiful" ". . . because it allows access to the highest bliss (*ānanda-atiśaya*)." (ibid.) Jayaratha afterwards discusses other types of *sparśa*, causing pain, etc.

The different layers of meaning which the word *sparśa* entails could explain its prominent place in Abhinavagupta's texts, especially in his later Tāntric works, the *TĀ* and *Parātrīśikāvivaraṇa*, representing the peak of his development of Kaula-/Krama-Tāntricism. With this polyvalent word, Abhinavagupta can, on the one hand, express the ultimate experience: the "touch of the power of the Self" (*Spandakārikā* 1.8) — the immediate "contact" with the core of reality, which he denotes as "the Highest" (*anuttara*) — and at the same time *sparśa*, in its sexual sense, can denote the heart of the Tāntric path: the discovery made by spiritual seekers that not necessarily only sexual abstinence and asceticism could lead

---

→ "physiological" connections between the sexual and the spiritual process: within the same centres in the body — *kanda, hṛt* (heart), *tālu* (palate; to be added here also are *trikoṇa* and *brahmarandhra*) — manifest the five main signs for the entering into the highest spiritual state, the "great pervasion" (*mahāvyāpti*, *TĀ* 5.105a): *ānanda* (bliss), *udbhava* (jump or bound), *kampa* (trembling), *nidrā* (yogic sleep) and *ghūrṇi* (vibrant whirling), cf. *MVT* XI.35. See *K* 71-75. Abhinavagupta quotes in *TĀ* 5.111 the *Triśirobhairavatantra*, which adjoins these signs of the spiritual rising (the rising of *kuṇḍalinī* through the subtle centres) to places in the subtle dimension of the body, in the following way: *ānanda/trikoṇa; udbhava/kanda; kampa/hṛt; nidrā/tālu; ghūrṇi/ūrdhvakuṇḍalinī.*

to the highest goal, but that it could also be sought through the interiorized sexual union, the most intensive sensual experience in a prolonged state of thoughtlessness (*nirvikalpa*). The contact, the union of man and woman, can in the end lead to the contact, and finally to the union with the "Highest." As a Western interpreter, after the "linguistic turn" and "demythologization," one should not walk into the trap of understanding this only as mere wordplay or metaphor. One should reckon with the possibility that the authors express clearly perceivable and concrete sensual experiences during meditation (e.g. the "touch of ants"), in their highest form being a real experience of contact with the "Nameless" (*nirnāma*, cf. *Mālinīślokavārttika* 1.20ab) — an experience in a very subtle dimension, which for them is best expressed with the notion "touch."

This is confined by the fact that the highest experience is also denoted with the same word "touch" in the Western spiritual traditions. The "touching" of God (Lat. *attingere*) is a basic term, which, starting from the Platonic literature runs through Western mysticism from its beginnings until modern times. The outstanding examples are Plotinus (CE 204/ 205-70),[73] the founder of antique Neo-Platonism, and Augustine (*c.* CE 354-73),[74] as well as Meister Eckhart in the Middle Ages and Nicolas of Cusa at the beginning of the modern era. If we are not inclined to view the expression "touched by God" as a mere *topos* of mystical literature but rather as an attempt of

---

73. See especially his famous, early *Ennead* VI 9,9; cf. VI 9,7,4; VI 7, 36, 4; V 3, 17, pp. 25f; VI 9, 4, 24-28; VI 9,9, 55; VI 9, 11, 24; *passim.*

74. See especially the famous passage in his *Confessions* (*Confessiones libri tredecim*), book IX, 10, 23-25, where he narrates his experience "to touch" [the eternal wisdom] in the moment of one heartbeat (. . . *attingimus eam [sapientiam aeternam] modice toto ictu cordis*).

people in different times and cultures to verbalize a real, concrete experience in a similar way, then this spiritual experience of "touch" — of an immediate contact with the core of reality, maybe only for one moment — seems to be an universal, "pure experience," independent from specific cultural patterns, "prejudices" and constructions. It could show the limitations of the standard thesis of the constructivists, that (religious) experience is *always* necessarily determined and constructed by the background (Wittgenstein: "Hintergrund") of a specific culture.[75] This thesis (in its dogmatic form) could turn out as one of the "myths," which are specifically determined by the European modern culture.

Non-dualistic Kashmir Śaivism describes the dimension of the "Highest" (*anuttara*) which can be experienced, as the power of pure, absolute Freedom (*svātantryaśakti*), the absolute New — and so experiencing Her is the contact with the New, the Freedom, absolute Creativity which breaks through the cultural, religious, individual patterns and the pre-conditions of perception, thinking and expression. It is exactly the essential nature of spiritual experience that transcends the "given background" (Wittgenstein: "das Gegebene"), the already known. Spiritual experience is *not always/not necessarily* a mere echo of symbols, signs, and motives which are stored

75. See the famous "Forman-Katz-debate" in the field of theory of mysticism: Steven T. Katz (ed.), *Mysticism and Religious Traditions*, Oxford: Oxford University Press, 1983; Robert K. C. Forman (ed.), *The Problem of Pure Consciousness: Mysticism and Philosophy*, New York/Oxford: Oxford University Press, 1990; id. (ed.), *The Innate Capacity*, New York/Oxford: Oxford University Press, 1998; id., *Mysticism, Mind, Consciousness*, Albany: State University of New York Press, 1999.

in a particular culture, religion and time.[76] There is the possibility that "the New" befalls, happens to somebody.

The Term Sparśa in Early Texts of Non-dualistic Kashmir Śaivism

The *Jayadrathayāmalatantra*, also known as "King of the Tantras" (*Tantrarājabhaṭṭāraka*), is one of the basic texts of the Krama-school of esoteric Śaivism of Kashmir. Manuscripts of it are still preserved, the oldest of them from the end of the twelfth century. Abhinavagupta quotes the Tantra as an authority; the text therefore must be dated before Abhinavagupta (tenth/eleventh century). Possibly, the *JY* is among the oldest Tantras (cf. *HTSL*, p. 45). In this text we find the term *sparśa*, among other meanings, in a significant context, in connection with *kuṇḍalinī (-śakti)*. This is important for the reconstruction of the role of the term *sparśa* in non-dualistic Kashmir Śaivism, as the touch of *kuṇḍalinī*:[77]

> *nāsikāntargataṁ sparśaṁ vahatas tasya yogavit* || 74 ||
> *pratyakṣaṁ kurute yas tu tasyādhyakṣaiśvarasthitiḥ* |
> *sparśād atītasaṁvittim astitvasthitilakṣitam* || 75 ||

> The touch within the energy of *nāsikā* [*kuṇḍalinī*] carries the knower of *yoga*. It makes visible his/her state as lord, who reigns above. By touch, the consciousness of that which has passed is experienced as the continuance of being.
>
> — *Jayadrathayāmala* 1.12.74-75

76. The argument is unfolded in my *Verstehen durch Berühren. Interreligiöse Hermeneutik am Beispiel des nichtdualistischen Śivaismus von Kaschmir*, Wien/Innsbruck: Tyrolia, 2006 (ch. IV 2: Spiritual Understanding).

77. I would like to thank Dr Mark S.G. Dyczkowski (Varanasi), who provided the following two passages of the unedited *JY* to me.

Interesting is here the expression *nāsikā*, which is understood as a synonym for *kuṇḍalinī*. Literally it means "nose" (cf. MW 538). What is the connection between the "nose" (*nāsā* or *nāsikā*) and *kuṇḍalinī*? In the *yoga* traditions, the concentration by which the externally-scattered energies of the senses are withdrawn, enabling the rise of the *kuṇḍalinī*-energy within the subtle body, is directed towards the nose. This might indicate the end of the nose (*nāsāgra*), upon which one's gaze is directed, so that any involuntary ocular movement comes to a rest. As the *Bhagavad-Gītā* (6.13) says: "He should look to the end of his nose (*nāsikāgra*) and not to every other direction." Or as Abhinavagupta expresses in a hymn: "With half-opened eyes, motionless thoughts, the gaze directed towards the end of the nose (*nāsāgra*) (. . .) the *yogī* reaches the highest reality."[78] Here it is important to clarify: "end of the nose" does not mean the tip, but the *root* of the nose: the point between the eyebrows, called *bhrūmadhya* or *bindu*. It is one of the *cakras*, which could be understood as "subtle energy centres" in the human body. As described by *Bhagavad-Gītā* 5.27: "They have excluded the outer touch, have directed the look on the midst between the eyebrows, they have equalized the ingoing and outgoing breaths, as they flow within the nose."

It is remarkable that in his commentary to this verse Abhinavagupta notes the difference between the "nose" (*nāsā*) — the place of the duality between the inhalation and the exhalation — and the "root of the nose," the point between the eyebrows (*bruvoḥ*), to express the difference between the modality of the normal, restless mind (*cittavṛttiḥ*) which moves

78. Abhinavagupta, *Anubhavanivedana*, Sanskrit text: Pandey, Abhinavagupta, op. cit., p. 953.

within the realm of duality and negative emotions like rage (*krodha*), and the mind which is concentrated at one point.[79]

The motive of the yogic concentration on the root of the nose appears also in one of the basic texts of non-dualistic Śaivism of Kashmir, the *Śivasūtra* (ninth century):[80]

> By concentration (*saṁyamāt*) on the inner centre [on the end] of the nose (*nāsikāntarmadhya*) — why [to say] more (*kimatra*) about "right," "left," [or] *suṣumnā*? — *Śivasūtra* III.44

This could be interpreted as saying that it is futile to speculate about the processes in the "subtle body," the rising movements of the "power" in the main "channels" or "courses" (*nāḍī*) — that is, *iḍā* (the left), *piṅgalā* (the right) and *suṣumnā* (the middle conduit) — for it happens on its own accord. Only the continuous, one-pointed awareness (*saṁyama*) on the middle point, the centre (*madhya*) matters — the concentration on the *cakra* between the eyebrows, at the end of the nose, which draws oneself into the centre and lets the "power" (i.e. *kuṇḍalinī-śakti*) arise in the "centre" (*suṣumnā*).

Now, in his commentary (*vimarśinī*) of this passage, Kṣemarāja (eleventh century) identifies *nāsikā* with *kuṇḍalinī*:

> In the most important of all courses (*nāḍī*), [that is], in the left, right and in *suṣumnā*, *nāsikā* [moves], [derived from] "*nasate*", "that which moves in a crooked way", that is the

79. Cf. *Abhinavagupta's Commentary on the Bhagavad-gītā: Gītārtha Saṁgraha.* Translated from Sanskrit with Introduction and Notes by Boris Marjanovic, Varanasi: Indica, 2002, p. 145.

80. *The Śivasūtravimarśinī of Kṣemarāja: Being a Commentary on the Śivasūtra of Vasugupta.* Edited by Jagadisha Chandra Chatterji (KSTS; 1) Srinagar 1911. Reprint, New Delhi: Bibliotheca Orientalia, 1990, p. 139. — I want to thank Pt. H.N. Chakravarty (Varanasi), who brought this reference to my notice.

power of the breath (*prāṇaśakti*).[81]

The notion "the crooked" for *kuṇḍalinī* seems to be based on the yogic experience that the "power" rises in a snake-motion or in an S-form up the spine,[82] and not only on the traditional Tāntric image that *kuṇḍālinī* in its potential form is coiled as a snake in three and a half turns at the base of the spine.[83]

At another passage of *Jayadrathayāmala*, the word *sparśa* appears in a significant way; the "touch of pure *cit*" is described as a quality of the highest Goddess (Kuṇḍalinī) herself:

pañcavyomāntarātīte cinmātrasparśalakṣaṇe | | 68 | |

[O Goddess, who is] beyond the five voids and whose characteristic is the touch of pure *cit*[84]!

— *Jayadrathayāmala* 2.1.68cd

A similar statement can be found in a later text of the Krama-school, in the *Mahānayaprakāśa* of Arṇasiṁha (*c.* CE 1050–1100):[85]

81. Ibid.

82. This fact could be the background for the prominent position of the letter SA (*sakāra*), as a code-letter for *kuṇḍalinī*, in the letter-speculation of the *TĀ*, e.g.: "The whole universe shines within the letter SA." (*TĀ* 3.165) About "SA" in the philosophy of Trika, see *Vāc*, pp. 301ff; pp. 417ff.

83. See for example *Tantrasadbhāva*, quoted by Jayaratha in the commentary to *TĀ* 3.67 (*TĀV*, vol. III, 429; English translation: *Vāc*, p. 128).

84. On *cit* see chapter II: Hermeneutical Reflections (1. Is *cit* "consciousness"?).

85. Arṇasiṁha, *Mahāyānaprakāśa*, National Archives Nepal, Mss. 5-5183/151 (A 150/6); ed. and tr. Mark S.G. Dyczkowski, unpublished manuscript, Sanskrit: 3, English translation: 4. — I am glad that I could study this text with Mark Dyczkowski in a group, in fall 2003.

> *itthaṁ devyo nirāveśamahāvarṇakramoditāḥ* ।
> *tattvataḥ sparśasaṁvittilaharyāmantaraṁ sphuṭam* ।।
>
> In this way the Goddess, arising from the sequence of the Great Letter [A], free from pervasion, is in reality clearly manifest within the wave of the touch of *saṁvit* (*sparśasaṁvitti*).[86] — *Mahānayaprakāśa* [A], verse 37

The goddess is *cinmātrasparśa*, who moves through the extension of I-ness (*aham; asmitācakra*) in the five voids (cf. verse 34). The five spheres of voidness are identified with five "powers" (*śaktis*): Vyomavāmeśvarī, Khecarī, Saṁhārabhakṣiṇī, Bhūcarī, and Raudreśvarī. About Vyomavāmeśvarī (literally: "she who emits the voids"), the highest of the five energies, the "void beyond the Great Void" (verse 40), the text says: "I adore her, who emits the divine transmission (*divyaugha*) and whose form is touch." Also Khecarī is denoted as "touch" (*sparśa*): "Khecarī is touch, the *mudrā*, which — free from all concealment and without any place (*nirniketanā*) — moves within the sphere of touch (*yā sparśa sparśagagane carantī nirniketanā sarvāvaraṇirmuktā mudrā sā khecarī smṛtā*)" (verse 102). *Mudrā*, literally "seal" or "gesture," is here used in the sense of *śakti*; the background is formed by the doctrine of Mudrā-Krama.[87]

Until now we have followed some traces of the concept of *sparśa* through the texts of the Krama-school. Unfortunately I could not examine other basic texts of Trika, e.g. *Tantrasadbhāva*, concerning the occurrence of the term *sparśa*. So at the moment

---

86. On *saṁvit* see chapter II: Hermeneutical Reflections (1. Is *cit* "consciousness"?).

87. See Navjivan Rastogi, *The Krama Tantricism of Kashmir. Vol. 1: Historical and General Sources*, Delhi: Motilal Banarsidass, 1979. Reprint 1996.

I can only provide a few evidential examples for the thesis that the usage of *sparśa* as a technical term within the Advaitic-Śaivite Kuṇḍalinī-Yoga entered into Trika through the Krama-school, which Abhinavagupta integrated into his synthesis.

In the *Spandakārikā* (ninth century), one of the basic texts of non-dualistic Kashmir Śaivism, the word *sparśa* appears in an important context:[88]

> *na hīcchānodanasyāyam prerakatvena vartate* |
> *api tvātmabalasparśāt puruṣastatsamo bhavet* ||

> The will (*icchā*) of the limited individual alone cannot impel the impulse of the will. But by the touch of the power (*bala*) of the Self (*ātma*), the human being (*puruṣa*) becomes equal (*sama*) to it (*tat*). — *Spandakārikā* 1.8[89]

After this verse, the commentator Kṣemarāja again refers to this verse in the introduction to *Spandakārikā* 1.9, when he wonders why the reality of the Self being identical with the "highest Lord" is imperceptible and hidden under everyday conditions.

> Why does the embodied Self not shine in its perfection, despite its being of the nature of the highest Lord? Why is the touch of the power of the inner Self necessary (*kasmād-antarmukhātma-bala-sparśam-apekṣat*)?[90]

---

88. *Spandakārikās of Vasugupta with the Nirṇaya by Kṣemarāja*, ed. Madhusudan Kaul (KSTS; 42) Srinagar, 1925, p. 21.

89. Cf. the translation of Jaideva Singh who uses the word "contact" for *sparśa*: "The empirical individual cannot drive the goad of desire. But by coming in contact with the power of the Self, he becomes equal to that principle." (*Spanda-Kārikās: The Divine Creative Pulsation — The Kārikās and the Spanda-nirṇaya*, trans. Jaideva Singh, Delhi: Motilal Banarsidass, 1980. Reprint 1994, p. 58).

90. *Spandakārikās of Vasugupta*, ed. M. Kaul, op. cit., p. 22.

Only through the touch, the immediate contact with the "power" (*bala,* one of the names of Śakti) of the inner Self (*ātma*), can the true nature (of humans/of all) be revealed as identical with the highest, unlimited light, the "highest lord" (Śiva). Or as Abhinavagupta puts it, also with the help of "touch":

> Only because of his limitations is he unable to touch his non-difference from Śiva (*kevalaṁ pārimityena śivābhedam-saṁspṛśan*).
> — *Tantrāloka* 9.91cd

Now we will find another use of *sparśa,* again in the context of the "touch of kuṇḍalinī": the term *pipīlikā-sparśa* (the touch of ants). Its technical application by Utpaladeva (tenth century) and Abhinavagupta (tenth/eleventh century) is preceded by a long tradition of use. This fact is shown, among other texts, by the *Vijñāna-Bhairava Tantra*:[91]

> *sarvaśrotonibandhena prāṇaśaktyordhvayā śanaiḥ* |
> *pipīlasparśaveḷāyām prathate paramaṁ sukham* ||

> Closing all the openings of the senses, by the slow upward rise of the Energy of Breath, one feels a sensation like the movement of ants. At that time the supreme joy is revealed.
> — *Vijñāna-Bhairava,* verse 67[92]

This Tantra presents itself as a part of the *Rudrayāmala,* and in any case — like all the *Yāmalas*[93] — must be dated before CE 900

---

91. *The Vijñāna-Bhairava with Commentary partly by Kṣemarāja and partly by Śivopādhyāya,* ed. with notes by Pt. Mukunda Rāma Śāstrī (KSTS; 8) Bombay, 1918, p. 54.

92. Translation by Bettina Bäumer (*Vijñāna-Bhairava: The Practice of Centring Awareness. Commentary by Swami Lakshman Joo,* Varanasi: Indica, 2002, p. 73).

93. *Yāmala,* literally "pair." Term for an important group of old Tāntric texts, which are badly preserved. See *HTSL,* pp. 39ff.

(cf. *HTSL*, p. 40). Certainly, the *Vijñāna-Bhairava* goes back to a long oral tradition of the *siddhas*, the "perfect" *yogī*s (*siddhamukhāmnāya*).[94]

The motif of the "touch of ants" also turns up in the *Mālinīvijayottara*,[95] which is the foremost Tantra according to Abhinavagupta.[96] It appears in the 14th chapter, within a series of yogic exercises with the "subtle elements" (*tanmātra*), starting from the *tanmātra* "smell" (*gandha*), then "taste" (*rasa*), "form" (*rūpa*), and finally "touch" (*sparśa*):

> Next, I now reveal to you another contemplation, [that of the Sensory Medium] of touch, whereby the Yogin becomes adamantine-bodied. [1.] One should contemplate oneself as seated within a hexagonal diagram; [one should imagine oneself to be] dry, black and overcome by twitching in every part of the body. Then, within ten days, O Goddess, the [crawling] sensation of ants arises everywhere on his skin. Then, contemplating that [sensation], he attains an adamantine body and the previously mentioned [rewards] as before. [2.-5.] Who can ward off him who contemplates the previously [visualized] form as the afore-mentioned diagram, and [thereby] attains the [esoteric] knowledge of the touch-realm. [6.-15.] One should contemplate the self without the diagram in order to achieve sovereignty of that

---

94. Cf. Raffaele Torella, "On Vāmanadatta," in: S.P. Narang/C.P. Bhatta (eds.), *Pandit N.R. Bhatt Felicitation Volume*, Delhi: Motilal Banarsidass, 1994, pp. 481-98; here: p. 492.

95. *Mālinivijayottara Tantram*, ed. Madhusudan Kaul (KSTS; 37) Bombay, 1922.

96. Cf. *Tantrāloka* 1.17-18: *Mālinīvijayottara* as the essence of the scriptures of Trika.

> [reality-level], by perfecting which, he will become a knower of all sensation.[97] — *MVT* 14.28-33

As we will see with the analysis of *Tantrāloka* 11.29-31, the term *pipīlikasparśa* is obviously used here in a different context than in the *Tantrāloka*.

The expression *sparśa* appears also in connection with the presentation of the rise of *kuṇḍalinī* in the twelve stages that represent twelve powers in the *Svacchandatantra* (*Svacchandatantra* 4.271-276 and 4.370-394).[98] In his commentary, Kṣemarāja connects this "touch" of the rising *kuṇḍalinī* at a particular stage with the "touch of ants" (*pipīlikā*);[99] in this way he refers to a tradition which compares this particular sensation with the crawling of ants.

This survey of the use of the word *sparśa* in Kashmir Śaiva texts prior to Abhinavagupta is far from complete. This has

---

97. Somadeva Vasudeva, *The Yoga of the Mālinīvijayottaratantra: Chapters 1-4, 7, 11-17*. Critical Edition, translation and notes (Collection Indologie; 97) Pondichéry: Institut Français de Pondichéry/École française d'Extrême-Orient, 2005, pp. 335f. — Vasudeva translates *pipīlikāsparśa* (verse 30) generally with "sensation of ants" and likewise *sparśa* with "sensation" (verse 32). A more literal translation would read: "he will become a knower of all touch (*sarvasparśavedī*)."— The term *pipīlikāsparśa* (in connection with a particular *cakra*, i.e. *brahmarandhra*) appears also in a text of Śaiva-Siddhānta (*Somaśambhupaddhati Nirvāṇadīkṣāvidhi* 235): *śaktiṁ ca brahmarandhrasthāṁ tyajed ittham anukramāt* । *divyaṁ pipīlikāsparśaṁ tasminn evanubhūya ca* ॥ Cf. Vasudeva, *Yoga of the Mālinīvijayottaratantra*, op. cit., p. 292, fn. 121.

98. *The Svacchandatantram with Commentary Udyota of Kṣemarāja*, ed. Vraj Vallabh Dwivedi, 2 vols., Delhi: Parimal Publications, 1985.

99. Kṣemarāja, *Svacchandatantroddyota* 4.384 (*yadvat pipīliketi saṁcarantīnām pipīlikānām*).

partly to do with the fact that the principal texts of the esoteric Śaiva tradition which have survived have not yet been edited — including the *Tantrasadbhāva,* the *Jayadrathayāmala* and the *Brahmayāmala.* Nevertheless, these fragments that we have discussed, drawn from their sources in the early Śaiva Tāntric literature, are able to show its importance within these schools of Trika-Śaivism that were related with the *Pūrvāmnāya,* the "Eastern Transmission."[100] It would be also fruitful to explore the use of the term in other traditions, like the Kubjikā-tradition, which belongs to the so-called *Paścimāmnāya,* the "Western Transmission."[101]

---

100. To the division of the Kula-related schools into four "transmissions" (*āmnāya*) see *Vāc,* pp. 61ff; *HTSL* 17; Mark S.G. Dyczkowski, *The Canon of the Śaivāgama and the Kubjikā Tantras of the Western Kaula Tradition,* Indian edition: Delhi: Motilal Banarsidass, 1989.

101. In this tradition *sparśa* is used to denote the Goddess itself. See, e.g. *Ciñcinīmatasārasamucchaya* (Nepal National Archives, Manuskripte 1/767, 1/199, 1/1560, 1/245), where the "highest [goddess]" is called "Sparśalakṣmī" ("wealth of touch"), ". . . contemplated by the wheel of passion (*raticakra*) . . ." (CMSS 1.3a). — About CMSS see Mark S.G. Dyczkowski, *The Canon of the Śaivāgama and the Kubjikā Tantras of the Western Kaula Tradition,* Indian edition: Delhi: Motilal Banarsidass, 1989, p. 175, fn. 93. The text was written before the thirteenth century (ibid., p. 184, fn. 157). I would like to thank Dr Dyczkowski, who brought this passage to my notice and mentioned the use of *sparśa* as a name of the Goddess in the Kubjikā-tradition.

2

Hermeneutical Reflections

Si vous voulez que je eroie en Dieu,
il faut que vous me le fassiez toucher.
If you want, that I believe in God,
you must let me touch him.
— The Blind Mathematician Sanderson
in: Denis Diderot, *Letter About the Blind* (1749)

It is an old tradition in the West, starting already with the Greek fathers, to begin a text with the reflection and clarification of some hermeneutic principles which are important for the understanding and interpretation of the following text. I use here "hermeneutics" in the general sense of a theory of understanding and interpreting. I wouldn't compare my enterprise with that of the early Greek fathers, but consider it useful to pose two hermeneutic questions in the beginning: does the English translation of the word *cit* — maybe the most important operative key term of Trika Śaivism — with "consciousness" comprise a correct interpretation? Also, how ought one to proceed through the multidimensional, metaphorical language of Abhinavagupta?

The question how to understand *cit* (or the synonym *saṁvit*) is relevant for our theme of *sparśa*, since we have seen that the texts talk about the "touch of *cit*," and we can understand this "touch" only in the light of an understanding of the central term *cit*.

Is Cit "Consciousness"?

The word *cit* is one of the key terms of Indian philosophy as well as of the Trika-system. In the Advaita Vedānta system of Śaṅkara (Śānta Brahmavāda) *cit* denotes the Divine Absolute (*Brahman*). Contrary to Śaṅkara's view of *cit* as inactive (*niṣkriya*) pure light (*prakāśa*), non-dualistic Kashmir Śaivism (Īśvarādvayavāda) stresses the Śakti-dimension of the Highest Reality (*anuttara*), its dynamism and activity (*kartṛtva*). For the Śaivites *cit* is not only pure light, but is simultaneously *prakāśa* and *vimarśa*, the "seeing" or cognizing of this light, symbolized by the non-separated yet differentiated pair "Śiva" and "Śakti." The highest Śakti (*parāśakti*, the supreme *kuṇḍalinī*) itself is *citi* (fem. of *cit*), the creative cause of the world: "The absolute *citi* is the cause of the emergence of the universe" (*Pratyabhijñā-hṛdaya*, *sūtra* 1). Here we specifically notice that Trika does not speak of the duality of Śiva as *cit* or *prakāśa* and Śakti as *vimarśa*, but rather that Śakti is identified with *cit* and *vimarśa*, possibly in an intentional contrast to the immobile, inactive *cit/Brahman* of Śaṅkara's Advaita Vedānta. Abhinavagupta therefore says at the beginning of his *Parātriśikāvivaraṇa*: "It is this supreme *saṁvit* (*parā saṁvit*) which is said to be the goddess (*devī*)."[1] This is also clarified by Kṣemarāja at the beginning of his *Parāprāveśika* (=*PP*):

> We adore *saṁvit*, which flashes forth (*sphurantīm*) in the form of the original Highest Śakti (*parāśakti*), the heart of the Highest Lord, she who consists of the world and transcends it. Here [in Trika] the Highest Lord is of the nature of light (*prakāśātmā*) and the light is of the nature of *vimarśa*. *Vimarśa* is the flashing forth (*visphuraṇam*), which is the uncreated "I" (*akṛtrima-aham*) in the form of the universe, of the light of

1. *PTV*, Sanskrit text: p. 3, translation: p. 9.

> the universe and of the dissolution of the universe. If it would be without *vimarśa*, then it would be without Lord, and lifeless (*jaḍa*). And that is, truly, *vimarśa: cit, caitanya*, the highest word (*parāvāk*), which arises from its own joy (*rasa*), autonomy (*svātantrya*), the original sovereignty (*aiśvarya*) of the highest Self (*paramātman*), agency (*kartṛtvam*), flashing forth (*sphurattā*), essence (*sāra*), heart (*hṛdayam*), vibration (*spanda*) — with these and other words is *vimarśa* proclaimed (*udghoṣyate*) in the Āgamas.[2]

At the same time, Abhinavagupta identifies *cit* with the Self, one's innermost nature:

> The Self (*ātman*), i.e. one's own nature (*svabhāva*), which is *cit* [à]. — *Tantrāloka* 5.127ab

Usually *cit* is translated in English as "consciousness" or "pure consciousness," "pure divine consciousness," or "absolute consciousness."[3] Torella generally translates *cit* or *citi* with just "consciousness" (cf. *Īśvarapratyabhijñākārikā* I. 3.7 *k*; I. 5.10 *v*, I. 5.13 *k*; *passim*), in the same way as do Dyczkowski[4] and others.

Let us have a closer look at a crucial passage within which Utpaladeva characterizes *citi*:

---

2. *Parāprāveśikā of Kṣemarāja*, ed. with Notes by Paṇḍit Mukunda Rāma Śāstrī (KSTS; 15) Bombay 1918, pp. 1ff. Translated by Bettina Bäumer.

3. See for example A. Padoux, "*Cit*": *Tāntrikābhidhānakośa* II, pp. 243-44 ("la pure conscience divine," "conscience absolue"); *Vāc* pp. 77, 454 ("consciousness"); pp. 88, 172, 235, 245 (pure consciousness); pp. 296 (supreme consciousness).

4. See for example Dyczkowski, *Doctrine of Vibration*, op. cit., pp. 43f, 125, *passim*.

(13) *Citi* has as its essential nature (*ātma*) reflective awareness (*pratyavamarśa*), the supreme word (*parāvāk*) arising from its own joy (*svarasoditā*).[5] It is freedom (*svātantrya*) in the eminent (*mukhya*) sense, the sovereignty (*aiśvaryam*) of the supreme Self (*paramātman*).

(14) It is the luminous vibrating (*sphurattā*), the great being (*mahāsattā*) unmodified by space and time; it is that which is said to be the heart (*hṛdayam*) of the supreme Lord, insofar as it is his essence (*sāra*).

— *Īśvarapratyabhijñākārikā* I. 5.13-14 *k*[6]

In this important passage, *citi* is equated with *parāvāk*.[7] Abhinavagupta identifies the "supreme word" (*parāvāk*) with the supreme Goddess of Trika, Parā.[8] He characterizes it at the beginning of *Parātriśikāvivaraṇa*, and so we receive a conception of *citi* (or *saṁvit*, or *anuttara*), alongside the characterization by Utpaladeva, wherein *parāvāk* shows a complete absence of difference, abiding in the "supreme I" (*paramāham*) beyond time and space.[9] It is the "non-dual *saṁvit* in all *sakala*-perceivers" (*sakalapramātṛsaṁvidadvayamayī*), that is, it is even present at the lowest of the seven levels of perception, in the *sakala*-state, in the realm of duality between objects and subjects of our everyday cognition — but usually we remain unaware of it. Abhinavagupta continues, stating

5. Torella does not translate the word *sva-rasa*, lit. "own (unadulterated) juice or essence" (MW 1276), but translates: ". . . that arises freely" (*ĪPK*, p. 120).

6. Especially in verse 13 I have modified the translation of Torella (*ĪPK*, pp. 120f).

7. Kṣemarāja affirms the identity of Parā, Vākśakti and the "light of Cit" (*citprakāśa*), cf. *PHṛ*, commentary *sūtra* 12 (*PHṛ*, p. 79).

8. Cf. *PTV*, Sanskrit text: p. 2, translation: p. 8.

9. Ibid.

that *parāvāk* is the nature (*svabhāva*) of the highest reality (*paramārtha*).[10] He characterizes it as "unconventional" (*asāṁketika*) and "uncreated" or "not made" (*akṛtaka*);[11] it vibrates/flashes (*sphurati*), resting in the light (*prakāśa*) of its own self, its own wonder (*svacamatkṛti*).[12]

In his translation, Torella renders *citi* (fem. form of *cit*) with the word "consciousness,"[13] in accord with the standard relation between the Sanskrit term *cit* and the English term "consciousness," based on a long translation-history in regard

---

10. *Paramārtha*: "highest truth, highest reality" (cf. MW 588). We meet the word from the title of Abhinavagupta's *Paramārthasāra*, in this text in verse 27: "Knowledge (*vijñāna*), inner ruler (*antaryāmī*), breath (*prāṇa*), cosmic body (*virāṭdeha*), species (*jāti*) and [individual] body (*piṇḍa*) are only [part of the] worldly existence (*vyavahāra*), but [with regard to] the highest reality (*paramārtha*) they are not." (*The Paramārthasāra by Abhinavagupta with the Commentary of Yogarāja*, ed. by Jagadisha Chandra Chatterji (KSTS; 7) Srinagar: Research Department of the Kashmir State, 1916). — J. Singh translates here as: ". . . the stage of *parā vāk* (. . .) is of the nature of the highest truth." (*PTV*, Sanskrit text: p. 2, translation: p. 9)

11. Jaideva Singh translates *akṛtaka* as "natural" (ibid.). — Abhinavagupta's description of *parāvāk* (= *citi*), the nature of Reality, as non-dual, full, unconventional (in opposition to the conventional, dualistic perception), not made, etc. reminds us of the characterization of "that-ness," the Real-as-such, in Nāgārjuna's *Mūlamadhyamakakārikā* 18.9: "Not dependent on another, peaceful and not fabricated by mental fabrication, not thought, without distinctions, that is the character of reality (that-ness)." (*The Fundamental Wisdom of the Middle Way: Nāgārjuna's Mūlamadhyamakakārikā*. Translation and commentary by Jay L. Garfield, New York/Oxford: Oxford University Press, 1995, p. 49).

12. *PTV*, Sanskrit text: p. 2, translation: p. 9.

13. Torella: *ĪPK*, op. cit., p. 120.

to *cit*. Anyhow, in my opinion, it is a very strong interpretative intervention, by which the whole passage — including the auto-commentary (*vṛtti*) — acquires a different meaning.

This is so because it is clear (especially from verse 14, but also from other texts like *PP*) that *cit* or *citi* — as well as *hṛdayam, sāra, sphurattā, spanda, ūrmi,* etc. — is one of the names of Śakti, and is identified with Her.[14] The crucial question is this: is the word "consciousness" able to express the dimensions of Śakti (*kuṇḍalinī*), its divine, cosmic, human wholeness according to Tāntric sources? Can the term "consciousness" express that *citi* — Śakti — is the *ground* and *root* of consciousness, and the *basis* of all life, "the life of all living beings" (*sarvajīvatāmjīvanaikarūpam*)?[15]

I am fully aware of the weight of the standardized translation-relation between *cit* and "consciousness," not only in view of the Trika texts, but of Indian philosophy in general, and to jeopardize this relation could seem as an act of academic Quixotism.

However, any translation as "consciousness" *in its usual modern usage* is reductive: it confines *cit* (a) to humans, and (b) to the lower level of *cit* in humans — in terms of the tradition to the contracted, limited condition of *cit*.[16] Its integral, divine-cosmic-human or "cosmotheandric" (Raimon Panikkar)

---

14. Cf. also *TĀ* 6.13, where Abhinavagupta uses the same names in the context of *prāṇaśakti*.

15. *PTV*, commentary *PT*, verse 1 (*PTV*, Sanskrit text: p. 4, translation: p. 15).

16. Cf. *PHṛ*, Commentary *sūtra* 5: "Individual consciousness (*citta*) is nothing else than *Citi*" (*PHṛ*, p. 59), which conceals its real nature and "[. . .] becomes contracted (*saṅkocinī*) in conformity with the objects of consciousness (*cetya*)." (*PHṛ*, *sūtra* 5)

dimension gets lost.[17] From this translation/interpretation arises the danger of interpreting the complex multi-dimensionality of the non-dualistic world-view of the Kashmir Śaivites — as for example in the case of an early work of Mark Dyczkowski — merely in the reductive framework of a "psychology of absolute consciousness."[18] This holds also true if the word "consciousness" is qualified by adjectives like "pure," "absolute" or "divine," since the word "consciousness" remains always the central term.

Already in 1922, John Woodroffe had directed our attention to the problem of the translation of *cit* into any European language:

> The fundamental peculiarity of the Advaita Vedānta and therefore of its Śākta form, is the distinction which it draws between Mind and Consciousness in the sense of *Cit*; a word for which there is no exact equivalent in any European Language.[19]

He characterizes *cit* as the

> [. . .] common source and basis of both Mind and Matter. Chit is the infinite Whole (Pūrna) in which all that is finite, whether as Mind or Matter, is. This is the Supreme Infinite Experience, free of all finitization which is Pure Spirit as distinguished from Mind and Body.[20]

---

17. See Raimon Panikkar, *The Cosmotheandric Experience: Emerging Religious Consciousness*, ed. Scott Eastham, Maryknoll, N.Y.: Orbis Books, 1993.

18. Mark S.G. Dyczkowski, *The Doctrine of Vibration: An Analysis of the Doctrines and Practices of Kashmir Shaivism*, Indian edition, Delhi: Motilal Banarsidass, 1989, p. 44.

19. John Woodroffe, *The World As Power: Power as Mind*, Madras: Ganesh & Co., 1922, intro., p. v.

20. Ibid., pp. v-vi.

This has remarkable correspondences with the understanding of the nature of reality in Tibetan Buddhism, which to briefly examine might be helpful for our attempt to understand *cit* in Trika. In Tibetan Buddhism, consciousness is divided into three stages: gross, subtle, and very subtle. These subtle levels appear when the processes of discursive thinking dissolve. The dimension of the "very subtle" consciousness again is divided into four stages, denoted as the "four voids" (Tib. *stong pa bzhi*): the stages of black, red, white appearance and finally the "clear light" (Tib. *'od gsal*). These four stages represent four grades of the state of emptiness. The highest dimension of consciousness is in the Guhyasamāja-circle denoted as "fundamental innate mind of clear light" (Tib. *gnyug ma lhan cig skyes pa'i 'od gsal gyi sems*), in the Kālacakra-circle as "all-pervading *vajra*-space" (*mkha'khyab mkha'i rdo rje*), and in the Dzogchen tradition as *rigpa*.[21]

Its descriptions — non-dualistic wholeness, purity, beyond time and space, etc. — as well as the methods described to attain it with the help of the more subtle level of the body (the subtle *vajra*-body), including the generation of the "inner flame" (Tib. *tummo*) in the Chakrasaṁvara system, correspond in principle with non-dualistic Tāntric Śaivism. We must note that the latter denotes *cit* or *saṁvit* as the "Heart" from which everything arises, as the "goddess" (Śakti, Kālī) or the "supreme Lord," underlining in this way its divine dimension with theistic terms, while Tāntric Buddhism seems to underline especially its fundamental emptiness.

21. Cf. Dalai Lama, "Hitting the Essence in Three Words," in: *Dzogchen. The Heart Essence of the Great Perfection. Dzogchen Teachings given in the West by His Holiness the Dalai Lama*. Translated by Geshe Thupten Jinpa and Richard Barron, ed. Patrick Gaffney, Ithaca, New York: Snow Lion Publications, 2000, pp. 37-92; here: p. 54.

> In the terminology of Nāgārjuna's and Āryadeva's commentary to Guhasamāja, clear light is all-void. Since the fact that clear light mind is a level of mind that is devoid of all fleeting levels, or devoid of being them, affirms that clear light mind is something else or something other than this, clear light mind, as an other-voidness, is an affirming nullification.[22]

But we should avoid a simplifying opposition and also note the status of voidness in Trika.[23] According to Abhinavagupta, Śiva Himself is of the nature of void (*kha*), besides being of the nature of "light," "sound," etc. (cf. *Tantrāloka* 1.63). In regard to the non-substantiality or emptiness of the phenomenal reality, we find this statement in *Vijñāna-Bhairava* 134:

> How can the immutable Self have any knowledge or activity? All external objects depend on our knowledge of them. Therefore this world is void (*śūnya*).[24]

Swami Lakshman Joo states in his commentary on *Vijñāna-Bhairava* 113:

---

22. Dalai Lama, "Discourse on the Auto-commentary," in id.: *The Gelug/Kagyü Tradition of Mahamudra*, Ithaca, New York: Snow Lions Publications, 1997, p. 235.

23. On the seven stages of voidness according to *SvT* see Lilian Silburn: "Les sept Vacuités d'après le çivaisme du Cachemire": *Hermés* 6 (1969) pp. 213-21; on the spiritual experience of voidness according to *VBh* see Bettina Bäumer: "Attaining the Form of the Void: Śūnya in Vijñāna-Bhairava," in: id./John R. Dupuche (eds.), *Void and Fullness in the Buddhist, Hindu and Christian Traditions: Śūnya — Pūrṇa — Plerôma*, New Delhi: D.K. Printworld, 2005, pp. 159-70.

24. *Vijñāna-Bhairava. The Practice of Centring Awareness*, op. cit., p. 158.

> Whatever you find in this world, whatever you see, whatever you perceive in these 118 worlds, it is *atattvam*, it has no essence, there is nothing in that. It is just like a joke.[25]

In reality there is only *cit* or *saṁvit*, which appears in the state of the world. *Citi*, the divine power, which moves in her highest form in the infinite space, takes the form of the slightly limited knower, called *khecarī*,[26] "that which moves about in void (*kha*)";[27] it is that power "which moves at the plane of 'awakening' (*bodha*)". The state of *cit* (or the Bhairava-state) consists in supreme voidness:[28] the melting of everything — body, breath, thought constructs — in absolute nothingness, described as entering into "the heart of the void (*śūnya*) of *anuttara*" (*Vijñāna-Bhairava* 32) or becoming "an abode of void (*śūnya*)" (*Vijñāna-Bhairava* 120). "Nothingness" is to be distinguished from "not-existing" in the sense of nihilism; rather, it is the Centre, "the light between being and not-being" (cf. *Tantrāloka* 1.84); *citi*, the "great being" (*mahāsattā*, *Īśvarapratyabhijñākārikā* I. 5.14), ". . . is not to be understood as the counterpart of non-being (*abhāvāpratiyoginī*), [for, rather] it also pervades non-being." (*Īśvarapratyabhijñākārikā* I. 5.14 *v*).

We have seen that John Woodroffe — already in 1922 — directs our attention to the problem of translating the word *cit*. Forty years later Woodroffe is followed by Jaideva Singh, who mentions the untranslatability of *cit*. He has translated the word with the English term "consciousness," but, he

---

25. Ibid., p. 157.

26. Cf. *K*, p. 8.

27. Cf. *PTV*, p. 5. — "One of the most ancient Sanskrit words for void is *kha*, which means the nave of the wheel, the empty space which makes movement and dynamism possible." (Bäumer: "Attaining the Form of the Void," op. cit., p. 160).

28. Ibid., p. 152.

explains, only because there is no better word. He stresses, however, that *cit* is *not* "consciousness":

> The word Consciousness connotes subject-object relation, knower-known duality. But *Cit* is not relational. It is just the changeless principle of all changing experience. It is Parāsaṁvit. It has, so to speak, the immediacy of feeling where neither the "I," nor the "This" is distinguished.[29]

The term "consciousness" is — within modern, post-Cartesian conditions — usually related with the individual, human consciousness, associated with "subjectivity," "self-awareness," "reason," and "thinking." The background of the term is the modern notion of the "subject," developed in the West over a long, complex process.[30] The central rank of "subjective consciousness" in the modern philosophy of the West forms an essential dimension of the eurocentric conditions of the encounter between India and the West — making it all the more important to see that *cit* is not limited to the human realm. In the "world-experience" of Trika, *citi* is the "Goddess" *herself*, Śakti, the flashing, shining, pulsating, blissful, conscious source and core of reality as a whole. This core is not separated from the individual human being, nor from any single plant, animal, drop of water, stone, song, atom, inspiration, spiral nebula, word, touch, star, etc. In the Advaitic experience of Trika, one's own nature "consists of this one nature, which is the nature of all things" (*Tantrāloka* 1.141), or also that the "deity," especially characterized by *cit* and *ānanda*, is the

---

29. *Pratyabhijñahṛdayam: The Secret of Self-recognition,* trans. Jaideva Singh [1963], Delhi: Motilal Banarsidass, 4th rev. edn. 1982; reprint 1998, intro., p. 5.

30. See the famous study of Charles Taylor, *Sources of the Self: The Making of Modern Identity,* Cambridge, 1989.

"wholeness of all entities" (*bhāvavrāta*, *Tantrāloka* 1.332). In the words of the *Vijñāna-Bhairava*:

> *Cit* is in all bodies (*sarvadeheṣu*); there is no differentiation among anything. Therefore, if a person realizes that everything is full of that [*cit*], he conquers the world of becoming. — *Vijñāna Bhairava* 100[31]

Therefore, in my view, the English expression "consciousness," loaded with anthropocentric and rationalistic layers of meaning, is not suitable to express the content of the keyword *cit* in the context of Trika. How to translate *cit*? Contrary to the position of scholars such as Jay Garfield,[32] I prefer the practical solution of translating by not translating. For this I follow a strong precedent: the great scholar and *yogī* from Banaras, M.M. Gopinath Kaviraj,[33] who does not translate

---

31. Bettina Bäumer translates: "The One which is characterized as Consciousness is residing in all the bodies" (*Vijñāna-Bhairava: The Practice of Centring Awareness*, op. cit., p. 119).

32. Jay Garfield, translator of *Nāgārjuna's Mūlamadhyamakakārikā*, states, after expounding the problem of the translation of the Tibetan *rang bzhin* (Skr. *svabhāva*), which he renders with the English philosophical term "essence": "Retaining the original term is worse, as it conveys nothing to the reader not already conversant with Tibetan, Sanskrit, and Buddhist philosophy." (*The Fundamental Wisdom of the Middle Way: Nāgārjuna's Mūlamadhyamakakārikā*. Translation and Commentary by Jay L. Garfield, New York/Oxford: Oxford University Press, 1995, p. 89, fn. 4). But he holds back a "middle way": to retain the original term in the translation and to add notes about the different layers of meaning and its respective philosophical background to this term, the possible renderings in another language, in this way helping the reader to come to her own conclusions.

33. See, e.g. Gopinath Kaviraj: "Śākta Philosophy," in: *Selected Writings of M.M. Gopinath Kaviraj*, ed. M.M. Gopinath Kaviraj Centenary Celebrations Committee, Varanasi 1990, pp. 46-88.

keywords like *saṁvīt, caitanya, cit, citta, ātman, vimarśa,* etc. into English.

This approach, based on theories of translation which are inclined to make evident the "otherness", the strangeness, the difference of the original text, is particularly represented by Lawrence Venuti. He argues against any approach which seeks to create an easily readable translation by ignoring the dissimilarities between languages, religions and cultures and which instead creates the "illusion of transparency."[34]

Let us summarize: to translate *cit* or *saṁvit* with "consciousness" within the framework of a "psychology of consciousness" would lead to a reductive and misleading interpretation and understanding of the whole system. Possibly, it is a reading which echoes Buddhist doctrines of consciousness (*vijñāna*) as from the Yogācāra school, and

---

34. See Lawrence Venuti (ed.), *Rethinking Translation: Discourse, Subjectivity, Ideology*, New York/London: Routledge, 1992; id., "Translation and Formation of Cultural Identities": *Cultural Functions of Translation: Current Issues in Language and Society* 1, no.3 (1994), pp. 201-17; id., *The Translator's Invisibility: A History of Translation*, London/New York: Routledge, 1995; id., *The Scandals of Translation: Towards an Ethics of Difference*, New York/London, 1998; (ed.), *The Translation Studies Reader*, London/New York 2000, 2nd edn., 2004. — To this post-modern theoretical approach to translation see Rainer Guldin: "The (Un)translatibility of Cultures," in: *Studies in Communication Sciences* 2 (2003), pp. 109-34; L. Lane-Mercier, "Translating the Untranslatable. The translator's aesthetic, ideological and political responsibility": *Target* 9, no.1 (1997), pp. 43-68; Roger Hart, "Translating the Untranslatable. From Copula to Incommensurable Worlds," in: Lydia Liu (ed.), *Tokens of Exchange. The Problem of Translation in Global Circulations*, Durham, NC: Duke University Press, 1999, pp. 45-73; Kaisa Koskinen, *Beyond Ambivalence: Postmodernity and the Ethics of Translation* (Acta Universitatis Tamperensis; p. 774) Tampere: Tampere University Press, 2000 (dissertation).

thereby fails to notice that the Trika conception is quite different. On the other hand, it would be a trap to read *cit* or *saṁvit* within the framework of a Judeo-Christian theocentric model based on the descriptions of *cit* as "highest reality" and "light itself" (cf. *Tantrālokaviveka*, vol. 2, 427), thereby constructing an analogy to "God," the "highest reality," "the light itself." If as Western readers and interpreters we (unconsciously) understand the theological keyterms of Trika within a theocentric paradigm, within the "background" ("Hintergrund," Ludwig Wittgenstein)[35] of Western Christianity, then we would be in danger of merely shifting our Christian terms of "God" and "the Absolute" over the Trika tradition.[36] The world-view of Trika would be understood within the philosophical, theological, ontological framework of Judeo-Christian monotheism. Trika would be subjugated to a "normalizing discourse" (Mary L. Pratt),[37] in

---

35. According to Wittgenstein I do not have my view of life (Weltbild), ". . . because I have proved its correctness, also not, because I am convinced about its correctness. Rather, it is the conventional background, on which I distinguish between true and false." [I do not have my view of the world, ". . . weil ich mich von seiner Richtigkeit überzeugt habe; auch nicht, weil ich von seiner Richtigkeit überzeugt bin. Sondern es ist der überkommene Hintergrund, auf welchem ich zwischen wahr und falsch unterscheide."] (Ludwig Wittgenstein, *Über Gewissheit*, Werkausgabe Bd. 8, Frankfurt a. M. 1984, §. 94).

36. See the remarks (in the context of dialogue between Christianity and Buddhism) of John B. Cobb Jr., *Beyond Dialogue: Toward a Mutual Transformation of Christianity and Buddhism*, Philadelphia: Fortress Press, 1982, pp. 41-44.

37. Cf. Mary Louise Pratt, "Scratches on the Face of the Country; or: What Mr. Barrow Saw in the Land of the Bushmen," in: Henry Louis Gates Jr. (ed.), *'Race', Writing, and Difference*, Chicago: University of Chicago Press, 1985, pp. 135-62; here: p. 139.

which its "otherness," the "alterity" would be invisibly eliminated, maybe even despite the best dialogical intention. In this way, exactly the important 'other' experience and other world-view of Trika would escape our notice. As Western readers we would fail to notice that the authors of Trika use the words *cit, saṁvit, anuttara, unmeṣa, pratibhā, parāvāk,* etc. to talk about something which is different from our usual concepts and categories, something which we did not imagine or expect. We would fail to encounter "the New." Maybe understanding could flow the other way round, so that Christians understand their own tradition in a new, transformed way, from the perspective of this newness of the Advaitic systems, as in the case of Swami Abhishiktananda (Henri Le Saux), who learned to see the biblical heritage in the light of the Advaitic experience.[38]

Is Vimarśa "Reflective Awareness"?

Vimarśa is another keyword of non-dualistic Śaivism of Kashmir. Kṣemarāja provides an important definition of *dhyāna* and at the same time of *vimarśa* in his commentary on *Netratantra* 8.15:

> . . . The great Lord (*parameśvara*), a condensation of *cit* and *ānanda* (*cidānandaghana*), is recognized by the wise people (*budhaḥ*), the realizer of reality (*tattvajñaḥ*), by *vimarśa* a (. . . *arthaccidānandaghanaṁ parameśvaraṁ dhyātvā vimarśya ye budhāstattvajñaste, tacceti tadvimarśātmaiva* . . .).[39]

---

38. See especially Abhishiktananda, *Ascent to the Depth of the Heart. The Spiritual Diary (1948-73) of Swami Abhishiktananda (Dom Henri Le Saux)*. A selection, edited with introduction and notes, by Raimon Panikkar. Transl. David Fleming/James Stuart, Delhi: ISPCK, 1998.

39. *Netratantra with the Commentary Uddyota by Kṣemarāja*, vol. 1 (KSTS; 46), Bombay 1926-1939, p. 184.

Any translation of *vimarśa* which would express the rational character of the act of *vimarśa* would not fit in this context, as the meaning would be that the "great Lord," the reality itself, is realized by a rational, intellectual act. In the context of the Yoga of the Śaivites it is clear that "the Reality," the true essence of the world and the ground of reason, is realized in a trans-rational dimension, above the rational faculties. In the Western mysticism of the middle ages this difference is expressed in the two human faculties called *ratio* (Lat. "reason") and *intellectus* (the faculty for a trans-rational cognition). These translations which interpret *vimarśa* within a rational framework, we find in the case of the Austrian indologist Erich Frauwallner who translates the word with the German terms "Betrachtung" (consideration, reflection) or "Urteil" (judgement), but also in the case of the common English translation "reflective awareness" (for example by Raffaele Torella or Mark Dyczkowski).[40] Words which are derived from "reflection" have the connotations of the functioning of reason (mental consideration, discussion). In fact Torella, as he informs us,[41] adopts the term "reflective awareness" from the philosopher Bimal Matilal who uses *vimarśa* for the translation of the term *anuvyavasāya* (inner perception).[42]

But *vimarśa* happens exactly when the activity of reason ceases. Utpaladeva states explicitly: The Self-recognition as the highest "I" (*aham*), the essence of Light, is not a thought-construct (*ahaṁpratyavamarśa yaḥ prakāśātmapi . . . nāsau vikalpaḥ*, *Īśvarapratyabhijñākārikā* I. 6.1). The highest form of *vimarśa* on

40. Cf. Torella, *ĪPK*, intro., p. xxiv, fn. 32.

41. Ibid.

42. Bimal Matilal, "Indian Theories of Knowledge and Truth. Review Article of J. Mohanty: Gaṅgeśa's Theory of Truth": *PEW* 18 (1968) p. 4; quoted in Torella, ibid.

the level of *cit* (*cittattvaṁ*) is clearly distinguished from the *vimarśa* of the (limited) cognizing subject, defined as a conceptual activity (*vikalpa*) which generates the distinction of subject and object (cf. *Īśvarapratyabhijñākārikā* I. 6.4-5).

Vimarśa in its highest form is defined by Utpaladeva as ". . . the primary essence of light" (*prakāśasya mukhya ātmā pratyavamarśaḥ*, *Īśvarapratyabhijñākārikā* I. 5.11 *v*) by which the Highest Light (*prakāśa*) — the Self (*ātma*), the true nature of everything (cf. 5.12) — is sensitive, lively, "conscious" (ibid., cf. 5.12) and recognizes itself as the "absolute subject," the highest "I" (*aham*). Utpaladeva takes a new run in the next verse: *vimarśa* is the essential nature of *citi*, the highest word (*citiḥ pratyavamarśātmā parāvāk svarasoditā*, I. 5.13a). It is the "luminous vibrating" (*sphurattā*), the "great being" (*mahāsattā*), beyond space and time, the "heart of the supreme Lord," insofar as it is His "essence" (*sā sphurattā mahāsattā deśakālaviśeṣiṇī* | *saiṣā sāratayā proktā hṛdayaṁ parameṣṭinaḥ*, 5.14). *Vimarśa* is the self-recognition of the Highest (the absolute Light),[43] identical with the act of the lightning, sudden, joyful astonishment (*camatkāra*) in which the Self realizes itself (cf. *Īśvarapratyabhijñākārikā* I. 5.11 *v*; *Pratyabhijñāhṛdaya*, Comm. *sūtra* 11).[44]

We can observe here the integration of two levels of *vimarśa* or of two perspectives on *vimarśa* which are ultimately non-dualistic:

(a) a "metaphysical" level, about the inner nature of the Highest (*anuttara*) as the union of the absolute One, pure unchanging Light (Śiva) and the absolute

---

43. Cf. Jaideva Singh, "the Self-Consciousness of the Supreme" (*PHṛ*, p. 171, glossary).

44. *PHṛ*, p. 77.

Dynamics and Power, the Recognition of the Light (Śakti); and

(b) on the level of the practitioner — the supreme spiritual state of the recognition of one's own true nature as the "condensed mass of *cit* and *ānanda*" and Light.

Torella seems to interpret these central statements in the *Īśvarapratyabhijñākārikā* within an epistemological framework, understanding *cit* as "consciousness" and *vimarśa* as "reflective awareness." He assumes an "analytical element in *vimarśa*"[45] and states the influence of the doctrine of the grammarian Bhartṛhari. The meaning of *vimarśa* in the context of limited cognition is also applied to *vimarśa* in its spiritual sense. These passages (*Īśvarapratyabhijñākārikā* I. 5.13 ff) unfold into a theory of perception and cognition, and the spiritual meaning gets lost. In my view the translation is based on a certain "prejudice," an implicit basic assumption in the sense of Gadamer's *Truth and Method*.[46] This prejudice is continuously confirmed by the translation of these keywords.

It seems that the translation/interpretation of the word *vimarśa* is an excellent example of the hermeneutical difficulties met when we, as representatives of the modern secularized Europe, encounter a spiritual-philosophical tradition of the Indian middle-ages. For centuries, the tradition of a mystical theology, philosophy and practice in Western Europe has been interrupted; the "life element" of these terms, ideas and practices does not exist any more, and so naturally modern European indologists interpret the "other reason" of the

45. Torella, *ĪPK*, intro., p. xxiv, fn. 32.

46. Cf. Hans-Georg Gadamer, *Wahrheit und Methode. Grundzüge einer philosophischen Hermeneutik* (Gesammelte Werke; 1) Tübingen: Mohr Siebeck, 1990, pp. 281 ff ("Prejudices as the condition to understand").

Śaivites within the framework of modern rationalistic thinking. It is absorbed by the background of the modern world-view. The challenge is to reconstruct the thought of the Śaivites against an already existing translation-history in the West.

Remarks on Tāntric Language and its Interpretation with the Example of Tantrāloka 5.94-95

One of the dominant characteristics of the language and rhetoric of Abhinavagupta in *Tantrāloka* (= *TĀ*) is his use of metaphor. Examples are:

— heart (*hṛdaya, hṛd*): *TĀ* 1.1; 1.176; 3.69.210.215.222; 4.199; 5.20.23.52.60; 26.65; 29.71 *passim*

— lotus (*kamala*): e.g. *TĀ* 29.151

— abode (*dhāman*): e.g. *TĀ* 2.44; 5.94-95; 3.111.133.143.166.171

— wave (*ūrmi*): e.g. *TĀ* 1.116; 3.103; 4.184

— mouth of the *yoginī* (*yoginīvaktra*): e.g. *TĀ* 3.94; 5.119; 29.40.124cd

— heart of the *yoginī* (*yoginīhṛdaya*): e.g. *TĀ* 5.73.121-122

— fire (*agni, vahni*): e.g. *TĀ* 3.227; 5.72

— sun (*sūrya*)

— moon (*candra, śaśadhara*): e.g. *TĀ* 29.153cd

— nectar (*amṛta*): e.g. *TĀ* 26.63

— triangle (*trikoṇa*): e.g. *TĀ* 3.95

— juice (*rasa*): e.g. *TĀ* 1.119.121; 26.61; 29.11.68

By using metaphors, Abhinavagupta refers to the language of the Tantras. He employs these words not only as single metaphors, but rather builds whole *Bild-Felder* (image-scapes), in which the resonances between the different images overlap each other and through this create whirring and vibrating patterns.

The interpretation of this metaphorical language proceeds from the underlying understanding of a "metaphor". While older opinions express the assumption that the "actual" meaning is replaced by the metaphorical expression (the replacement-model of the metaphor), in recent metaphor theory the specific, intrinsic value of the metaphor itself is stressed. Therefore, does Peter Szondi underline that literary metaphorism would represent an independent "mode of experience of reality."[47]

Applied to Abhinavagupta, one could say that the multidimensionality of his language is an adequate expression of the experience of the multidimensionality of reality from a yogic perspective. This becomes especially visible in the case of the pervasion of spiritual and sexual experience. Here it would be a reductive understanding of the metaphor to conceive it as mere code; then the point would be only to decode the "actual" (e.g. sexual) meaning. Conversely, it would also be a mistake to dig out the spiritual dimension of every word or sentence as the "true" meaning. The actual task is to dissolve the tension in neither direction, but rather to accept as intentional that the several layers of meaning do not merely overlay each other, but rather pervade each other. One could use the image of a studio, wherein a multi-channel recording system allows the digital separation and respective treatment of the individual instruments or voices. This would be a metaphor for the artificial separation of the particular lines of meaning, in which one — according to one's own pre-understanding and "prejudice" in the sense of Gadamer — one would fade out a track and intensify another. The hermeneutic attitude which I would prefer would be — to

47. Peter Szondi, *Einführung in die literarische Hermeneutik*, Frankfurt a. M. 1975, p. 89.

remain within this *Bild-Feld* — a live concert in which one hears all the instruments and voices together as an integrated sound-event.

To hear and to accept as intentional the integral sound of the language of Abhinavagupta in his *Tantrāloka* would, in my opinion, correspond with the general principle of understanding, the principle of "hermeneutic equity" ("hermeneutische Billigkeit," *aequitas hermeneutica*).[48] It is one of the basic principles of classical Western hermeneutics: on the one hand the assumption of the consistency, appropriateness and truth of the statements of Abhinavagupta with regard to the "perfection of the signs" (*Vollkommenheit der Zeichen*), and on the other hand, the assumption that the author is able to express that which is appropriate in an adequate form with regard to the "perfection of the originator of the signs"(*Vollkommenheit des Urhebers der Zeichen*). The opposite of the application of this hermeneutic principle would be an attitude towards the text of Abhinavagupta which presupposes that he wasn't really able to name the "actual thing," and that it is now the duty of the interpreter to work out what he "really" wanted to say — be it towards the "mystical," the "rational-philosophical," or the "sexual." Since all these levels overlap within the *Tantrāloka*, every interpreter will find proofs for their own interpretative paradigm in the text. Instead of interpreting Abhinavagupta's text according to one's own expectations or to decode it according to one's own pre-understanding, the task would be to accept

48. Georg Friedrich Meier, *Anfangsgründe aller schönen Wissenschaften*, Halle im Magdeburgischen, 2. verb. Auflage, 1754-1759, § 516; quoted from: Oliver Scholz, *Verstehen und Rationalität. Untersuchungen zu den Grundlagen von Hermeneutik und Sprachphilosophie* (Philosophische Abhandlungen; 76) Frankfurt a. M. 1999; 2nd edn., 2001, p. 55.

Abhinava's language to be intentionally composed. The new, illuminating cognition awaits precisely within his particular use of language — something which one did not expect.

In particular, Tāntric literature is a prominent field for reductive, one-sided interpretations — as in the case of John Woodroffe *alias* Arthur Avalon, one of the most read researchers of tantrism in the twentieth century — which ignore all morally offensive passages or difficult parts and try to domesticate, "deodorize," rationalize and clean the texts.[49] Partly it is a reaction to an already reductive reading in the opposite direction, in which Tāntric texts are disparaged as morally reprehensible and decadent by British orientalists, travellers or missionaries.[50]

A prominent contemporary example for this lust to discover — in the manner of a detective — that which

49. Cf. Hugh B. Urban, "The Extreme Orient: The Construction of Tantrism as a Category in the Orientalist Imagination": *Religion* 29 (1999), pp. 123-46; here: pp. 124f. — On John Woodroffe see R.K. Dasgupta, "A British Worshipper of the Mother": *The Statesman*, Puja Supplement (2 October 1959); J. Duncan Derrett, "A Juridical Fabrication of early British India: The Mahānirvāṇa Tantra", in: id., *Essays in Classical and Modern Hindu Law. Vol. 2: Consequences of the Intellectual Exchange with the Foreign Powers*, Leiden: Brill, 1977, pp. 197-242; Hugh B. Urban: "The Strategic Uses of an Esoteric Text: The Mahānirvāṇa Tantra": *South Asia* 18 (1995), pp. 55-82; Kathleen Taylor, *Sir John Woodroffe, Tantra and Bengal: 'An Indian Soul in an European Body'*? Richmond, Surrey: Curzon, 2001; Jeffrey Kripal, "Being John Woodroffe: Mythical Reflections on the Postcolonial Study of the Hindu Tantra", in: José Ignacio Cabezón/Sheila Devaney (eds.), *Anxious Subjectivities: Personal Identity, Truth, and the Study of Religion*, New York: Routledge, 2004.

50. Cf. Urban, *The Extreme Orient*, op. cit., pp. 124f.

ostensibly is "essential" in the texts of Trika are the theses of David Gordon White:[51] he elaborately defends the idea that the ritual with sexual fluids would constitute the "true" nucleus of the whole system, while the whole philosophical and theological presentation (what he calls "Tāntric mysticism") would be a mere "superstructure" (*Überbau*) to legitimate the ritual in the Brāhmanical surrounding, reduced to mere "second-order reflections."[52] In his view,

> . . . it was sexual practice and in particular the ritualized consumption of sexual fluids that gave medieval South Asian Tantra its specificity — in other words, that differentiated Tantra from all other forms of religious practice of the period.[53]

He interprets the approach of Abhinavagupta and other authors as a "sublimation" of this "hard core" Tāntric practice ". . . into a type of meditative asceticism whose aim it was to realize a transcendent subjectivity."[54] This transformation was, in his view, a strategy of elite Brāhmanical circles to win a bigger support base among the high-caste householders in Kashmir — a transformation "which often systematically distorts the meaning of the original practice itself."[55] Its extensive repetition cannot conceal the fact that his thesis of an "original practice" — the oral consumption of sexual fluids

---

51. Cf. David Gordon White, "Transformations in the Art of Love: Kāmakalā Practices in Hindu Tantric and Kaula Traditions": *History of Religions* 38, no.2 (1998), pp. 172-98; id.: *Kiss of the Yogini: 'Tantric Sex' in its South Asian Context*, Chicago: The University of Chicago Press, 2003.
52. White, *Kiss of the Yoginī*, op. cit., p. 13.
53. Ibid., p. 219.
54. Ibid., p. 16.
55. Ibid.; cf. p. xii.

as power substances forming the core of Tantrism, of which the approach of Trika Śaivism would be a distortion — is mere speculation. Without doubt Abhinavagupta and his Trika school represents a peak in the development of Hindu Tantrism over the ages; the distinctive character of his Tāntric philosophy is exactly the inseparable pervasion of the spiritual and sexual dimensions, as the *Tantrāloka* demonstrates from its benedictory verse to the end. To impute to Abhinavagupta a "meditative asceticism" does no justice to his work at all, as we will see in ch. 3 especially in the context of chapter 29 of the *Tantrāloka* regarding the sexual ritual. This imputation can be only understood as a stratagem of ideological argumentation, i.e. an argumentation where one's interest (to demonstrate the ritual with sexual fluids as core of Tantrism, or, on another level, to make manifest a revolutionary thesis in the field of academic research on Hindu Tantrism) governs cognition. White does not grow weary of criticizing a reductive approach towards Tantrism, especially by contemporary Westerners.[56] But it is obvious that his thesis — "Tāntric sex" in the sense of oral consumption of sexual fluids as the core of the system — represents itself a blatant reduction which simultaneously reflects and legitimates the reductive approach of many Western Tāntric circles.

As a specific example of Abhinavagupta's literary style found throughout the *Tantrāloka*, I submit two verses from chapter 5 (*TĀ* 5.94-95), wherein the textual mechanics become especially visible. The Sanskrit text shall be given first, to give an impression of its poetic concentration and condensation (as it consists almost entirely of forms of the word *dhāman*), followed by a translation. *Dhāman* means "dwelling-place, house, abode, domain, especially seat of the gods; favourite

56. See ibid., preface.

thing or person; power, strength, majesty, glory, splendour, light" (cf. MW 514). Silburn translates *dhāman* as "realm, domain"; she distinguishes two domains to which the sexual act can lead: a "worldly" union leads to the lower domain (*adhodhāman*), while a "mystical" union leads to the superior domain (*ūrdhvadhāman*) when the awakened *kuṇḍalinī* draws the secondary energies of the senses to the "centre," the median channel, called *madhyacakra* or *suṣumnā*.[57] In their French translation of the *TĀ*, Padoux and Silburn render *dhāman* as "manifestation lumineuse de l'energie"[58] and quote Gonda's translation of *dhāman*: "a holder and container of numinous potency."[59] In verse *TĀ* 5.94cd-95 they therefore translate *dhāman* as "la puissance" (power, dominion).[60] Pt. H.N. Chakravarty connects the aspects of "power," "abode" and "light" and translates *dhāman* as "glory of light" or "glorious abode of light."[61] Therefore, the verse could be translated like this:

> *dhāmasthaṁ dhāmamadhyasthaṁ dhāmodaraputīkṛtam* ॥ 94cd ॥
> *dhāmnā tu bodhayeddhāma dhāma dhāmantagaṁ kuru* ।
> *taddhāma dhāmagatyā tuṁ bhedyaṁ dhāmāntamāntaram* ॥ 95 ॥

> Established in the abode of light (*dhāmasthaṁ*), established in the centre of the abode of light (*dhāmamadhyasthaṁ*), enclosed (*puṭīkṛtam*) by the belly (*udara*) of the abode of light one shall awake (*bodhayet*) in the abode of light through the abode of light. Then one shall contrive (*kuru*) the abode of light to enter into the abode of light. That (*tad*) abode of light

---

57. Cf. *K*, p. 186.
58. *Lumiére*, p. 169, fn. 46.
59. Jan Gonda, *The Meaning of the Sanskrit Term "dhāman"*, Amsterdam 1967; quoted in: ibid.
60. *Lumiére*, p. 286.
61. Oral information, Varanasi (31 October, 2004).

> should be entered into (*bhedyaṁ*) by the movement (*gatyā*) of the abode of light, [till one is] at the end (*antam*) in the interior (*antara*) of the abode of light. — *Tantrāloka* 5.94-95

At first sight it is obvious that it is impossible to render the brevity of the Sanskrit text into English. What does the passage mean? The keyword is obviously the word *dhāman*. It unites the following strata of meaning:

— abode, house, realm;

— might, power, glory, majesty;

— light, brilliance; and

— seat of the gods.

But the literal meanings of the word do not help our understanding so long as we do not know in which precise sense the word is used in this context, to which "abode" it refers to or to whose "majesty" or "might," etc. On the other hand, the choice of the meaning "seat of the gods" would be arbitrary; a formulation as "enclosed by the belly of the seat of the gods" is unintelligible. So, at the first glance the two verses look like a play, a riddle.

A key for the interpretation is that Abhinavagupta imitates a verse from a tantra, the *Nityaṣoḍaśikārṇava* (*NSA*),[62] one of the most important and oldest preserved Śrīvidyā texts, commented upon by Jayaratha under the title *Vāmakeśvarīmatam*.[63] The verse reads:[64]

62. I would like to thank Pt. H. N. Chakravarty for this discovery. He has supported Louise M. Finn in her translation of the Tantra into English in the eighties in Varanasi (see fn. 65).

63. *Vāmakeśvarīmatam with Rājānaka Jayaratha's Commentary* (KSTS; 66) Srinagar 1945.

64. *Nityaśoḍaśikārṇava with two Commentaries*, ed. V.V. Dvivedi (Yoga-Tantra-Granthamālā; 1) Varanasi 1968, p. 242.

> *kāmasthaṁ kāmamadhyasthaṁ kāmodaraputīkṛtam* ।
> *kāmena kāmayet kāmaṁ kāmeṣu nikṣipet* ॥ — *NSA* 4.45

Finn translates the verse in the following way:

> Through desire one should lead to the goal desirably that abiding in the middle of desire established in desire enfolded in the womb of desire. One should cast desire into the desires. Making it desirable with desire, the one who is abiding in desire may throw the universe into turmoil.[65]

Abhinavagupta replaces the word *kāma* by *dhāman*. *Kāma* means "desire, wish, longing; love, especially sexual love or sensuality, affection, object of desire or of love or of pleasure" etc. (cf. MW 271). Jayaratha comments: "in *kāma*" means "in the *mūlādhāra*," the centre of power (*cakra*) in the realm of the sexual organs, and "residing in the centre of *kāma*" means "in the vagina (*yoni*)." Afterwards he mentions the expression *sparśa-liṅga*, which is interpreted by Finn as the male sexual organ.[66]

We assume that Abhinavagupta could presuppose that the original gleams through the palimpsest. But even if we interpret *dhāman* before the background of the original verse and its meaning and assign a sexual meaning to *dhāman*, still the meaning of the passage is not clear. Abhinavagupta is obviously indicating two different "glorious, powerful, illuminating abodes" when he says "One should contrive the abode of light to enter into the abode of light" and "In that abode of light it should be entered by the movement of the abode of light." What are these two realms?

---

65. *The Kulacūḍāmaṇi Tantra and the Vāmakeśvara Tantra with the Jayaratha Commentary*. Introduced, translated and annotated by Louise M. Finn, Wiesbaden: Harrassowitz, 1986, p. 344.

66. Ibid., p. 345, fn. 121.

In his detailed commentary Jayaratha gives us the next key for the interpretation of the two verses *TĀ* 5.94-95:[67]

— First he mentions that the supreme achievement of a *yogī* is freedom (*svātantrya*).

— Afterwards he explains *udara* (belly) with: "the own reality of that" (*svatattvaṁtena*).[68]

— *puṭīkṛtam* = "enclosed from all sides; to unite inseparably (*nityāviyuktam*)."

— *dhāmnā* = "the limitation, which is constantly re-established and manifests itself."

— *dhāma* = "one should awake (*bodhayet*) the Self (*ātmānaṁ*)."

— *dhāmnā* = "the root of *kula* (*kulamūla*), the base of birth (*janmādhāra*, the female sexual organ), which is established in the centre (*madhye sthitaṁ*)."

---

67. *TĀV*, vol. III, p. 1022.

68. *Udara* probably is an allusion to the expression "the belly of the fish" (*matsyadarīmata*), which denotes a certain condition in which one rests at the origin of the two movements of emanation and resorption of the universe (the spontaneous *kramamudrā*), as the belly of a fish automatically contracts and expands. At the same time it refers to the contraction and expansion of the sexual organs in the sexual act (cf. *K*, p. 58).

The metaphor "the belly of the fish" occurs in *PTlv* in a quotation at the end of commentary on verse 16: "*kulabījakam asyāntarbhogaḥ kālam kṛṣādiṣu*" (*La Parātrīśikālaghuvṛtti de Abhinavagupta. Texte traduit et annoté par André Padoux* [Publications de l'Institut de Civilisation Indienne, Série IN-8, Fasc. 38] Paris 1975; Sanskrit text: pp. 49-63; here: p. 56). Muller-Ortega translates the quotation like this: "The *kula*-seed is within the belly of the fish. Its fruition, that is, the Kaula, is available during the *kṛta-yuga* — the Golden Age — and so on." (Muller-Ortega, *Triadic Heart*, op. cit., p. 217 [Appendix: "The Short Gloss on the Supreme, The Queen of the Three"]).

— *dhāma* = "the power of *prāṇa* (*prāṇaśakti*)."

— *dhāmnā* = "by sexual passion (*rati*) and attachment (*āsaktyā*)."

— *dhāmnā* = "*citi* should be driven on to attain the realm (*pada*) beyond the fourth (*turyātīta*)."

— "the end" (*anta*) = "the attainment of supreme excellence (*kāṣṭā*) in the form of direct perception (*sākṣāt*), because one becomes one with it (*ekarūpatayā*)."

— *āntaram* = "the subject (*pramātṛ*) is the object most to attain."

— *dhāmāntam* = "the last realm, empty (*śūnya*) of all accidental qualities (*upādhi*) of knowledge of the subject and of cognizable objects, of the nature of the power of will (*icchāśakti*), nothing but *vimarśa*. One shall take refuge (*āśrayet*) in it, so that it develops itself (*praroha*)."

The commentary itself is encoded and not immediately clear. But it articulates in which way the dimension of the interiorized sexual act and the dimension of the awakening and unfolding of the Self — the states of the "fourth" (*turīya*) and then "beyond the fourth" (*turyātīta*), "beyond every state"[69] — pervade each other in an indissoluble way. The

---

69. *K*, p. 216 (glossary). One attains this state "beyond every state" after the experience of *sparśa*, the stage of Self-pervasion (*ātmavyāpti*), the "fourth state" (*turīya*), evoked by the piercing of the *cakra* at the skull cap (*brahmarandhra* or inner *dvādaśānta*), when the Power (*kuṇḍalinī*) rises higher and pierces the supreme or cosmic *dvādaśānta* or *sahasrāra*, twelve fingers above *brahmarandhra*, consisting of the fusion (*sāmarasya*) of Śiva and power (Śakti), "two aspects of the absolute Reality that are light on the one hand and the vibrating resonance on the other." (*K*, →

point of the passage is the pervasion of these dimensions; it is precisely this that this way of speaking strives to express. The fluidity and transluminescence of the language reflects the experience that, during the spiritual ascent, the apparently solid reality of the body, the "I," and the phenomenal world melts, becomes more and more light and transparent, more and more fluid, until only its core remains — the vibrating, shining resonance of the Power — and finally merges, fuses, flows into the One, the "Supreme Śiva" (Parama-Śiva).

One would miss this point if one would try to dissolve this complete immersion (*sāmarasya*) of the two dimensions, be it by the reduction to the sexual or to the spiritual level. At the same time we see from this passage the step which Abhinavagupta takes in evolution from the *NSA*. While there, according to Jayaratha, we simply find an encrypted sexual meaning, Abhinavagupta integrates in a more complex way a sexual and a spiritual process — the core of the *kulayāga*. Seen in this light, the fundamental statement of the two verses *TĀ* 5.94-95 is this: one shall, by means of the union within the *dhāman* (= vagina), enter into the *dhāman* (= the light of the awakened Self), or: one shall induce the awakening of the mighty, illuminating *dhāman* of the Self by the mighty *dhāman* of the "base of birth." The radical and provoking Tāntric

---

→ p. 31). This realm of innumerable energies, represented by the picture of a "thousand-spoked wheel," ". . . cannot be attained through any amount of self-effort, for it is the very nature of things (*svābhāvika*)" (ibid.). Someone who reaches "beyond the fourth," the divine pervasion (*śivavyāpti*) ". . . is no other than Divine life, Bliss, and true Love" (*K*, p. 64). Here one finds ". . . all things fusing into Parama-Śiva. This is *turiyātīta*, beyond the Fourth state, where the divine essence is perceived as all-pervading . . . at the heart of this one-savoured unity [*sāmarasya*], Self and universe merge into the Whole in perfect harmony." (*K*, p. 167)

hermeneutics consists in that both — the female sexual organ and the realm of the Self — are denoted by the same term "abode of light" (*dhāman*), since one can reach the supreme plane by means of the interiorized union within "the base of birth." One can reach the "Heart" (*hṛdaya*) of Reality, the "heart of the *yoginī*" (*yoginīhṛdaya*), "the heart of supreme repose" (*viśrānti*, cf. *TĀ* 5.120cd), "when one's entire life becomes nothing but divine energy (*kula*)"[70] via the "heart of the *yoginī*" (= vagina, cf. *TĀ* 5.121).

Jayaratha gives a hint regarding the way this happens: through *prāṇaśakti*. In his commentary on *TĀ* 3.94-95ab, where Abhinavagupta talks about the "triangle" (*trikoṇa*), Jayaratha connects the female sexual organ (*yoginīvaktra*, "the mouth of the *yoginī*," or *janmādhāra*) with "the power of *prāṇa*" (life, life force, vital breath). *Prāṇaśakti* begins to rise as *kuṇḍalinī* and finally brings about the state of the "fourth" (*turīya*) and "beyond the fourth" (*turyātīta*): "From there the supreme Śakti ascends. As it was said: 'She of crooked form (*kuṭilarūpiṇī*) arises from *śṛṁgāṭapīṭha*.' "[71] In the ascent of *kuṇḍalinī*, the lower triangle of energies in the realm of the sexual organs moves up to the upper triangle of energies in the uppermost *cakra*, *brahmarandhra*.[72] Afterwards Abhinavagupta alludes to this process, when he says: one shall contrive *dhāman* to move into the *dhāman*. The "centre" of the *dhāman* could indicate the "point" (*bindu*) in the centre of the lower triangle (*trikoṇa*, *mūlādhāra*), around which the "crooked" is coiled in three-and-a-half windings and from where she ascends, up to the *bindu* in *brahmarandhra*. The "enclosing" (cf. *puṭīkṛtam*) could refer to it, and at the same time to the enclosing of the male

70. K, p. 168.

71. *TĀV*, vol. II, p. 456. — On *śṛṁgāṭapīṭha* see ch. 3 fn. 330.

72. Cf. K, p. 33.

sexual organ, the penis, by the *dhāman* (the vagina), which are compared with the moving, pulsating "belly of the fish." All these possible interpretations underline the very dense — and to some extent, impenetrable — texture (*tantra*) of meanings.[73]

---

73. Another prominent and important example for this superimposition of dimensions would be *Tantrāloka* 1.1, the first *Maṅgalaśloka*. The importance of the verse is demonstrated by the fact that Abhinavagupta uses it also as the opening verse of *PTV* and *MVV*, as well as of *TS*, a shortened presentation of the content of *TĀ*, and of *Tantroccaya*, a short version of *TS* [*editio princeps*: Raniero Gnoli, Raniero and Raffaele Torella: "The Tantroccaya of Abhinavagupta," in: P. Daffinā (ed.), *Indo Sino Tibetica. Studi in onore di Luciano Petech* (Studia Orientali; 9) Roma 1990, pp. 153-59; an English translation was made by Francesco Sferra, "The Tantroccaya by Abhinavagupta. An English Translation": *AION* 59 (1999), pp. 109-33]. About the verse Jayaratha says that it embodies the whole Trika doctrine, which he (Abhinavagupta) then unfolds in the *TĀ* (cf. *TĀV*, vol. II, p. 3). On this verse see Alexis Sanderson, "A Commentary on the Opening Verses of the Tantrasāra of Abhinavagupta," in: Sadananda Das/Ernst Fürlinger (eds.), *Sāmarasya: Studies in Indian Arts, Philosophy and Interreligious Dialogue — in Honour of Bettina Bäumer*, New Delhi: D.K. Printworld, 2005, pp. 89-148. Here is an attempt to translate this verse:

    "May my heart (*hṛdaya*) completely flash up (*saṁsphuratāt*), embodying (*kula*) the nectar (*amṛta*) of the Highest (*anuttara*), one (*mayam*) with the state (*bhāva*) of emission (*visarga*), manifested (*sphurita*) by the union (*yāmala*) of both (*tadubhaya*): The mother (*jananī*), grounded (*āśraya*) in the pure (*vimalā*) energy (*kalā*), shining (*mahā*) in the ever-new (*abhinava*) emanation (*sṛṣṭi*); The father (*janakaḥ*), whose nature (*tanuśca*) is full (*bharita*), who shines (*rucir*), hidden through five faces (*pañcamukhagupta*)."

    A second meaning of the first part of the verse is implied, similar to a palimpsest:

    "Vimalā, my mother, whose greatest joy was my birth, and Siṁhagupta, my father, [both] all-embracing." (*TĀ*, 1.1)

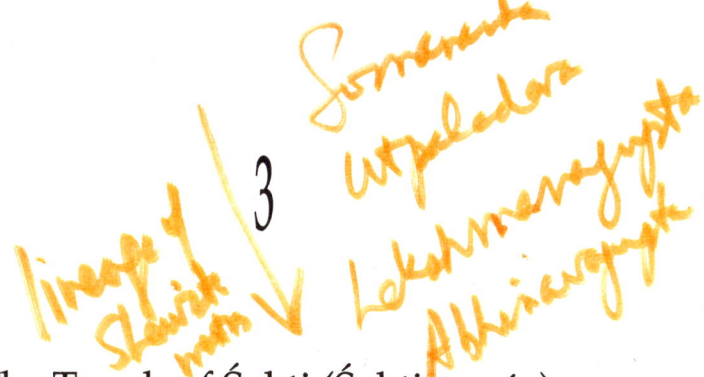

3

The Touch of Śakti (Śaktisparśa)

Selected Texts of Non-dualistic Śaivism of Kashmir

O God! Let me become like a drum, silent in myself,
ever awaiting your divine touch.
An instrument only of your will,
ever ready to resonate with your song.
— Swami Lakshman Joo
(Ishvar Ashram, Srinagar, 1979)[1]

Utpaladeva: Śivastotrāvalī with the Commentary (Vivṛtti) by Kṣemarāja

Introduction

Utpaladeva (tenth century) represents the non-dualistic traditions within Śaivism in Kashmir, especially the so-called Pratyabhijñā-school, one of the main streams of Kashmir Śaivism at this time. This school gets its name from his main work, the *Īśvarapratyabhijñākārikā*, the "Verses about the Recognition of the Lord."[2] The first work of this school is the *Śivadṛṣṭi* of Utpaladeva's teacher Somānanda (ninth/tenth

---

1. Quoted in: *The Mālinī*, July 1998, p. 29.

2. *The Īśvarapratyabhijñākārikā of Utpaladeva with the Author's Vṛtti* (= *ĪPK*). Critical edition and annotated translation by Raffaele Torella, corrected edition, Delhi: Motilal Banarsidass, 2002.

century).[3] Utpaladeva is the teacher of Lakṣmaṇagupta, who is Abhinavagupta's teacher of the Pratyabhijñā philosophy. At the beginning of his *Tantrāloka* (1.10-11), Abhinavagupta pays respect to the line of his teachers: Somānanda, Utpaladeva, Lakṣmaṇagupta. He talks about his "grand-teacher" Utpaladeva with great respect as "the master" (cf. *Tantrāloka* 9.279ab).

Utpaladeva's works consist of a commentary to the book of his teacher Somānanda, the *Śivadṛṣṭivṛtti*, as well as the *Sambandhasiddhi* and its auto-commentary, a text about the traditional philosophical problem of "relation" (*sambandha*), discussing Buddhist theories of "relation," especially Dharmakīrti's *Sambandhaparīkṣā*.[4] In addition, his short philosophical works are *Ajaḍapramātṛsiddhi*, developing his concept of subjectivity, and the *Īśvarasiddhi*, about the question of a "highest knowing subject."[5] Utpaladeva has also written two commentaries to his *Īśvarapratyabhijñākārikā*; the short commentary (*Vṛtti*) is preserved, the longer (*Vivṛtti*) is known only from fragments.[6]

---

3. *Śivadṛṣṭi of Somānanda, with Utpaladeva's Vṛtti* (KSTS; 54) Srinagar, 1934.

4. Cf. R. Torella, *Īśvarapratyabhijñākārikā*, op. cit., p. 95, fn. 21. — On the problem of "relation" in Indian philosophies see V.N. Jha, *The Philosophy of Relations* (Bibliotheca Indo-Buddhica Series; 66) Delhi 1990; id. (ed.), *Relations in Indian Philosophy* (Sri Garib Dass Oriental Series; 147) Delhi: Sri Satguru Publications, 1992.

5. The three works *Saṁbandhasiddhi*, *Ajaḍapramātṛsiddhi* and *Īśvarasiddhi* are published in: *The Siddhitrayī and the Pratyabhijñā-kārikā-vṛtti of Rājānaka Utpaladeva*, ed. with notes by Pt. Madhusudan Kaul (KSTS; 34) Srinagar, 1921.

6. Raffaele Torella, "A Fragment of Utpaladeva's Īśvarapratyabhijñā-vivṛti": *East and West* 38 (1988) pp. 137-44.

The hymns, collected later as the *Śivastotrāvalī* (*ŚSĀ*),[7] stand out among his works. In the *Īśvarapratyabhijñākārikā*, Utpaladeva develops a brilliant rational argumentation, especially in the discussion with Buddhist authors, founding the non-dualism of the Kashmir Śaivites in a theoretical way and formulating the philosophical base of Trika Śaivism in its classical form. However, in his hymns, the atmosphere changes completely: here Utpaladeva talks poetically and ecstatically, as a *bhakta*, free from the controlled character of philosophical argumentation. Thus, much of his personality and spiritual experiences seems to be condensed within his hymns. In their conciseness and intensity the hymns seem like spontaneous exclamations with the colours, moods and times of different *rāgas*. The commentator Kṣemarāja discloses that the individual hymns were written sporadically and had been collected afterwards by two of his disciples, Śrī-Rāma and Ādityarāja.[8] In both the *Īśvarapratyabhijñākārikā* and in the *Śivastotrāvalī* he talks as somebody who has reached the goal of "this new, easy path" (*Īśvarapratyabhijñākārikā* IV. 16), the highest perfection (*siddhi*, cf. IV. 18) — but while in the *Īśvarapratyabhijñākārikā* he argues as a philosopher who defends

7. Text and commentary are quoted from *The Śivastotrāvalī of Utpaladevācārya. With the Sanskrit Commentary of Kṣemarāja.* Edited with Hindi commentary by Rājānaka Lakṣmaṇa (Chowkhamba Sanskrit Series; 15) Varanasi: Chowkhamba Sanskrit Series Office, 1964.—The text is not edited in the KSTS. This fact is astonishing, considering the great popularity of the hymns among the Kashmir Śaivites till present days. This popularity becomes evident from the strikingly great number of manuscripts of *ŚSĀ*, preserved in the manuscript-collection of the "Iqbal-Library," University of Srinagar.

8. Cf. Jan Gonda, *Medieval Religious Literature in Sanskrit* (A History of Indian Literature; vol. II, Fasc. 1) Wiesbaden: Harrassowitz, 1977, pp. 32ff.

this way with logic, in the *Śivastotrāvalī* he teaches as a spiritual master to those who are already on this path, identifying himself with them by the poetical "I" of the hymns. The difference in the atmosphere of the two texts belonging to different genres should not mislead one to cleave too sharp a division between the philosopher and the mystic. In the first verse of the *Īśvarapratyabhijñākārikā*, Utpaladeva clarifies that he writes this philosophical text as somebody who has "in some way (*kathaṁcid*) attained the state of a servant" of the Supreme Lord (*Īśvarapratyabhijñākārikā* I. 1.1), the state of "recognition" (*pratyabhijñā*) of the Lord that is one's own nature as identical to Śiva — "a state which is very difficult to achieve" (I. 1.1, *vṛtti*). Also, the purpose of the work is a spiritual one: he wants to "make possible the awakening of the recognition of the Lord" as a service "to the whole of mankind" (I. 1.1). He has explained this recognition of the Lord "with argumentations" (*upapādita*, last verse of the *Śivastotrāvalī*, IV. 18), so "that the ordinary man too can attain perfection effortlessly" (ibid.). And also the motive of *bhakti* is mentioned in the *Īśvarapratyabhijñākārikā*: Utpaladeva illustrates the "recognition of the Lord" with the famous metaphor of the loving woman who feels joy towards the foreign man in front of her only when she recognizes him as her beloved (cf. IV. 17). On the other hand, the *Śivastotrāvalī* also presents many philosophical and theological topics, as for example the relation between the transcendence and the immanence of the Divine (2.5; 2.8; 12.2). These topics do not unfold out of argumentation, but rather arise almost playfully, like haikus.

So it is not surprising that it is in this part of his writings where we meet *sparśa*, a word of experience, in different contexts. Its use within different derivations in the *Śivastotrāvalī* is so numerous and striking that is astonishing that

Constantina Rhodes Bailly does not mention it in her study of the *Śivastotrāvalī*, though she quotes the respective verses (e.g. 5.26; 14.6; 15.19) in her introduction.[9]

Utpaladeva uses the noun *sparśa* as well as other derivations of the verbal root *spṛś* in the following verses of the *Śivastotrāvalī*:

(a) *sparśa*: 4.23; 5.11; 5.26; 9.1; 9.16; 10.15; 10.20; 13.14; 16.12; 17.4; 17.28

(b) *saṁsparśa*:[10] 5.5; 5.12; 7.6; 14.8

(c) *asaṁspṛṣṭa*, "not touched" (in a figurative sense): 1.17

(d) *spṛśyate*: "he/she/it is touched": 13.6

In addition, Utpaladeva uses different synonyms for *sparśa*:

(a) *saṅgama*: 8.9; *saṅga*: 8.12

(b) *samparka*: 5.1

I will only treat those passages where the word is used in an especially significant way.

***

The word arises for the first time in a marked way in the fourth *stotra*:

> O Lord of the gods (*amareśvara*)! Even if I would have the sovereignty (*ādhipatya*) over all the three worlds (*triloka*) —

---

9. *Shaiva Devotional Songs of Kashmir: A Translation and Study of Utpaladeva's Shivastotravali* by Constantina Rhodes Bailly, Indian edition, Delhi: Sri Satguru Publications, 1990, 20 and 22.

10. *Sa*, connected with *saha* or *sam*, is a prefix expressing "junction", "conjunction," "possession," "similarity," "equality" (cf. MW, p. 1111). It has an intensifying function: *saṁsparśa* denotes the "close or mutual contact, touch, conjunction, mixture . . ." (MW, p. 1122).

> all this would be joyless (*nīrasa*) without the joy (*rasa*) of the nectar (*amṛta*) of the touch (*sparśana*) of your feet.
>
> — *Śivastotrāvalī* 4.23

Utpaladeva stresses the significance of the "touch of the feet" of the "highest Lord." Even the command over the entire world — according to Indian cosmology the earth, middle-world and the heavens — would be useless (*nīrasa*, literally: "juiceless," "without essence") without it. But what does he mean by this expression? The commentator Kṣemarāja gives the first hint: He interprets "feet" as *marīci* ("ray", *Śivastotrāvalī*, p. 69). "Rays" is a current image for the divine powers (*Śakti*). In *TĀ* 1.202-205ab, Abhinavagupta quotes the *Mataṅgatantra*:

> The abode of the highest master are the rays of his energy — luminous, radiating, unchangeable. This is the highest point, subtle, omnipresent, of the nature of nectar, free from obscuration, peaceful, desirous of pure existence, wise, devoid of beginning and end, metaphorically denoted as the "body" (*mūrti*),[11] the manifest aspect [of the highest deity].

The encoded meaning of the expression lies under the obvious meaning of the bowing down to touch the feet of an elder, respected person with the fingers (or even with the head),

---

11. *Mūrti* is derived from the root *mūrch-*, "to thicken, solidify." The word denotes the material form, the body, the visible image, especially the worshipped image. As the body is the solid, manifest form which surrounds the true nature, the *ātman*, and the worshipped object is the outer, perceivable wrap of the invisibly present deity, in the same way the "energies" (*śakti*) are the manifest, perceivable, accessible dimension of the highest Reality. As the *Vijñāna-Bhairava* says: Śakti is the mouth (*mukham*), the entrance to Śiva (cf. *VBh* 20); "Just as parts of space are known by . . . the rays of the sun, in the same way, o dear one, Śiva is known through Śakti" (*VBh* 21).

even until now the primary expression of respect, reverence and humility in India. Combining these two layers of meaning, we are reminded of his opening verse of the *Īśvarapratyabhijñākārikā* where he describes the highest state attainable by a human being with an equal expression of humility: he has ". . . somehow reached the state of a servant of the great Lord" (I.1.1). The highest experience — the "touch of the Goddess" (Śakti), the diving into Śiva by his "power" — requires complete surrender and humility (touching the feet).

The motif of "touching the feet" appears again in verse 5.1. However, here Utpaladeva uses the similar expression *samparka* instead of *sparśa*:

> O Lord (*nātha*)! By the mere contact (*samparka*) with your lotus feet (*pādapadma*) along with complete enjoyment (*saṁbhoga*), let me enter (*praveśya*) into your own realm (*svaveśma*) by the "foot on the neck" (*galepādika*).
>
> — *Śivastotrāvalī* 5.1

Kṣemarāja again interprets "feet" (*pāda*) as "rays" (*marīci*), the enjoyment through the contact as a "taste (*āsvāda*) of the diving (or entering, immersion, ingress, *samāveśa*)." *Galepādika* (the foot on the neck) is understood by the commentary as: "by the process of the violent downward fall of the energy (*haṭhaśaktipātakrama*)." "Own realm" (or kingdom) he understands as "the abode of the nature of pure *cit*" (*citsvarūpa*).[12]

Here Bailly does not translate literally, but in her rendering of *galepādika* refers to the commentary, interpreting *Śaktipātakrama* as "by the touch of the *guru*" who transfers the power of Śakti. One can surmise that the background of her interpretation, which places the spiritual master in the centre,

12. Cf. *ŚSā*, p. 72.

is the specific view of the Siddhayoga movement,[13] which stresses the primary role of the *guru* for receiving "divine grace" (*śaktipāta*), the spontaneous awakening of *kuṇḍalinī* — whereas Utpaladeva (and later, Abhinavagupta) emphasizes the spontaneous, *completely* free and unpredictable operation of the "Power" itself as the primary phenomenon.

Thereby does Bailly ignore the question of why Utpaladeva uses precisely this peculiar expression "*galepādika*". Obviously he plays with the double use of the motif of "feet": he relates "the touch of the feet" of the highest Lord, i.e. contact with the divine power, to the touch (the kick) of a foot — of course, a rather violent (*haṭha*) touch. One could interpret it as meaning to grasp somebody's neck (*galehastikayā*) and to push him into the "realm," e.g. into the state of pure, thought-free, timeless consciousness, or into the sudden contact with the "Highest" (*anuttara*) through the experience of his energy. However, Utpaladeva uses an expression which describes an even more humiliating act: to put one's feet on the neck of somebody who lies deep before them — at their feet. The expression "with his feet on my neck" reminds us of archaic wrestling matches, in which the winner finally puts his feet on his opponent's neck or back as a sign of subjugation. This would fit the approach of Utpaladeva, as we have already seen, to combine the highest state with expressions of highest humility, as with "servant" or "touching of feet." This would also correspond with our passage: to connect the experience of grace ("the touch of the power," "the descent of grace," *śaktipāta*) with the expression "a foot on the neck." Utpaladeva expresses it in this way: it arises not from one's own merit,

13. The Siddhayoga movement is traced back to Swami Muktananda. C.R. Bailly is connected with this movement.

but from pure grace — leaving no reason for any spiritual arrogance.

Sometimes the term "grace," in everyday religious use, implies something over-sweet. But here the violent aspect is expressed in a very realistic manner — the violence, which is associated with the falling, the overtaking of grace, the sudden contact with the divine power which can be shocking, which can overwhelm a person and overthrow their earlier, sophisticated ideas about reality, which can throw one off balance, throw one out of one's routine, and which puts its "foot on your neck."

The sudden violence which happens to a person reminds one of the phenomenon of possession, until now an important element of the religious life in India, especially of tribal traditions. A deity or the spirit of a dead person instantaneously occupies a person's consciousness, and violently and abruptly takes possession of them. Actually, the Sanskrit term for "possession" is the same word *samāveśa* (derived from the root *viś*-), the "complete entering," "diving in" (the "Highest" through His "power"), which is used as the central expression for the spiritual state in the texts of non-dualistic Kashmir Śaivism. But there exists more than a mere linguistic relationship, if one considers the so-called "five signs" — reactions in the practitioner which occur as a result of the growing "touch with the plenitude" (*pūrṇatāsparśa*, cf. *K*, p. 73), the rising and unfolding of *kuṇḍalinī-śakti*. Lilian Silburn describes the "jump" (*udbhava*) as startling, and *kampa* in the following way: ". . . as *kuṇḍalinī* reaches the heart there occurs a violent trembling" (*K*, p. 73).

Important in this context is how Kṣemarāja characterizes the effect of the "touching of the feet" — it is the "tasting of absorption (*samāveśa*)."

Samāveśa as a Key-word of Tāntric Śaivism

Samāveśa (cf. *āveśa*) means "entering, penetration, absorption into" (cf. MW 1162). The expression reflects earlier stages of Tāntric Śaivism, e.g. the Kāpālika cults at the burning places, associated with possession by terrible deities.[14] Like *sparśa*, the word *samāveśa* also integrates the spiritual and the sexual dimension, since it denotes the main spiritual aim and simultaneously includes a sexual layer of meaning: *samāveśana* means "the consummation of marriage" (cf. MW 1162). The sexual meaning is clear, as it is for example in the unknown text quoted by Jayaratha in his commentary on *Tantrāloka* 3.146-148. The context is the definition of *kāmatattva*.

> The mind is driven onwards by the extremely pleasing penetration (*samāveśa*); they continuously recite [the unclear uttered letter, located in the throat of the beloved, cf. *Tantrāloka* 3.146f] at the festival of the sexual union with women. The lords of *yoga* (*yogīśvara*), with their mind fixed [on it], attain the highest *yoga*. — *Tantrālokaviveka*, vol. 2, p. 503

In *Tantrāloka* 5.71 Abhinavagupta uses the expression *kulāveśa*, "the absorption in *kula*." Silburn translates this word as "absorption dans la pure énergie sexuelle."[15]

Samāveśa denotes diving into the "power" of the "Highest" (*anuttara*) and being permeated by it. It is the aim of all the three "spiritual ways" (*upāya*) of which Trika teaches (cf. *Tantrāloka* 1.167-170): the "immersion" (*samāveśa*) on the grounds of an intensive "awakening" (*prabodhataḥ*) on "the way of Śambhu" (*śāmbhavopāya*),[16] the merely mental immersion

---

14. Cf. R. Torella, *ĪPK*, op. cit., intro., pp. XXXIIf.

15. Lilian Silburn, *La Vijñāna Bhairava*, Paris: Ed. de Boccard, 1983, p. 210.

16. Śambhu, the kind, benevolent one, is one of the names of Śiva, according to the *Mahābhārata* (cf. MW, p. 1055).

in "the way of the power" (*śāktopāya*) and the immersion by various means, like meditation or rituals, etc. in the case of "the way of the limited individual" (*āṇavopāya*).

Hence it is difficult to follow Torella's judgement that for Trika, and especially for Kṣemarāja, *samāveśa* became only ". . . a technical term . . . which has lost any specific identity."[17] Torella's statement is only based on a passage in Kṣemarāja's *Pratyabhijñāhṛdaya* (=*PHṛ*), i.e. his commentary to *sūtra* 18, in which he lists *samāveśa* next to *samāpatti* as a synonym for *samādhi* (*samāveśasamāpattyādiparyāyaḥ samādhi*).[18] It is true that Kṣemarāja uses the word as synonymous with *samādhi*, especially in his commentary to *sūtra* 19, where *samāveśa* appears seven times. However, if you consider the whole text of the *Pratyabhijñāhṛdaya*, then the outstanding theological and spiritual significance of the word *samāveśa* becomes clear: at the beginning of the *Pratyabhijñāhṛdaya*, Kṣemarāja declares that the purpose of the work is to give a short explanation for people who haven't studied difficult logical works and still "intensely desire for *samāveśa* with the highest Lord."[19] The "supreme *yogī*" (*paramayogī*) is denoted as *samāviṣṭa*, defined as somebody who "has directly experienced the [shining and effulgent] unfolding of the highest Śakti" (*sākṣāt-kṛta parāśakti-sphāra*).[20] With the help of these descriptions, the characteristics of *samāveśa* become clearer.

---

17. Torella, *ĪPK*, op. cit., intro, p. XXXIII and fn. 50.

18. Kṣemarāja, *Pratyabhijñāhṛdayam*, ed. Mukunda Ram Shastri (KSTS 3) Srinagar 1918, p. 45; English translation: *Pratyabhijñahṛdayam. The Secret of Self-recognition*, trans. Jaideva Singh (1963), Delhi: Motilal Banarsidass, 4th rev. edn., reprint 1998, pp. 102f.

19. *PHṛ*, op. cit., p. 46.

20. Commentary *sūtra* 19; *PHṛ*, op. cit., p. 104.

In his commentary of the *Śivasūtras* (=*ŚSV*),[21] Kṣemarāja adopts the description of *samāveśa* as the goal of all three "spiritual ways": *samāveśa* in *śāmbhava* (*Śivasūtras* I.2), in *śāktopaya* (I.6 comm.) and *āṇavopāya* (II.6 comm.). The prominent rank of the term couldn't be explained if it had already "lost its specific identity" at the time of Kṣemarāja.

The root *viś-*, from which *samāveśa* is derived, can be understood in both a transitive and an intransitive way: as "to enter, immerse, penetrate, take possession" or as "to be entered, permeated, possessed."[22] Therefore, the word is especially suited to express the non-dualistic experience which is at the same time an absorption into the nature of the "Highest," full of light (through his "power") — "the [shining and effulgent] unfolding of the highest Śakti" — and which is also being permeated by "Śiva." Stated more clearly: it is a realization of the uninterrupted non-different "me" and "Śiva." Thus, Somānanda (ninth/tenth century) opens his *Śivadṛṣṭi* with the exclamation:

> Let Śiva, who is co-penetrated (*samāviṣṭa*) with my own being (identified with me) praise Śiva in his extended form through his own power, Śiva who obscures Himself by Himself!
>
> — *Śivadṛṣṭi* 1.1[23]

---

21. *The Śivasūtravimarśinī of Kṣemarāja. Being a Commentary on The Śivasūtra of Vasugupta,* ed. Jagadisha Chandra Chatterji (KSTS; 1) Srinagar 1911. Reprint, New Delhi: Bibliotheca Orientalia, 1990.

22. Cf. Torella, *ĪPK*, op. cit., intro., p. XXXIII.

23. Translation by Raniero Gnoli, "Śivadṛṣṭi by Somānanda" : *East and West* 8 (1957), no. 1, pp. 16-22, here p. 19. — Abhinavagupta quotes this verse in his *PTV* (*Parātrīśikā-Vivaraṇa: The Secret of Tantric Mysticism.* English translation with notes and running exposition by Jaideva Singh. Edited by Bettina Bäumer, Delhi: Motilal Banarsidass 1988, reprint 2000, p. 56 [Sanskrit text]). →

Torella indicates that Utpaladeva uses *āviś-* in the first of the three last verses of the *Īśvarapratyabhijñākārikā* in the active sense,[24] saying that one who "enters the nature of Śiva will be liberated in this life" (*Īśvarapratyabhijñākārikā* IV. 16 *v*). Alexis Sanderson mentions the *Īśvarapratyabhijñāvivṛttivimarśinī* (vol. 3, 326, 22-23) to *Īśvarapratyabhijñākārikā* 3.2.12, where Abhinavagupta describes *samāveśa* as the active entering (into one's own true nature). But Sanderson stresses the fact that this use is outweighed by the principle of this system that the "agency," the authority to act (*kartṛtā*), befits only the deity itself.[25]

On the other hand, Swami Lakshman Joo in his definition of *samāveśa* stresses the passive aspect of being touched:

> The penetrative state of trance (*samāveśa*) is called *śāmbhava samāveśa*; [it] is that when once it shines before you there is no way to escape from it; (. . .) this trance has digested you.[26]

→ Jaideva Singh translates the verse, as usual, already including his interpretation: "May Śiva who has entered into us as the Subject (as *śodhaka*) make obeisance by Himself (in the form of *mantra* as *śodhana*), to Śiva who is extended as the universe, by means of *parā* who is His own Śakti in order to remove all obstacles which are but Himself." (ibid., p. 156).

24. Torella, *ĪPK*, op. cit., intro., p. XXXIII.

25. Cf. Alexis Sanderson, "Maṇḍala and Āgamic Identity in the Trika of Kashmir," in: André Padoux, *Mantras et Diagrammes Rituelles dans l'Hindouisme*, Paris: Éditions du Centre National de la Recherche Scientifique, 1986, pp. 169-214; here: p. 177, fn. 33. — In part 3 (176f) of his article Sanderson treats the four levels of *samāveśa*, which he translates as "possession."

26. Swami Lakshman Joo, *Shiva Sūtras: The Supreme Awakening* (Audio Study Set), Culver City, CA: Universal Shaiva Fellowship, 2002; CD 1 (commentary to *sūtra* 5); not included in the book-version.

Obviously, it is at the same time an act of permeating and being permeated — like the sexual act, or each form of touch, which is at the same time an active touching and a passive being touched. Touch is always mutual, a "together-touch" (Lat. *con-tactus*), in that the touching and the touched touch each other. It is always a double sensation of the body,[27] a unique relationship which exists only in the case of touch, not in the case of any other sense.

However, Abhinavagupta makes it completely clear that the absorption is not primarily an effort of the human being, but rather it arises from Śiva's initiative:

> The entering (*āveśa*) is the identification with Śiva, which consists of the immersion (*nimajjana*) of one's own unfree (*asvatantra*) state, caused by the original (*ādya*) Śambhu by His energies. — *Tantrāloka* 1.173b-174

Jayaratha illustrates this slow immersion, diving, sinking down, dissolving, this transformation of the limited and contracted state of the individual in his commentary to *Tantrāloka* 2.35 with an impressive metaphor:

---

27. "(. . .) einerseits ist er [der Leib] physisches Ding, Materie . . . , andererseits finde ich auf ihm, und empfinde ich ‚auf' ihm und ‚in' ihm: die Wärme auf dem Handrücken, die Kälte in den Füβen, die Berührungsempfindungen an den Fingerspitzen." [On the one hand it [the body] is a physical thing, matter . . . , on the other hand, I find on it, and I feel "on" it and "in" it: the warmth on back of the hand, coldness in the feet, the sensations of touch at the finger-tips] — Edmund Husserl, *Ideen zu einer reinen Phänomenologie und phänomenologischen Philosophie. Zweites Buch: Phänomenologische Untersuchungen zur Konstitution* (Husserliana Bd. 4) Den Haag 1952, p. 145. See also Maurice Merleau-Ponty, "Der Philosoph und sein Schatten," in: id., *Das Auge und der Geist*, ed. and trans. H. W. Arndt, Hamburg 1984, p. 52.

> As wood, leaves, little shards of stone, etc. which have fallen into a salt lake transform into salt, in the same way all entities which are different from the Self enter into (*āveśa*) *cit.*[28]

The metaphor "the immersion into the lake" can already be found in the *Śivasūtras* (ninth century):

> *āsanasthaḥ sukhaṁ hrade nimajjati* ll
>
> Established in his seat, the *yogī* easily merges into the lake.
>
> — *Śivasūtras* 3.16

In his commentary Kṣemarāja interprets "to merge into": "All impressions (*saṁskāra*) of the contraction (*saṁkoca*) of the body, etc. merge into (*nimajjati*)." Swami Lakshman Joo explains in his paraphrase of Kṣemarāja's commentary:

> In diving into the ocean of nectar, he lets the impressions of the body (*deha*), of the breath (*prāṇa*), of the eight constituents (*pūryaṣṭaka*)[29] and of the void (*śūnya*) sink into that ocean and becomes one with that nectar. This is the real way to dive.[30]

In the Trika view, the contraction of the one, true, highest reality (Śiva) manifests itself — under the influence of *māyā* — with the impressions of the solid body, the breath, the eightfold psychic body and the void. Now, in the process of "diving" into one's own true nature/the true nature of everything, this

---

28. *TĀV*, vol. 2, p. 340.

29. Torella translates *pūryaṣṭaka* as "eightfold" (*ĪPK* p. 204, fn. 24), Pandey with "group of eight" (*ĪPV*, vol. III, p. 15), Dyczkowski with "city of eight" (*Stanzas on Vibration. The Spandakārikā with four Commentaries*, translated with an Introduction and Exposition by Mark S.G. Dyczkowski, Varanasi: Dilip Kumar Publishers, 1994, p. xviii, passim).

30. Lakshman Joo, *Shiva Sūtras*, op. cit. (fn. 25).

contraction dissolves. One returns to the "place of the nature of pure *cit*" (*citsvarūpa, Śivastotrāvalī* 5.1, comm.). *Śivasūtra* 3.4 expresses it concisely, calling it the "dissolution of the circles in the body" (*śarīre saṁhāraḥ kalānām*).[31] During the process of meditation, the physical body (*sthūla śarīra*), having emerged from the five elements (cf. *Tantrāloka* 4.118), enters the "subtle body" (*pūryaṣṭaka*), and the subtle body enters the "most subtle body" (*sūkṣma śarīra*).[32] The solidifying, thickening, hardening (cf. *mūrti*) of the true, luminous Reality happens gradually:

— the "fourth" state (*turīya*)

— the void

— *pūryaṣṭaka*

---

31. Swami Lakshman Joo interprets *kalānāṁ* in the sense of the five cosmic sub-divisions *nivṛtti kalā, pratiṣṭhā kalā, vidyā kalā, śāntā kalā* and *śāntitā kalā* (ibid.). About the "way of *kalās*" (*kalādhvan*) see *TĀ* p. 11; *Vāc*, pp. 357-64. Other translations do not connect *ŚS* 3.4 with *kalādhvan*: Dyczkowski translates *kalānāṁ* as "forces" (*The Aphorisms of Śiva. The Śiva Sūtra with Bhāskara's Commentary, the Vārttika.* Translated with Expositions and Notes by Mark S.G. Dyczkowski, Varanasi: Indica, 1998, p. 100), J. Singh as "various parts" (*Śiva Sūtras. The Yoga of Supreme Identity. Text of the Sūtras and the Commentary Vimarśinī of Kṣemarāja*, trans. Jaideva Singh, Delhi: Motilal Banarsidass, 1979; reprint 2000, p. 134).

32. Cf. Lakshman Joo, *Shiva Sūtras*, op. cit. From his commentary it becomes clear that it is a matter of different forms of meditation (*dhāraṇās*), called "meditation of dissolution" (*laya bhāvanā*), as described, for example, in *VBh* 56 (quoted *ŚSV* 3.4): "One should meditate successively on the entire universe in the form of stages (*adhvan*) of *bhuvana* (world) and others, in their condition of gross, subtle and supreme, and in the end the mind will dissolve." (*Vijñāna-Bhairava: The Practice of Centring Awareness*, op. cit., pp. 60f). — See Bettina Bäumer, *Vijñāna-Bhairava. Das göttliche Bewusstsein. 112 Weisen der mystischen Erfahrung im Śivaismus von Kaschmir*, Grafing (Germany): Edition Adyar, 2003, pp. 106-08; M. Dyczkowski, *Doctrine of Vibration*, op. cit., pp. 210f.

— the breath

— the physical body

And in the opposite direction, this contraction becomes gradually dissolved through the process of meditation, until the "highest Self" (*parātmā*) shines without limits.[33] In this way, the goal of all ways, described by Trika, is attained:

> But when the cognizable is entirely dissolved within him and there is the full consciousness of the I, the state of Śiva is attained. — *Īśvarapratyabhijñākārikā* IV. 14 *v*

***

The "immersion," associated with *sparśa*, forms the core of the following verse:

> O, how wonderful! May the immersion (*nimajjana*) in the lake (*saras*) of the nectar (*sudhā*) of the touch (*saṁsparśa*) of your feet be always the enjoyment (*saṁbhoga*) above all enjoyments for me. — *Śivastotrāvalī* 5.12

In the commentary Kṣemarāja again associates — as in his interpretation of *Śivastotrāvalī* 5.1 — *sparśa* with *samāveśa*. He interprets "the touch of your feet" as: "entering (*samāveśa*) into *rudraśakti*,"[34] and continues: "Exactly this is the essence (*sāra*) of the nectar — the ocean of joy (*rasāyanābdhi*)." While Kṣemarāja in his comment to 5.1 has explained *sparśa* simply as the "tasting of *samāveśa*," he says now that it is the entering,

---

33. Cf. *PTV*, commentary of *PT* 9-18; Sanskrit: p. 82; translation: p. 218; *ĪPV*, *Kriyādhikāra*, ch. III: The subject is limited by body, breath, *pūryaṣṭaka* and void (*ĪPV*, vol. III, p. 162).

34. Rudra: "crying, howling, roaring, dreadful, terrific, terrible, horrible . . ." (MW, p. 883). In the Vedas, "Rudra" is the name of the god of storms and father and ruler of the Rudras and Maruts. Originally, "Śiva" ("benevolent," "auspicious") is an epithet of Rudra, later becomes a real name (cf. ibid.).

the immersion into the Śakti of Rudra (= Śiva). Why does he introduce here the name "Rudra," seen here in *rudraśakti*? By doing so, Kṣemarāja gives us an important hint at the meaning of *sparśa* in this spiritual context: *rudraśaktisamāveśa* is an expression which has already been used in the *Mālinīvijayottara Tantra* (= *MVT*), a prominent Tantra of Trika Śaivism.

> Somebody who is permeated by the *Śakti* of Rudra (*rudraśaktisamāviṣṭa*), impelled by the will of Śiva, will be led to an authentic teacher (*sadguru*) to obtain enjoyment (*bhukti*) and liberation (*mukti*). — *Mālinīvijayottara Tantra* 1.44[35]

Peculiar here is that the Tantra uses the passive voice — it stresses the "being permeated, entered, possessed" by the *rudraśakti*, while Kṣemarāja uses the active form. Here we find the important observation for any spiritual way, that finding an authentic spiritual teacher is not the result of one's own efforts or intelligence, but rather the fruit of grace.

Already in this Tantra itself we can find Kṣemarāja's combination of "touch" and *samāveśa* by *śakti*; the two preceding verses of the *Mālinīvijayottara Tantra* (1.42-43) talk about the "contact with *śakti*." However, it is not the word *sparśa* which is used here, but *sambandha*, "close connection, relation, uniting, binding."[36] In this context, we meet an important level of meaning of the *sparśa* of *śakti* (*śaktisparśa*): contact with *śakti* (cf.

---

35. *Mālinīvijayottaratantram*, ed. by Madhusudan Kaul (KSTS; 37) Bombay, 1922, 6. Cf. *MVT* 2.17: "The pervasion by *rudraśakti* is fivefold, because of the differentiation into elements (*bhūta*), principles (*tattva*), Self (*ātmā*), *mantra* and *śakti*." Jayaratha quotes this verse in *TĀV* 1.186cd-187ab.

36. Abhinavagupta quotes *MVT* 1.44, a bit shortened, in *TĀ* 13.241 and in 21.2. J quotes the verse in *TĀV* 21.1. The references in the index of the edition of N. Rastogi and R.C. Dwivedi are not correct (cf. *TĀ*, vol. VIII, p. 3768).

MVT 1.42-43) or the pervasion by *śakti* (cf. *MVT* 1.44) is seen as *śaktipāta*, literally the "falling down" of *śakti*. Therefore, *samāveśa* is not only to be understood as the slow absorption into the "ocean of joy," especially within the context of meditation, but also as the lightning-quick,[37] abrupt dissolving of the veil and the unveiling of one's own true nature as an "ocean of joy," maybe only for a moment, which can happen at any place, in any situation of everyday life (*śaktipāta*). *Śaktipāta*, the "falling down" of *śakti*, understood as the immersion into *rudraśakti*, into the core (*hṛdaya*), the essence (*sāra*) of all: the shining, pulsating "ocean of joy."[38] Regarding the traditional division of three stages of intensity of *śaktipāta*, which are again respectively divided into three degrees, *rudraśaktisamāveśa* is the third intensity of *śaktipāta*, i.e. *tīvramanda śaktipāta*, the "lowest of the highest descent" of *śakti*. Its experience results in the discovery of a "true spiritual teacher" (*sadguru*); a person who experienced this type of *śaktipāta* is afterwards guided (by the will of Śiva) to a *sadguru*. He can awake the "sleeping *kuṇḍalinī*" in a person by the touch of his hand or by the mere sight of him.

This direct contact with the "ocean of joy," the "essence of the *nectar*," is characterized by Utpaladeva in verse 5.12 as "enjoyment which exceeds all enjoyments." Kṣemarāja specifies in his comment: "all" means, that this enjoyment ". . . excels all enjoyments up to Sadāśiva" (*Śivastotrāvalī*, p. 78), this

37. Rudra, the god of storm, throws the lightnings; cf. Hermann Grassmann, *Wörterbuch zum Ṛgveda*, Wiesbaden 1964, p. 1174.

38. In the texts of Trika we meet enumerations of characterizations of the "Highest" (*anuttara*) in its "accessible" dimension (= *śakti*). These specifications combine theological terms (e.g. *parāvāk*, *svātantrya*, *kartṛtvaṁ*) with metaphors (e.g. *hṛdayam*, *sāra*) and aspects of the human experience of this reality (e.g. *spanda*, *sphurattā*, *viśrānti*). For these lists see *PP*; *ĪPK* I.5.14; *TĀ* 6.13, etc.

encompassing every experience which is associated with the 34 *tattvas*.[39] In this, we receive an important datum for our topic, because Kṣemarāja indirectly indicates the spiritual plane, the level in the rise of *kuṇḍalinī* at which *sparśa* is experienced: that is, at the dimension of the 35th *tattva*, called "Śakti," which leads to the highest, 36th *tattva*, called "Śiva." This last *tattva* is beyond "experience," cannot be experienced, because there is no more objectivity which could be experienced in the duality of "experiencer" and "experienced"; the opposites coincide.[40] Later we will see — in the context of the analysis of *Tantrāloka* 11.29-32 or in the context of "*uccāra* of *OṀ*" — what it implies, and if other texts confirm this statement that *sparśa* is experienced at the level of *śakti*.

Here a clarification could be useful: already now, at the beginning of our examination, it becomes clear that the same term (*śakti-*) *sparśa* can be used for different forms of experiences of the contact with *śakti*, at different places in the (subtle) body. When we will analyse the motive of *sparśa* in the texts of Abhinavagupta, we will again meet other forms of "contact" with *śakti* and its particular bodily reactions (e.g. "the touch of ants"). This might sound confusing. It has to do with the nature of *śakti*, the dynamism of the "Highest"

---

39. *Tattva*: "principles" or "levels of reality" from the "earth" up to "Sadāśiva," i.e. the elements, the senses, but also experiences in the "non-objective" realm (beginning with the level of *śuddha vidyā*, "pure wisdom"). — "Level of reality" is the translation for *tattva* by Somadeva Vasudeva: *The Yoga of the Mālinīvijayottaratantra.* Chapters 1-4, 7, 11-17. Critical Edition, translation and notes (Collection Indologie Pondichéry; 97) Pondichéry: Institut Français de Pondichéry/École française d'Extrême-Orient, 2005.

40. Cf. the definition of *aham*, "I," highest subjectivity, by J in his commentary to *TĀ* 3.173cd-174 (vol. II, p. 525).

(*anuttara*): one of her principal names is *svātantrya*, "complete autonomy, independence, freedom." Her appearance, awakening, "work," dynamics, revealing or forms can neither be calculated nor properly categorized.

Now, Kṣemarāja again combines the motifs of "feet" and of *śaktipāta*, which are related by Utpaladeva in verse 5.1 in such a powerful way, in his comment on verse 5.2. Here he theologically interprets the expression "by the dust of your lotus-feet" from the verse in the following way: "by the lotus-dust (*kamalaparāgeṇa*) of the highest *śakti* (*parāśakti*), activated (*pravṛtta*) by grace (*anugraha*)."[41] The word "dust" in the context of *śakti* might be employed because the same word (*kiraṇa*) also means "rays" (cf. MW 283), in addition to the general background of the metaphor in India, that one wants to touch with one's forehead even the dust which was trod upon by the feet of a saint or a god like Kṛṣṇa. While in verse 5.1 the order of "touch" and "grace" remains open, Kṣemarāja clearly states that grace is the condition for the activity and dynamism of the highest *śakti*. At the same time, the concrete experience of "touch" — e.g. in the form of "entering (*samāveśa*) into *rudraśakti*," maybe only for a moment — is the evidence for having received grace.

Unto the present, the expression "lotus-feet" is a common epithet in India. The lotus (*padma, kamala*; in the *Śivastotrāvalī ambuja*, lit. "water-born"), since long a central symbol of India's religious traditions, embodies purity and beauty. It grows out of mud yet rises above it. In the same way, the "feet" of the "Highest Lord" are the point of His contact with earth, dust, the material world — a contact which does not reduce His purity.

---

41. *ŚSĀ*, p. 73.

In verse 5.1 of the *Śivastotrāvalī*, Utpaladeva again uses the expression "the touch of your lotus-feet." In this verse, which is especially important for our topic, he hints for the first time at the spiritual (yogic) process which is produced by the "touch of *śakti*" (*śaktisparśa*). This process will be further clarified by Kṣemarāja's comment.

> My eyes (*locana*) completely closed (*parimīlita*) at the touch (*saṁsparśa*) of your lotus-feet — may I blossom out (*vijṛmbheya*), whirling (*ghūrṇita*) drunken (*mada*) from the wine (*madirā*) of your love (*bhakti*). — *Śivastotrāvalī* 5.5

The eyes here represent all five senses, which are completely closed. At first sight one could interpret this expression as *pratyāhāra*, "the withdrawal of the senses,"[42] as one of the means which lead to the unfolding of the "centre" (*madhya*) and the contact with (*kuṇḍalinī-*) *śakti* rising within it. But Kṣemarāja explains in the commentary that it is exactly the opposite: "By the bliss (*ānanda*) of your *śakti*, the instruments (*karaṇa*, sense-organs) [are] turned inwards" (*Śivastotrāvalī*, p. 74). In other words, the complete interiorization of the sense-energies is *itself* an effect of the *śakti* rising in the subtle dimension of the body, for example, during the process of meditation. The keyword *ānanda* in the comment together with the participle of *ghūrṇati*, "to move to and fro, shake, be agitated, roll about" (MW 378) in the verse indicates the context, the five major "signs" or phases of the rise of the *kuṇḍalinī*, i.e. *ānanda* (bliss), *udbhava* (jumping), *kampa*

42. *Pratyāhāra* is defined in Patañjali's *Yogasūtra* as the separation of the senses from their corresponding objects (restraining of the sense-organs), cf. *YS* II.54 (Swāmī Hariharānanda Āraṇya, *Yoga Philosophy of Patañjali with Bhāsvatī* (1963), Calcutta: University of Calcutta, 3rd rev. edn. 1981, 3rd enl. edn. 2000, p. 245).

(trembling), *nidrā* (yogic sleep), and *ghūrṇi* (vibrant whirling).[43] These spiritual phenomena are brought about by the touch (*sparśa*) of *kuṇḍalinī-śakti* with the corresponding "subtle centres" (*cakra*) in the body: *ānanda* by her touch at the lowest centre, at the base of the spine, called *mūlādhāra*, and *ghūrṇi* by her touch at the highest of the five main centres, at the skullcap, called *brahmarandhra* (cf. *K*, pp. 72 and 74). Lilian Silburn describes the state of *ghūrṇi* as follows: "(. . .) it consists of a specific mystical whirling, a vibration moving in all directions so intense as to defy the imagination" (*K*, p. 74).

The desire, expressed by Utpaladeva in the verse "may I blossom out, whirling (*ghūrṇita*)" and so on, is therefore related to one of the highest stages of this spiritual process, denoted by Trika with the expression *mahāvyāpti* (great pervasion). The practitioner attains the state of "universal consciousness"; he remembers, recognizes again his identity with the core of the whole reality. Abhinavagupta identifies this "great pervasion," after describing the other "signs" of the rising of *kuṇḍalinī*, with the state of *ghūrṇi*:

> Then, risen (*rūḍha*) into the realm of truth (*satyapada*), [he] remembers (*smṛtā*) *saṁvit*[44] as the universe, and he "whirls," because "whirling" is called the great pervasion
>
> — *TĀ* 5.104cd-105ab

---

43. Cf. *MVT* 11.35; *TĀ* 5.100b-105a; see *K* 71-75.

44. In many cases the word *saṁvit* seems to be used as a synonym for *cit*. But sometimes there is a subtle differentiation between *cinmātra* and *saṁvit*, e.g. in *TĀ* 6.179b-181, where Abhinavagupta talks about the relation between *prāṇa* ("life," "life-force," "principle of life," "vital breath," "consciousness," cf. *K* 39), *saṁvit* and *cit*: "Truly (*evam*), emanation (*visṛṣṭi*) and dissolution (*pralaya*) are together (*ekatra*) based (*niṣṭitā*) on *prāṇa*, that on *saṁvit*, and *saṁvit* on pure *cit* (*cinmātra*)." Pure *cit* is identified with the Goddess (*devī*) itself, the "highest heart" (cf. *TĀ* 6.171ab). Likewise,

→

With the same view, Kṣemarāja interprets the verse *Śivastotrāvalī* 5.5:

> How does it happen? By direct perception (*sākṣātkṛte*); this *bhakti* is the enjoying (*āseva*) of the intoxication by the wine (*madirāmada*), the astonishment (*camatkāra*) caused by the Kadamba-liquor (*kādambarī*),[45] due to which he whirls around (*ghūrṇita*), moved (*lambhita*) by the great pervasion (*mahāvyāpti*). — *Śivastotrāvalī*, p. 74

At the level of *mahāvyāpti* one finds the point of transition from the "absorption with closed eyes" (*nimīlanasamādhi*, cf. *parimīlita* in the verse) to the "absorption with open eyes" (*unmīlanasamādhi*).

→ at the beginning of Kṣemarāja's *PP* we find this association of *saṁvit* and Śakti as the "heart of the highest Lord": "We adore *saṁvit*, which flashes forth (*sphurantīm*) in the form of the original Parāśakti, the heart of the highest Lord (. . .)." (*Parāprāveśikā of Kṣemarāja*, op. cit., 1). Abhinavagupta says about *saṁvit*: "This [*saṁvit*] is found, veiling itself, at the level of the insentient (*jaḍapada*); in its half-veiled and half-revealed form it takes the form of living beings, starting from the gods down to the plane of plants. Each of these, in its sentient and insentient form, is wonderfully manifold." (*TĀ* 1.134b-135; see also 138). If we take *saṁvit* as a synonym with *cit*, then this passage underlines again that a translation as "consciousness" would be misleading, since it would be rather eccentric to attribute "consciousness" in its usual understanding to an insentient rock or a piece of glass. In contrast to this interpretation, in my understanding it would be more appropriate to have the connection of *saṁvit* and Parāśakti (*kuṇḍalinī*) in view. Then one could understand *saṁvit* maybe as the innermost, pulsating, vibrating, shining core of reality, the true, highest nature of everything (*including* of the human consciousness), as an aspect of Śakti.

45. Liquor, extracted from the flowers of the *kadamba* tree (cf. MW p. 270).

The verb *vijṛmbhate* in the verse means "to open, expand, become expanded or developed or exhibited, spread out, blossom, (. . .) to arise, appear, awake" (MW 960). While Bailly renders the word very freely with "May I rejoice," it is translated here as "blossom out" (or: "burst into blossom," "open," "bloom"), so that the connection with the symbol of the lotus is evident. As the diurnal lotus opens and expands and unfolds by the rays of the sun, in the same way the "heart-lotus" blossoms out by the touch of the rays of grace;[46] the centre (*madhya*) unfolds until one experiences the state of the original unity of everything, or recognizes this unity again (cf. *TĀ* 5.104cd-105ab), within the "great pervasion" (*mahāvyāpti*). Like with the expression *samāveśa*, it is primary that something *happens* to a person: One is "moved" or "touched" by *mahāvyāpti*; one cannot reach this stage by any yogic practice or through one's own effort. Therefore, Kṣemarāja, as a spiritual master, stresses that only at the beginning of this process may there be a yogic exercise like *pratyāhāra* — for the complete interiorization of all senses and its energies occurs through "the touch of *śakti*," by the dynamism of the "power," and not the other way round — and this "touch" is, as we have seen, grace itself (cf. *Śivastotrāvalī* 5.1; 5.2 commentary; 5.12).

Of particular theological importance is the fact that Utpaladeva understands this highest state of *mahāvyāpti* — the pervasion of Highest Self, individual Self, and the Self of

46. Precisely in this sense Abhinavagupta uses the metaphor of the lotus: "But unless the heart-lotus (*hṛtkuśeśaya*) of people, who are like bound animals (*paśujana*), is made to blossom out (*avikasite*) by the rays (*kiraṇa*) of grace, which fall down from the highest lord (*parameśaśaktipāta*), then even hundreds of my words (. . .) can neither open [the heart-lotus] nor [help] to attain [the goal]." *PTV*, Sanskrit text: p. 46.

all as essentially one — not as an anonymous experience of unity, but as the experience of "love" (*bhakti*) of the "Highest Lord." It reminds us of the ecstatic lyric verses of the sūfīs as Utpaladeva explains the state of mystic "whirling," "twisting" with the intoxication by the "wine of love" of the highest lord.

It is remarkable: the highest state of non-duality (*advaita*), the attaining of the "state of Śiva" (*śivatālābha*, *Īśvarapratyabhijñākārikā* IV. 16 *v*), is understood as the *bhakti* of the "highest lord" — "love," which includes a duality of lover and beloved.

What happens in this process? Kṣemarāja mentions in his comment an important word: "direct perception" (*sākṣātkṛte*). The ablative form *sākṣāt* is derived from *sa* and *akṣa*, literally "with eye," and means "with the eyes, through the eyes" (cf. MW 3). "Eye" represents here all the senses. In a figurative sense, the word means "evident, clear, direct, and immediate." *Sākṣātkāra* denotes "an evident perception." The background of this use of the word is the commonsensical conviction that sensual perception guarantees direct, immediate contact with the outer reality and represents a doubtless ground for its cognition. This pre-philosophical view is epistemologically represented and philosophically defended by the "naïve" or "direct" realism, and in the Indian context by Nyāya-realism: we see, we touch the physical, three-dimensional objects comprised in part by their visual (*rūpatanmātra*) and tactile (*sparśatanmātra*) qualities, which are viewed as a part of physical reality, *in a direct way*. The question of direct perception forms the central issue in the twelve-century long dispute between Nyāya and Buddhism.[47] The Buddhists hold the

47. See Bimal Krishna Matilal, *Perception. An Essay on Classical Indian Theories of Knowledge* (1986), Delhi: Oxford University Press, reprint 2002.

position that we touch a flower not directly, but rather that we touch only its touchability, its tactile quality — only these appearances of the phenomena (*gandha, rasa, rūpa, sparśa, śabda*) are real, and from them we construct stable, solid physical objects.

From this background, the point of Kṣemarāja's statement becomes clearer: these spiritual stages — from the first "joy" (*nijānanda*) up to the "great pervasion" (*mahāvyāpti*) — occur through "the touch of *śakti*," and this experience is the direct perception of the "essence" (*sāra*), of the "heart" (*hṛdaya*) of reality. Utpaladeva so describes the highest *śakti* of Parameśvara, here denoted with one of her names, *citi* (fem. of *cit*):

> It [*citi*] is the luminous vibrating (*sphurattā*), the absolute being (*mahāsattā*), unmodified by space and time; it is which is said to be the heart (*hṛdayam*) of the supreme Lord, insofar as it is his essence (*sāra*).
>
> — *Īśvarapratyabhijñākārikā* I 5.14

Kṣemarāja refers precisely to "direct perception," the foundation of cognition for the materialists, as the foundation of cognition of the shining, pulsating essence of matter, which in the last analysis is real. He gives us a hint as to what could have been the reason to choose the word *sparśa* for the experience of contact with the highest *śakti*, which is the dynamism and the accessible dimension of the "Highest" (*anuttara*): among the senses, *sparśa* represents *immediate* experience. Now, the aim of all spiritual paths is "the direct perception of one's own Self (*svātmasākṣātkāra*)" (*Tantrālokaviveka* 5.22cd-23ab). Following this, all the other sensual expressions used by Utpaladeva and his commentator obtain a significant meaning:

- — the complete enjoyment (*saṁbhoga*) of touch (*Śivastotrāvalī* 5.1);
- — the taste, the tasting (*āsvāda*)[48] of absorption (comm. 5.1);
- — the taste (*rasa*) of the nectar of touch (4.23); and
- — the pleasure which excels all other pleasures (5.12).

Here these expressions are not understood as mere mystical metaphors, but as attempts to describe direct, sensual perceptions at a subtle level of the body and the senses. In these cases the energies of the senses are not directed outwards, but inwards; not towards physical objects, but to their origin.

In verse 5.26 we find the same metaphors — "the touch of feet," "the lake of nectar" — as in *Śivastotrāvalī* 5.12:

> O Lord, sometimes, at the touch (*sparśa*) of the sole of your foot, something extraordinary flares up (*sphurati*) in [my] mind, whereupon (*yatra*) this whole world dissolves (*galati*) in a lake of nectar — show me [this] forever!
>
> — *Śivastotrāvalī* 5.26

To touch the soles of the feet, the lowest parts of one's body, seems to be the most humble form of respect. Kṣemarāja interprets the expression as follows: "those who participate in the touch of your *śakti* (*tvadbhavaśaktisparśaśālinā*)." A comment of *kimapi* follows the verse: "*kimapi*: an extraordinary state flares up in one's mind." "Dissolves" he interprets as "unite," and "lake of nectar" as "the ocean of highest bliss." And he concludes: "Show me forever such an experience: grant

48. *Rasāsvāda* (the tasting of *rasa*) denotes the aesthetic enjoyment, the aesthetic experience (Bäumer, "Brahman," in: *KTK* I, op. cit., p. 21).

me [this], so that I may always remain within the dense (*ghana*) joy of union (*samāveśa*)."

Bailly translates the verse in the following way:

> When I touch the soles of your feet, it sometimes flashes in my mind that this whole world has merged into a lake of nectar. Lord! Grant me this always![49]

Thus, she interprets the effect of the "touch" as an idea, an image which flares in the mind, i.e. that the whole world has dissolved in a lake of nectar. But why should somebody request the Lord to grant "this" (this conception) incessantly?

A different meaning results in understanding *yatra* ("where," "whereupon") as an opening of a causal clause: by the touch of *śakti*, the whole world dissolves in a lake of nectar.

How can we understand the "dissolution of the world," the cosmic dissolution (*pralaya*)? Unlike the destruction of the whole world (*mahāpralaya*) at the end of a Kalpa,[50] it is limited in duration, a short-term dissolution of the objective outer reality. Utpaladeva compares it with the state of deep sleep (*suṣupti*), "the state of the void of the recognizable" (*jñeyaśūnyatā*, *Īśvarapratyabhijñākārikā* III. 2.13), the level of the identification of the I "[. . .] with the negation (*niṣedha*) of the intellect (*buddhi*), the breath (*prāṇa*), etc." (*Īśvarapratyabhijñākārikā* III. 2.13 *v*). It is the state of *apavedyasauṣupta* (deep sleep without any cognition), in which the objects of cognition, including intellect and breath, are dissolved.[51] Or, expressed differently, the "projection" (*sṛṣṭi*)

49. Bailly, *Shaiva Devotional Songs*, op. cit., p. 51.

50. *Kalpa*: a cosmic age for a mythical period of time (a day of Brahmā; one thousand *yugas* or 320 million years of us mortals), cf. MW p. 262.

51. Cf. Torella, *ĪPK*, op. cit., p. 203, fn. 20.

of the outer reality, which takes place through the function of the three inner senses (*buddhi, manas, ahaṁkāra*) and the ten outer senses and which constitutes the state of wakefulness (*jāgrat*, cf. *Īśvarapratyabhijñākārikā* III. 2.17), ends for a certain period. But this is not the type of dissolution which is sought. As Utpaladeva clarifies in his *Īśvarapratyabhijñākārikā*: the states of wakefulness, dream and deep sleep should be abandoned, because in them the false identifications of the breath, etc. with the self still prevail, and also because one's freedom is reduced in these states (cf. *Īśvarapratyabhijñākārikā* III. 2.18). The point is to attain a different type of dissolution of the cognizable reality: the "fourth" (*turīya*) state, beyond wakefulness, dream and deep sleep. Utpaladeva briefly describes this state:

> Flowing upwards through the middle path, the breath is called *udāna*; it is in the fourth state and is made of fire [. . .].
>
> — *Īśvarapratyabhijñākārikā* III. 2.20

Abhinavagupta adds in his commentary of Utpaladeva's *Īśvarapratyabhijñākārikā*: the rising movement of the inner power of breath in the "median way" (*suṣumnā*) "causes all duality (*bheda*) to melt like ghee."[52] The power of breath, rising in *suṣumnā*, is fire, which burns all duality — of inhalation (*apāna*) and exhalation (*prāṇa*), of day and night, of projection and dissolution, of birth and death[53] — the whole world which

52. *Bhāskarī: A Commentary on the Īśvarapratyabhijñāvimarśinī of Ācārya Abhinavagupta*, ed. K.A. Subramania Iyer/K.C. Pandey, vol. II (1950): Delhi: Motilal Banarsidass, 2nd edn. 1986, p. 274 (= *ĪPV*). — translation: *Bhāskarī*, vol. III: An English translation by K.C. Pandey, Varanasi (1954), 2nd edn. 1998, pp. 217f.

53. Cf. *Īśvarapratyabhijñāvivṛttivimarśinī of Abhinavagupta*, vols. I-III (KSTS 60, 62, 65), Bombay, 1938-1943. Reprint: Delhi, 1987. Here: vol. III, pp. 350f.

exists in time and space and consists of dualities and differentiations.

Now it becomes more clear, what Utpaladeva and Kṣemarāja express in the code language of that esoteric tradition: "the touch of *śakti*" (*śaktisparśa*) results in the "fourth" state — a certain (higher) state of consciousness, usually within the process of meditation, where the outer, objective world is (subjectively) dissolved. This state consists of a specific state of *prāṇa*.

The word *prāṇa* is derived from the verbal form *prāṇ-* (*prā*, "filling," cf. MW 701, and the root *an-*, "to breathe, respire, gasp; to live [. . .]; to move, go", MW 24). *Prāṇa* is "the breath of life, breath, respiration, spirit, vitality, (. . .) wind, vigour, energy, power" (MW 705). According to Trika, the universal, pure *cit*, the highest reality of conscious light, manifests in its first creative vibration as *prāṇa*. Kallaṭa, author of the *Spandavṛtti* (ninth century), the commentary to *Spandakārikā*,[54] coined the famous phrase:

prāk saṁvit prāṇe pariṇatā
Prāṇa is the first (*prāk*) development (*pariṇati*)[55] of *saṁvit*.[56]

---

54. *Stanzas on Vibration: The Spandakārikā with four Commentaries*, translated with an Introduction and Exposition by Mark S.G. Dyczkowski, Varanasi: Dilip Kumar Publishers, 1994.

55. From *pariṇam* — *pari*, "round, around, about, fully, towards, . . ." and root *nam*, "to bend or bow, to turn towards, to yield or give way" (cf. MW, p. 528) — "to bend down, stoop, change or be transformed into, to develop, become ripe or mature, . . ." (MW, p. 594).

56. Cf. M. Dyczkowski's translation: "The vital breath is the first transformation of consciousness" (Dyczkowski, *Doctrine of Vibration*, op. cit., p. 266, notes). Since *prāṇa* includes more than the meaning "vital breath," I prefer not to translate this key-

→

Pandit Hemendra Nath Chakravarty says in this regard: "*Prāṇa*, so to say, mediates between Consciousness and the external manifestation in space and time."[57] Abhinavagupta quotes this sentence of Kallaṭa when he describes this important connection between *prāṇa* and *saṁvit*, in the context of the explanation of means (*upāya*) to enter into *anuttara*, more precisely: "the means as related to time" (*kālopāya*, cf. *Tantrāloka* 1.279ab):

> (9) *Saṁvit* alone, very pure and of the highest reality of light (*prakāśaparamārthaka*), detaching objectivity from itself, shines as the sky (*nabha*) free (*vivikta*) [from all things]. (10) It is proclaimed to be of the form of voidness (*śūnyarūpatva*), the highest state (*parā daśā*) which *yogī*s [attain] through *vimarśa* [with the attitude of] *neti, neti* (not so, not so).[58] (11) It is precisely this void self (*khātmā*) which is called *prāṇa*, "vibration" (*spanda*), wave (*ūrmi*); by virtue of its inner outpouring (*samucchalatattva*) it descends (*patana*) to the differentiation, which is separated from it, to take possession

---

→ term (similar to *cit*, *saṁvit*, etc.) to avoid a reduction of these terms to its merely human dimensions ("breath," "consciousness"), or, in other words: to avoid a modern anthropocentric interpretation. Cf. the more interpreting translation by H.N. Chakravarty, "Consciousness in its first creative upsurge manifests itself as *prāṇa*." (Hemendra Nath Chakravarty, "Prāṇa," in: *KTK* I, op. cit., pp. 123-53; here p. 141).

57. Ibid.

58. *neti neti*: in the Upaniṣads, the classical "negative Bezeichnung des Ātman oder Brahman, weil es mit keiner sinnlichen oder vorgestellten Wirklichkeit identifiziert werden kann" [negative characterization of *ātman* and *Brahman*, because it cannot be identified with any sensual or imagined reality] (Bettina Bäumer, *Befreiung zum Sein. Auswahl aus den Upanishaden* [Klassiker der östlichen Meditation. Spiritualität Indiens] Zürich/ Einsiedeln/ Köln, 1986, p. 254).

> of it. (12) Therefore it is said: "*prāṇa* is the first development of *saṁvit*,"[59] and that the breath (*vāyu*) becomes the refuge (*śrayāta*) of the principle (*tattva*) of the inner organ (*antaḥkaraṇa*). (13) This innate power of *prāṇana* (*prāṇanaśakti*), the intensive desire (*dohada*)[60] for an inner act (*antara udyoga*) [of *saṁvit* to develop, evolve into the dimension of differentiation], this is called "pulsation" (*spanda*), "effulgent vibrating" (*sphurattā*), "repose" (*viśrānti*), "life" (*jīva*), "heart" (*hṛt*), "intuition" (*pratibhā*).
>
> — *Tantrāloka* 6.9-13

Important for our understanding of *prāṇa* is that here the names for *prāṇaśakti* are the names of the highest, divine Śakti: *sphurattā, hṛt, pratibhā*.[61] Yet from this passage it becomes clear that *prāṇa* cannot be simply reduced to the empirical breath.

---

59. According to this context the statement could be understood as: *prāṇa* is the first manifestation or development of *saṁvit*, "which is of the nature of highest light," within the dimension of differentiation, objectivity, time and space. This dimension is, in a non-dualistic view, not separated from or opposite to the "Absolute"/"highest state," which is of the nature of the highest light, but a form of it, a particular manner of its appearance or its cognition. This is expressed with the expression "inner act" (*antara udyoga, TĀ* 6.13): this act of that Reality, "which is of the nature of the highest light," to develop and evolve into its cosmic form, into the realm of differentiation (e.g. time), happens *within* this (non-differentiated, timeless) Reality, and not in the form of a separation.

60. *Dohada* denotes "the longing of a pregnant woman for particular objects; (. . .) pregnancy" (MW, p. 499).

61. Cf. *ĪPK* I 5.14 (*sphurattā, hṛt*); *PHṛ* 83, Komm. *sūtra* 12 (*sphurattā*); *Parāprāveśikā*: "heart of the highest lord" (*hṛdayam parameśituḥ*); *TĀV* 3.67: *Kuṇḍalinī* (*kaulikī*) is the essence, the heart, the highest emission (*visarga*) of the lord; *MVV* 1.17cd-20ab: The "highest face" of Maheśvara, the "seed of the universe" is called "heart, vibration, knowledge (*dṛk*), the highest, essence, nameless (*nirnāma*), wave, etc."

Rather, the duality of the movement of the ingoing and outgoing breaths is, in the perspective of Trika, one of the microcosmic dimensions of *śakti*, in which it limits itself and "descends" (*patana*) into the realm of objectivity and differentiation (*bheda*). Abhinavagupta therefore uses for "breathing" a different expression, i.e. *vāyu* (wind, air). It becomes the "refuge" of the "inner organ" (*manas, buddhi, ahaṁkāra*), that falsely identifies with it and forgets its true nature (cf. *ĪPK* I.4-5; *TĀ* 6.15) — i.e. "of the nature of the light of the highest reality."

It now becomes clear as to what may be the background of Utpaladeva's expression in the first part of our verse, *Śivastotrāvalī* 5.26: "Sometimes something extraordinary flares up (*sphurati*) in [my] mind at the touch of the soles of your feet." The word *sphurati* brings us to an important, frequently used group of words in Trika Śaivism, derived from the root *sphur-*. On the one hand, it means "to tremble, throb, quiver, palpitate, twitch," on the other hand, "to flash, glitter, gleam, glisten, twinkle, sparkle, shine," but also "to burst out, come into view, to break forth, be evident or manifest" (cf. MW 1270). The qualities of "Parāśakti," the "Goddess" or the "Highest *kuṇḍalinī*" are condensed in this one word, and, since it forms the core of Trika, the core of its experience and understanding of reality is expressed in it, i.e. the pervasion (gr. *perichoresis*) of the threefoldness (in Christian theological terms: "triunity," "trinity") of "Śiva" (the Highest, transcendence), "Śakti" (divine dynamics of the Highest, immanence) and "Nara" (world): The all-permeating, sparkling, effulgent, vibrating, pulsating essence of the whole reality bursts forth — in a timeless flashing up — from its groundless ground, the highest light (*prakāśa*), in the form of the world, one with the light and its dynamic power, "her" "body" (*vapus*) full of light, but at the same time transcending it: "It is the Goddess *Cit* alone (*cideva bhagavatī*), who spontaneously and freely flares up (*sphurati*) in the form of innumerable worlds."[62]

> Again, in the highest Śiva (*paramaśiva*) — who transcends (*viśvottīrṇa*) the universe and is immanent (*viśvātmaka*) in it, consisting of the highest joy (*paramānanda*) of the condensation of light (*prakāśakaghana*) — effervesces (*sphurati*) the whole universe in non-difference (*abheda*) [of Him].[63]

Thus, *sphurattā* is the name for the "Highest word" (*parāvāk*), the highest *śakti*, the vibrating, pulsating, effulgent, throbbing ". . . heart of the supreme Lord, insofar as it is his essence" (*Īśvarapratyabhijñākārikā* I. 5.14).

> We adore *saṁvit*, which flashes forth (*sphurantīm*) in the form of the original highest Śakti (*parāśakti*), the heart of the highest Lord, she who consists of the world and transcends it.
>
> — *Parāprāveśikā*[64]

Important for our topic is that *śakti* can be understood as the "touchable" dimension of the transcendent-immanent "Highest," and in fact, *śakti* is identified with *vimarśa* (derived from the root *mṛś*, "to touch"), the "self-awareness"[65] of the highest light (*prakāśa*):

> Here [in Trika] the Highest Lord is of the nature of light (*prakāśātmā*) and the light is of the nature of *vimarśa*. *Vimarśa* is the flashing forth (*visphuraṇam*), which is the uncreated

---

62. Kṣemarāja, *PHṛ*, op. cit., *sūtra* 1 (commentary), p. 48. — Jaideva Singh translates *cideva bhagavatī* as: "divine consciousness alone."

63. Kṣemarāja, *PHṛ*, op. cit., *sūtra* 3 commentary, p. 54.

64. Kṣemarāja, *PP*, op. cit., p. 1.

65. Cf. *Vāc*, p. 77.

> "I" (*akṛtrima-aham*) in the form of the universe, of the light of the universe and of the dissolution of the universe.[66]

All these names — *sphurattā*, *śakti*, the essence, the heart, *parāvāk*, the highest emission — refer to each other, denote different aspects, and are at the same time names of *kuṇḍalinī* (cf. *TĀV* 3.69), even if the authors of Trika use that expression in only a few places.

In my opinion, this is the background for Utpaladeva's exclamation: "Sometimes something extraordinary flashes (*sphurati*) in [my] mind at the touch of the soles of your feet."

In the quoted texts of the Trika school, the word *sphurattā* is a central element of the revelation of the nature of the divine power and dynamism.[67] These passages show the cosmic, cosmogonic dimension of Śakti: The whole universe emerges — essentially and in every moment — in the form of the flashing of Śakti within the "Highest" (*anuttara*), which is of the nature of the highest light (*prakāśa*). However, here in this verse of Utpaladeva we meet the touch of the *kuṇḍalinī*-power (*udānaśakti*) as the contact with the effulgent and vibrating power at the *individual* level — nevertheless, the macrocosmic, microcosmic, divine, human dimensions of the same reality must be integrated. They permeate each other, "touch" each other, as in a metaphor of Utpaladeva: "like day and night at the equinox (*viṣuvatīva*)" (*ĪPK* III. 2.19 *v*), when the duality of day and night is removed. Divine or cosmic dimensions of Śakti (*kuṇḍalinī*) aren't to be set against the human dimension, the concrete experience of *sphurattā* as a result of the "touch" of *kuṇḍalinī* at the individual level as described by Utpaladeva (something extraordinary flashes in my mind) or, in our times,

---

66. Kṣemarāja, *PP*, op. cit., p. 1.

67. For *sphurattā* see Torella, *ĪPK*, op. cit., p. 121, fn. 28.

by Lilian Silburn. She paraphrases this experience of *sphurattā* as "a vibrant, gushing act of awareness" (*K* 219, index) or as "luminous vibrations, the flashing forth of consciousness" (*K* 6). And at the same time, one has to keep in mind that *sphurattā* is not merely an "effect" of the touch of Śakti, but — as Utpaladeva underlines in his auto-commentary of *Īśvarapratyabhijñākārikā* I. 5.14 — Śakti (here denoted with her name *citi*) "is, by nature, luminous vibrating, it is the subject[68] of this luminous vibrating" (*sphuradrūpatā sphuraṇakartṛtā*, *ĪPK* I. 5.14 *v*).

It is now clear that the meaning of the verse is deeper than expressed by the translation of Bailly (that an image flashes in the mind).

In verse 8.9 the metaphor of nectar is directly connected with "touch":

> Even if I am only once (*kadācana*) touched — just a little bit (*tanīyasa*) — by the drops (*kaṇa*) of the nectar (*amṛta*) of your touch (*saṅgama*), I would avert my face from all worldly pleasures (*lokasukheṣu*).
>
> Why then am I deprived of (*cyuta*) both (*ubhaya*)?
>
> —*Śivastotrāvalī* 8.9

It is the complaint of somebody who has experienced the highest joy, i.e. who came into contact or was touched by the dynamism of that "Highest," "consisting of the highest joy (*paramānanda*) of the condensation of light (*prakāśakaghana*)"[69] — maybe just for a moment, "just a little bit." But this was enough to feel all worldly joys compared to it as flat, insipid and

68. *Kartṛtā*: "the state of being the agent of an action" (MW, p. 258); "agency"; cf. *kartrī*, "one who makes or does or acts or effects, a doer, maker, agent, author" (MW, p. 257).

69. Kṣemarāja, *PHṛ*, op. cit., *sūtra* 3 commentary, p. 54.

provisional. And now, as the joys of this world became relative for this person, also the experience of this true, highest joy is withheld — because this is the touch of the absolutely free and independent, of *svātantrya* (absolute freedom, autonomy). It hides itself, and unexpectedly it suddenly appears and touches one, in the centre of one's heart, with an unspeakable kind of presence — like in the play of lovers in a baroque labyrinth, in which they grasp at each other, kiss (touch), then slip away and hide.

However, Kṣemarāja has a different touch in mind, for he explains *saṅgama* with "union with you" (*tvat samāveśa*); accordingly, the "sprinkling with nectar" with "immersed into nectar." In his commentary of "all worldly pleasures" he quotes the end of *Yogasūtra* 2.15: "For the discriminating persons everything is sorrow" (*sarvaṁ duḥkhaṁ vivekinaḥ*). Those having attained the discriminating cognition (*viveka*), cognize the clinging, the attachment to provisional, temporary joys as the cause of sorrow.[70] Kṣemarāja continues after this quotation: "According to this truth the world has to be abandoned." However, he clarifies at this point, that he does not take this position, rather presents here the specific view of non-dualistic Tāntric Śaivism. It represents exactly the opposite: not "to abandon the world." Accordingly, he interprets "by the sprinkling with the highest nectar I have averted my face" with:

> Thus I will turn towards (*sammukha eva bhaviṣyāmi*).[71] How? "Averted from both" — from that which has to be abandoned

---

70. For the meaning of *viveka* see *YS* 2.26-29 (Hariharānanda Āraṇya: *Yoga Philosophy of Patañjali*, op. cit., pp. 198ff).

71. *Sam-mukha:* "facing, fronting, confronting, being face to face or in front of; directed or turned towards; towards, near to" (cf. MW, p. 1180).

> or to be accepted; the meaning is: one should view everything without difference (*abhedena*).[72]

Kṣemarāja alters the perspective of the verse: while Utpaladeva says that the experience of the "nectar of touch" leads to an aversion towards common pleasures, Kṣemarāja states that the result of this experience is that one "will turn towards" the world and "face" the world. The result of the immediate contact with the "highest joy" is not an ascetic turning away from the world, an abandonment of the world, but a turning towards all — a "facing," maybe including the new power "to see what is," instead of a repression of the frightening aspects of the actual (political, economic, social . . .) reality. At the same time, Kṣemarāja explains in which attitude this "facing" happens (How?): One views everything "without difference," without differentiation. In my opinion it refers not to a moral demand that one ought to view everything without judging, in an attitude of a spiritual indifference. Rather, it refers to the highest state, in which the duality of "seer" and "seen," subject and object, "high" and "low," "worldly" and "spiritual" is removed and the unity of reality is recognized — a state which afterwards will affect one's daily perception. In a sense Kṣemarāja corrects the statement of his great-grand *guru* Utpaladeva: even between the "spiritual" joy and the "worldly" joy there is, in the last sense, no duality — both have the same source and essence.

The lament of verse 8.9 corresponds to the longing exclamation in 9.1:

> Longing (*utsuka*) for the taste (*āsvāda*) of the complete enjoyment (*saṁbhoga*) of the ever-new (*nava*), fresh (*ārdra*) experience (*rasa*), and having abandoned (*vihāya*) the other

72. *ŚSĀ*, p. 111.

(*anyan*), when (*kadā*) will my mind (*mama manaḥ*) transform (*pravarteta*) itself at your touch (*tvadsparśane*)?

— *Śivastotrāvalī* 9.1

A peculiar expression in this verse is *ārdra*, which means "liquid," as well as "moved, soft, wet, fluid, juicy, flowing, melted," etc. Together with *rasa* (lit. "juice") obviously the experience described concerns becoming soft, fluid, melting, where something stiff becomes soft and movable. In this way, Swami Lakshman Joo translates this part of the verse in Hindi as: "longing for the wonder of the excellent enjoyment (in the form of the complete immersion into) the utmost soft nectar of love."[73] The gerund *vihāya* is here literally rendered as "having abandoned" — in this way the translation tries to express that it doesn't refer to a condition (after he had abandoned the other) but to a simultaneous result of the transformation of the mind by the "touch": the duality of "this" and "other" dissolves. With the explanation within the brackets Swami Lakshman Joo gives a hint as to where and when this "complete enjoyment" occurs: in the immersion, diving and plunging (*samāveśa*). What happens with the mind through the "touch"? Utpaladeva says: *pravarteta*, which is translated here as "transform." Swami Lakshman Joo translates into Hindi as *lagā*, "to attach, strengthen," which may be/could be interpreted as "deepen."

Kṣemarāja comments on "through a new experience" (*navarasena*) with: "through a new unfolding (*prasara*) of your love (*bhakti*)." *Ārdra* he explains with: "of the utmost affability, attractive (*spṛhaṇīya*)." "To transform at your touch" he interprets as: "May it [my mind] be full of your immersion (*tvat samāveśa-mayaṁ-bhavet*)." Theologically important is the

73. *ŚSĀ*, p. 115. For the translation from Hindi I would like to thank Dr Bettina Bäumer.

keyword *bhakti* in his commentary: it becomes clear that it is not a matter of the experience of an anonymous force, but rather is the experience of love, the touch of a "you," of the embrace (*samāśleṣa*, cf. *Śivastotrāvalī* 13.6, comm.) of the Goddess in her form as *kuṇḍalinī*. Therefore, Swami Lakshman Joo says about the experience of *kuṇḍalinī*:

> This is full of love, full of bliss, intensity of love rises here in *kuṇḍalinī*, in both *prāṇa-* and *cit-kuṇḍalinī*. It is the embodiment of love, of real love. Love is full of life, without love you are dead. You don't live if there is no love. I don't mean sexual love, I mean real love. Real love exists in *kuṇḍalinī*.[74]

These statements make dubious the stereotypical idea — based on a long tradition of prejudices and devaluations — of an opposition between a personal mysticism in Christianity, in which the love of God is in the centre, and an apersonal experience in Hindu religions which is seen as a lower form by Christian theologians.

The overwhelming result, caused by the experience of "touch," is expressed by Utpaladeva in the following verse:

> When will I feel the essence of your touch (*tvadsparśarasa*), [so that] my stream of tears of joy (*ānandabāṣpapūra*) will make me stammer (*gadgada*), my voice will break and my face (*vadana*) will blossom out (*ullāsita*) with laughter (*hāsa*)?
>
> — *Śivastotrāvalī* 9.16

Again Kṣemarāja clarifies in his commentary that the place of "touch" is the "inner absorption" (*antaḥ samāveśa*), the slow immersion into the "ground" of the self and of all things, which

74. Swami Lakshman Joo, *Kashmir Śaivism. The Secret Supreme* (Audio Study Set), Culver City, CA: Universal Shaiva Fellowship, 2002, ch. 17 (CD no. 12).

is nothing other than supreme joy. "Full with tears of joy," the result of "touch," he explains with: "tears, due to the joy of the inner absorption (*antaḥ samāveśa*)."[75] Therefore, one could understand the interrelation of *sparśa* and *rasa* within the word *sparśa rasa* in the verse differently: "When will I attain the touch of your joyful essence (*rasa*) . . . ?" The supreme joy is not merely a result of touch, but it is the touch of the Supreme Joy itself, of the pure joy, the essence of the "Highest" (*anuttara*) described by Kṣemarāja in his *Pratyabhijñāhṛdaya*:

> Again, within the highest Śiva (*paramaśiva*) — who transcends (*viśvottīrṇa*) the universe and is immanent (*viśvātmaka*) in it, consisting of the highest joy (*paramānanda*) of the condensation of light (*prakāśakaghana*) — flashes (*sphurati*) the whole universe in non-difference (*abheda*) [of Him].[76]

In the commentary of *Śivastotrāvalī* 9.16 Kṣemarāja explains "stammer" (*gadgada*) as: "inarticulate sounds" (*aspaṣṭākṣara*) and *akranda* as "the great sound" (*mahānāda*); one could understand these in the way that uttering inarticulate sounds and one's voice breaking are expressions of the "great sound." "By laughing" (*hāsena*) he interprets with: "to blossom out by unfolding (*vikāsa*)."

The expression *vikāsa* and its counterpart *saṁkoca* (contraction) refer in this system — among many other usages — to two movements of *prāṇakuṇḍalinī* (cf. *K* 64ff):

— *saṁkoca* to the descent of the innate power of breath (*prāṇa-śakti*) from *tālu*[77] down to the lowest *cakra*

---

75. *ŚSĀ*, p. 127.

76. Kṣemarāja, *PHṛ*, op. cit., *sūtra* 3 commentary, p. 54.

77. *Tālu*: point within the subtle body, "at the back of the vault of the palate," called as well *lambikā, uvala* or *catuṣpada* (*K*, p. 28).

(*mūlādhāra*), after the movement of breath having stopped at the point between ingoing and outgoing breath for half a minute, and its rushing into the "median way" (*suṣumnā*); this form of *prāṇa-kuṇḍalinī* is called the "lower *kuṇḍalinī*" (*adhaḥkuṇḍalinī*) and is connected with an interiorization, a withdrawal (*saṁkoca*) of the power and an absorption with closed eyes; and

— *vikāsa* to the rising of the innate power of breath through the "median way" in the form of the "rising breath" (*udāna*); this form of *prāṇa-kuṇḍalinī* is called the "ascending *kuṇḍalinī*" (*ūrdhvakuṇḍalinī*) and is connected with the unfolding and expansion (*vikāsa*) of the power until the "all-pervasion" or "great pervasion" (*mahāvyāpti*) and an absorption with open eyes.

In this way, the term *vikāsa* in the commentary gives us a hint at the context in which the "touch" is experienced: the complete "immersion" (*samādhi* or *samāveśa*) by the ascending of the power of breath (*prāṇa-śakti*) in *suṣumnā* and its transformation into *kuṇḍalinī*, which rises from *cakra* to *cakra* within the subtle body and leads finally to a dissolution of discursive thinking, including duality, and to the direct cognition of the Self, which consists in supreme joy.

Kṣemarāja clarifies that this experience belongs to the "way of *śakti*" (*śāktopāya*), saying: this is for one "who is on the way of *śakti* (*śaktimārga*)." Therefore, it is said: "one whose face is beautiful (*śobhitaṁ*) by the liberating laughter."[78] He hints that these phenomena — tears of joy, etc. — are characteristic for the "way of *śakti*." Sushri Prabha Devi, the disciple of Lakshman

---

78. *ŚSĀ*, p. 127.

Joo, said about him with regard to this verse: "Precisely this was his state, very often."[79]

That *sparśa* denotes the highest possible experience, which is desired by spiritual practitioners, is also made clear by the following verse:

> Even if I have seen (*dṛṣṭe*) You, of the nature of the nectar of highest joy, the Self of the world (*jagadātmani*), with utmost intensity (*atyantatara*) I [nevertheless] long for (*utkaṇṭhitaḥasmi*) the joyful experience (*rasa*) of your touch (*sparśa*).
> — *Śivastotrāvalī* 10.15

Regarding our topic of *sparśa*, this verse is very important: here it becomes clear that the "touch" of that reality whose nature is described by Utpaladeva as the "essence of the highest joy" denotes a higher stage in the spiritual ascension than does "seeing" the Highest. Touch consists of an immediate contact, while seeing still implies a distance. Here, in this realm, a reversal of the traditional hierarchy of senses — Western as well as Indian — takes place, which normally ascribe the first rank to the sense of seeing and the last rank to the tactile. This hierarchy is reflected in the metaphors for the experience of God in Christian mysticism, which is primarily described as "vision" (Lat. *visio*).

Again Utpaladeva uses the word *sparśa* in connection with the expression *rasa* (lit. "juice," "liquid"). Maybe he wants to indicate that the spiritual process leads to a "liquefaction," "becoming liquid," a fluidity of the stiff and rigid I-identity of the "solidified" self in the form of body, breath, etc. of the borders between self and other — up to the experience of pervasion (*vyāpti*) of the self by all, and of the all by the self.

79. Personal information (Faridabad, Haryana, 27 February 2004).

Kṣemarāja interprets this verse in the following way: he expounds "after having seen you in the form of the self of the universe, in the form of blue (*nīla*) and yellow (*pīta*), etc." as: "nevertheless I have recognized (*pratyabhijñate*) you in this form in the common consciousness (*vyutthāna*)." Thus, he describes the experience of "seeing" of the Self of the world as a temporary, provisional experience, for it occurs in the normal everyday consciousness which is characterized by perceiving the duality of subject and object. Therefore, he longs for the immediate "touch" of the divine power, for the state "beyond the fourth" (*turīyātīta*), in which all duality and separation have vanished. Kṣemarāja interprets *sparśarase* with: "in the expansion (*prasare*) of the touch (*sparśa*) of the deep entering (*gāḍha-samāveśa*) — this I long for."[80] Here object-consciousness (*vyutthāna*) and absorption (*samāveśa*) form an opposition, while the state of *krama-mudrā* integrates both: one moves from the complete absorption into the Self towards the outside, towards the sensual perception of the outer reality and immerses oneself again into the highest Self, and so on. Abhinavagupta compares this twofold movement of inward withdrawal and outward expansion with the natural movement of the belly of a fish (cf. *TĀ* 5.58cd-60ab). Swami Lakshman Joo indicates that the experience of *krama-mudrā* is an element of the interiorized sexual act (*caryākrama*): "Under such influence even a *kaulayogī*, at the time of *siddha yoginīs* (. . .) possesses the supreme and unstained state."[81]

---

80. *ŚSĀ*, p. 127.

81. Jankinath Kaul "Kamal" (ed.), *The Awakening of Supreme Consciousness. Lectures of Swami Lakshman Joo,* Srinagar/Jammu/Delhi: Ishwara Ashrama Trust/Delhi: Utpal Publications, 1998, 96. — About *krama-mudrā* as a part of the interiorized sexual union see *K*, pp. 170f.

The most important verse for our theme — the meaning of *sparśa* in the *Śivastotrāvalī* — we find in chapter 13:

> Where the supreme Lord (*parameśvara*) Himself (*svayam*) is meditated upon (*dhyāyate*), thereafter (*tadanu*) being seen (*dṛśyate*) and then (*tataḥ*) touched (*spṛśyate*) — there (*yatra*), where You are experienced (*bhavato 'nubhāvataḥ*),[82] may the great festival of Your worship (*pūjanamahotsavaḥ*) always occur to me (*sa me*). — *Śivastotrāvalī* 13.6[83]

Here Utpaladeva underlines that "meditation," "vision" and "touch" refer to stages of experiences of the Supreme Lord. This description of a sequence of stages gets lost in Bailly's translation, which omits the temporal terms (afterwards):

> Let there be that great festival of worship
> Where the Supreme Lord himself
> Is meditated upon, seen, and touched.
> Be always mine through your grace.[84]

But Utpaladeva actually stresses this temporal order, by using two times a temporal term (*tadanu* and *tataḥ*), in a striking manner. In this way he underlines a fact which we already discovered in verse 10.15: it is a matter of sequential and progressive stages of nearness which gradually intensifies until the immediate contact (*sparśa*). What comes "afterwards"? Each form of feeling (at the higher, subtle level) of "a touching

---

82. *Anubhāva*, from: prefix *anu* ("alongside," "near to," "with"; cf. MW, p. 31) and root *bhū*, "to become, to be" (cf. English: "be," German: "bin"; MW, p. 760), therefore it means: to be near, "to enclose, embrace" (MW, p. 36). In this way, Utpaladeva uses in the verse, after "is touched," again a "tactile" expression, and maybe we could translate also: ". . . there, where you are embraced . . .."

83. *ŚSĀ*, p. 127.

84. Bailly, *Shaiva Devotional Songs*, op. cit., p. 77.

reality," a "touch" and somebody who is "touched" dissolves, and one melts with "that." Or, in other words, one realizes or recognizes the original unity. In this perspective, *sparśa* seems to be the highest possible experience before one is carried into a state where there is no more any subject of experience, any experience or any experienced object. We will come across these stages of proximity again in Abhinavagupta's *Tantrāloka*, where he assigns the experience of *sparśa* to a precise stage in the ascent of "the power of *oṁ*."

The translation of this verse into Hindi by Swami Lakshman Joo is revealing:

> O Lord! Where the Lord itself (that is, without effort, *anāyāsa hī*) is meditated upon, is thereafter seen (in *samāveśa*) and after that is touched of itself (spontaneously), exactly there let this great festival of your worship be always attained by me through your might (*prabhāva*).[85]

Thus, Swami Lakshman Joo specifies the context of the "seeing of the supreme Lord" to be the complete absorption or immersion (*samāveśa*). On the other hand, he translates *anubhavataḥ* not as "experience," but according to the general meaning of the word: "might," "power," "authority," "result' etc. He underlines that it is a meditation (*dhyāna*) "without effort." This statement is typical for the interiorized form of *yoga* of the Kashmir Śaivites, which at first consists in awareness on one's breath, then in the one-pointed concentration during the ascent of the innate power of breath (*prāṇa-śakti*). *Dhyāna* denotes that moment at which — because of the uninterrupted awareness on the point between ingoing and outgoing breath (at the end of exhaling, at the beginning

85. *ŚSĀ*, p. 197. Translation Bettina Bäumer.

of inhaling) — the breath stops, for half a minute.[86] In the context of the twelve stages of the ascent of the energy of *oṁ* (*uccāra* of *oṁ*) it is that stage of the ascent of *kuṇḍalinī* which is denoted as *ardhacandra* (half-moon).[87] As we have seen in the case of the interpretation of *Śivastotrāvalī* 9.16, this stage leads to the rushing of the power of breath towards the lowest *cakra*, into the "median path" (*suṣumnā*) associated with the complete immersion (*samāveśa*). Swami Lakshman Joo assigns the "seeing of the supreme Lord" to this state. "Afterwards" (*tataḥ*) the touch is experienced, or, as Utpaladeva expresses it in the active form: the supreme Lord is touched (*spṛśyate*). Now, in which state, at which stage of the ascent of *kuṇḍalinī* in the subtle body does *sparśa* occur? As we have seen in the other verses, this experience takes place precisely in the state of *samāveśa*. Maybe we could conclude that the "touching," contrary to "seeing," occurs in a later moment of the ascent of *kuṇḍalinī*. In the second part of this chapter, in the analysis of *sparśa* in the *Tantrāloka*, we will see that the experience of *sparśa* is actually associated with the penetration of the uppermost *cakra* (*brahmarandhra*) and the emergence of the ascending subtle power from the body.

In the perspective of the *upāyas*, one could be inclined to connect the three stages of *dhyāna*, *darśana* and *sparśa* with the three stages of "the way of the limited soul" (*āṇavopāya*), "the way of the power" (*śāktopāya*) and "the way of Śambhu" (*śāmbhavopāya*). However, Swami Lakshman Joo clarifies that even the stages *before* "meditation" (*dhyāna*) — the uninterrupted awareness on the middle point between

86. Kaul "Kamal" (ed.), *Awakening of Supreme Consciousness*, op. cit., pp. 30f (fourth lecture by Swami Lakshman Joo, 31 May 1980).

87. Cf. *Vijñāna-Bhairava: The Practice of Centring Awareness*, op. cit., p. 5.

exhalation and inhalation (cf. *Netratantra* 8.12f; *Vijñāna-Bhairava* śl. 61) — do not belong to *āṇavopāya* (or *kriyopāya*), but rather to *śāktopāya*, inasmuch as no "action" is required:

> It is not *āṇavopāya* because you have only to maintain awareness. With no recitation of *mantra*, you have only to inhale and exhale and to see where the two voids are, between the outgoing and the incoming breaths.[88]

Śāktopāya — the gliding transition from discursive thinking (*vikalpa*) to a higher, non-discursive state within the process of the ascent of *kuṇḍalinī* — leads to *śāmbhavopāya*, the persistence of this state, and finally to the pervasion of self and universe. In other words, the awareness of the void between inhaling and exhaling leads to the state of voidness, in which finally the "Highest" is "touched."

Now it becomes clearer as to what Swami Lakshman Joo means by *dhyāna* "without effort"; only the initial stages (*prāṇāyāma* and *pratyāhāra*) are based on concentration (upon the breath), while a process starts after the stage of *dhyāna* (or *ardhacandra*), after the cessation of the breath, which cannot be directed by one's own will, but happens by itself.[89] It is not based on one's own yogic achievement, but only depends on grace, as Swami Lakshman Joo states precisely about the stage of *dhyāna*:

> It is the grace of God which carries you from the lowest point to the highest point. You are automatically carried after you cross the boundary of *māyā*; however, His grace has been with you throughout the whole of your journey.

---

88. Lakshman Joo, *Vijñāna-Bhairava*, op. cit., p. 22 (commentary to *VBh*, śl. 25).

89. Cf. Kaul "Kamal" (ed.), *Awakening of Supreme Consciousness*, op. cit., p. 30.

> His grace is always there in the background, for if it were not there you could not do anything.[90]

How does Kṣemarāja comment on this verse from the *Śivastotrāvalī* (13.6)? At first sight it can be seen that he comments on this verse in great detail, to underline its importance. First he quotes a part of a verse in the *Mālinīvijayottaratantra*: "The reality (*vastu*) which is meditated upon (*vicintayan*) without the utterance (*uccāra*) [of a *mantra*], but with the mind (*cetas*) alone." (*MVT* 2.22).[91] Then he says: "In this state one meditates." In this way, Kṣemarāja seems to emphasize that this form of "meditation" (*dhyāna*) refers to the stage of *śāktopāya* — to a subtle yogic process of the power of breath, and not to a voluntarily meditative practice of concentration, imagination, recitation or the like. He continues: "And afterwards he is seen — he shines due to the complete immersion (*samāveśa prakāśate*)." It becomes clear that this experience in *samāveśa*, which precedes the experience of touch, has to do with light. It is the experience of the Highest (*anuttara*), which is of the nature of light, as Abhinavagupta says in the *Tantrāloka*:

> The highest reality (*param tattvam*) of the cognizable (*jñeya*) is Śiva, of the nature of light (*prakāśātmaka*), for that which is not of the form of light (*nahyaprakāśarūpa*) can neither be illuminated (*prākāśyam*) nor does it have real existence (*vastutā*).
>
> — *TĀ* 1.52

It is the unfolding or flashing of one's own true nature, the light of the Self, or, from another perspective, it is the state of union with the true nature of all which is light, as Abhinavagupta puts it in his *Paramārthasāra*:

---

90. Swami Lakshman Joo, quoted in *The Mālinī* (15 April 1996), p. 17.
91. *ŚSĀ*, p. 197.

> Awakened (*pratibuddha*) in this way, [the person] sacrifices all thought-constructs (*vikalpāḥ*) in the light of the Self, illuminated (*dīpta*) by the touch (*samīra*) of realization (*bhāvanā*), and becomes full of light.
>
> — *Paramārthasāra*, verse 68[92]

Samīra means "air, breeze, wind," also "touch," from *sam-* ("with," "together," expressing "conjunction," "union," "intensity") and the root *īr*, "to go, move, rise," etc. in this way meaning "to join together." So this verse also combines the experiences of light and touch: one experiences the "touch of realization" (of the light of the Self) after having dissolved all thought-constructs and discursive thinking. The touch is here in the centre: it kindles the "light of the Self," in the sense of making it visible or uncovered.

The way of describing this process of the highest experience (in the state of *samāveśa*) and its stages by Utpaladeva and Kṣemarāja corresponds with a statement by Abhinavagupta [redacted] 29, though Abhinavagu[redacted]*rśa*, but a synonym: [redacted]

> The supreme Bhairava [redacted]herein as sound (*nāda*), with eight aspects (*aṣṭavidha*), of [redacted] nature of light (*jyoti*), of resonance (*dhvani*) and of touch (*samīra*), is known as the highest pervasion (*vyāptirucyate paramā*) of Māntrī.
>
> — *TĀ* 29.159cd-160

This important passage will be examined at a later point in our study; here we should only note that Kṣemarāja does not mention the stage of the experience of "sound" or "resonance"

---

92. *The Paramārtha-Sāra by Abhinavagupta with the Commentary of Yogarāja*, ed. Jagadisha Chandra Chatterji (KSTS; 7) Srinagar: Research Department of the Kashmir State, 1916.

(*dhvani*) — probably because his commentary follows the verse of Utpaladeva and denotes the expression "seeing" as the experience of supreme light which precedes the experience of supreme touch. We should also note that there is no trace of the context in which Abhinavagupta describes these stages of the highest experience, the sexual ritual (*kulayāga*). Kṣemarāja would not have had any clue regarding the verse of Utpaladeva, belonging as he did to a stream of Trika which was different from the Kaula Tantrism of the *Tantrāloka*. This underlines that the highest experience is not limited to this one form of "sacrifice" (cf. *TĀ* 29.7, where Abhinavagupta mentions six forms of "sacrifice").

Kṣemarāja continues the commentary with an essential statement for our topic of *sparśa*:

> Afterwards he is touched (*tatopi spṛśyate*) — becoming one (*ekīkriyate*) by a more and more intense (*gāḍha gāḍha*) embrace (*samāśleṣa*).

Contact passes into a union — as the sexual touch and embrace can lead to the dissolution of the duality of the two partners, at least for a few moments. The description is concrete, seemingly based on his own experience: the touch, the embrace becomes "more and more intense."

At this point we are able to record an important result of our study of *sparśa* in the *Śivastotrāvalī*: it denotes the highest spiritual experience, after or above the experience of supreme light.

Gāḍha is derived from *gāh*, "to dive into, bathe in, enter deeply, to be absorbed," and means "to be dived into, entered deeply, firm, strong, excessively, intensive," etc. (cf. MW 354). Thus, the word combines the aspects of "immersion" (*samāveśa*) and of a very close and intense contact. The repetition of *gāḍha* marks a process, a continually intensifying contact, an ever-deepening submersion, a more complete melting, until all duality is dissolved. The word *samāśleṣa*, "a close and firm embrace" (MW 1163) also denotes an intensity of nearness and of contact. It reminds us of the last verse of the *Vijñāna-Bhairava*:

> *ityuktvānanditā devī kaṇṭhe lagnā śivasya tu* | |
>
> Having said this, the Goddess, full of bliss, embraced Śiva.
>
> — *Vijñāna-Bhairava*, *śl*. 163[93]

Laganā also means "touching" and expresses a close, intense contact. Insofar as this embrace or union with "Śiva" forms the end of the Tantra, it is underlined that this is the goal of all preceding exercises (*dhāraṇā*s). Swami Lakshman Joo comments upon these stages of the highest joy, touch and unification as follows:

> So, there ends the language of transcendental love which we have learned. This is the language of transcendental love.[94]

Now, Kṣemarāja discusses *svayam* (itself) in detail:

> Not dependent from other means like utterance (*uccāra*), [bodily] means (*karaṇa*), etc. [rather] through the "beautiful body" (*vapus*) [consisting] of pure *cit* (*cinmayena*) without succession (*naupacitena*), characterized by being not different (*ananya*).

As in the commentary of Swami Lakshman Joo on *svayam*, in his gloss of "the supreme Lord himself" Kṣemarāja

---

93. *Vijñāna-Bhairava: The Practice of Centring Awareness*, op. cit., p. 185.

94. Ibid.

characterizes the type of "meditation" by which the "Lord is seen" and afterwards "touched." It is not a meditation in the common sense; it does not take place with means like the ritual utterance of a *mantra* (*japa*) or certain bodily postures (*karaṇa*, cf. *TĀ* 1.170.220; 5.128-131). It, therefore, does not belong to the "way of the limited individual" (*āṇavopāya*). What happens cannot be directed voluntarily or consciously; it takes place in a different dimension of the body called *vapus*. The word *vapus* generally means "form," "body," especially "beautiful form," "beauty," as well as "essence," "nature" (cf. MW 920). One could therefore render *vapus* with "the beautiful body," the "essence" (of the body). Padoux and Silburn translate *vapus* in *Tantrāloka* 3.104.110 as "le corps cosmique."[95] Kṣemarāja himself clarifies how we should understand *vapus*:

— *Vapus* is "without succession" and *ananya* (lit. "no other"), "not different"/"without a second"; maybe we can interpret it as beyond the conditions of time, the objective reality, qualified by duality; and

— *vapus* consists of "pure *cit*."

Here, Kṣemarāja provides a very important hint about how we can understand the experience of "touching"/"being touched by" the Supreme in the state of *samāveśa*. It takes place within the "beautiful body" (*vapus*).

It is striking that Kṣemarāja does not simply state that the supreme Lord is touched and seen through pure *cit*, the subtlest, immaterial level of consciousness. Rather, he uses

95. Abhinavagupta, *La Lumiére sur les Tantras. Chapitres 1 à 5 du Tantrāloka.* Traduits et commentés par Lilian Silburn et André Padoux (Collége de France. Publications de l'Institute de Civilisation Indienne, Série in-8, fasc. 66) Paris: Édition-Diffusion de Boccard, 1998, pp. 162f (quoted as *Lumière* and page number); cf. index: "*corps cosmique de la divinite*" (ibid., p. 311).

the word *vapus* — the Supreme is touched and seen through a body, though at its subtlest level, consisting of pure *cit*. This may explain why the authors frequently use sensual terms — "seeing," "touching" — to denote the contact with the Highest which is beyond the realm of the common, physical senses. Though pure *cit*, *vapus* is provided with sensual faculties, although in its subtlest form, which allows it to touch/feel the touch of the Supreme. Therefore, the phenomenon of *vapus* may explain how we can understand these experiences of "seeing," "hearing" or "touching" as concrete, real sensual experiences, and not merely as metaphors or analogies for the human contact with the Absolute. The reality of a supreme form of senses — we could say the "*cit*-dimension" or "deep dimension" of the physical senses — corresponds to the phenomenon of "spiritual senses" in Western mysticism,[96]

96. *Survey*: Mariette Canévet, "Sens spirituel," in: DSp 14 (1990) pp. 598-617; Hans Urs von Balthasar, "Die geistlichen Sinne," in: id.: *Herrlichkeit. Eine theologische Ästhetik, Bd. 1: Schau der Gestalt*, Einsiedeln 1961, pp. 352-93; Karl Rahner, "Die Lehre von den 'geistlichen Sinnen' im Mittelalter," in: id., *Schriften zur Theologie*, Bd. 12, pp. 111-72. — *On particular authors*: Henri Crouzel, *Origène et la 'connaissance mystique'* (Museum Lessianum; Section théologique) 1961; Ulrich Köpf: *Religiöse Erfahrung in der Theologie Bernhards von Clairvaux* (*BHTh*; 61) 1980; Fridolin Marxer: *Die inneren geistlichen Sinne. Ein Beitrag zur Deutung ignatianischer Mystik*, Freiburg i. Br.: Herder, 1963; Karl Rahner, "Die geistlichen Sinne nach Origenes," in: id.: *Schriften zur Theologie*, Bd. 12, Zürich/Einsiedeln/Köln: Benziger, 1975, pp. 111-36; Margot Schmidt: "Elemente der Schau bei Mechthild von Magdeburg und Mechthild von Hackeborn. Zur Bedeutung der geistlichen Sinne," in: Peter Dinzelbacher/Dieter R. Bauer (Hg.), *Frauenmystik im Mittelalter*, Ostfildern 1985, pp. 123-51; Margot Schmidt, "Versinnlichte Transzendenz bei Mechthild von Magdeburg," in: *Minnichlichiu gotes erkennusse. Studien zur frühen abendländischen Mystiktradition. Heidelberger Mystiksymposium vom*

→

understood as the sensory faculties of the "inner man" (*homo interior*): The ears hear the voice of God, the eyes see the divine light, one tastes divine food and feels the embrace of God, as found, for example, in Augustine.[97] One must note, however, that the standard interpretation of the "spiritual senses" by Western theologians in modern times consists in an understanding of them as a metaphorical expression, a mere language of analogies.

How can we understand the reality of *vapus*? Here we might consider an important statement by Abhinavagupta in his *Tantrāloka*. According to him, each entity has two aspects: one aspect corresponds with the nature of *māyā*, which "offers resistance," and the other consists of "pure knowledge" (*śuddha vidyā*) and offers no resistance. Śiva appears within each entity in a twofold way: as the "(original) image" (*bimba*) and as the "reflection" (*pratibimba*) of this image (cf. *TĀ* 3.10-11). Accordingly, maybe we could say that *vapus* represents the

---

→ *16. Januar 1989*, hg. Dietrich Schmidtke, Stuttgart/Bad Cannstatt: Frommann-Holzboog, 1990, pp. 61-88; P. Doyere, *Sainte Gertrude et les sens spirituels*: *Revue d'ascétique et mystique* 36 (1960), pp. 445ff; id.: "Zur Bedeutung der geistlichen Sinne bei Hildegard von Bingen," in: *Tiefe des Gotteswissens — Schönheit der Sprachgestalt bei Hildegard von Bingen. Internationales Symposium in der Katholischen Akademie Rabanus Maurus, Wiesbaden-Naurod vom 9. bis 12. September 1994*, hg. Margot Schmidt (Mystik in Geschichte und Gegenwart; 1/10), Stuttgart/Bad Cannstatt: Frommann-Holzboog, 1995, pp. 117-42.

97. See Carol Harrison, "Senses, Spiritual," in: *Augustin through the Ages: An Encyclopedia*, ed. Allan D. Fitzgerald, Grand Rapids, Mich./Cambridge, U.K.: Eerdmans, 1999, pp. 767-68; P.L. Landsberg, *Les sens spirituel chez saint Augustin*: Dieu Vivant 11 (1948), pp. 83ff. — On the "inner man" in Augustine see Aimé Solignac, "Homme intérieur. 1. Saint Paul, 2. L'âge patristique": *DSp* 7/1 (1969) col. 650-658.

non-phenomenal dimension of the body, consisting of the "pure category" (*śuddha tattva*) above the category of *māyā*, i.e. "pure knowledge," contrary to the phenomenal, empirical dimension of the body within the realm of *māyā*.

Kṣemarāja continues his commentary: he expounds upon the statement of place, *yatra* (there) in the verse, with "in the great festival of worship (*pūjanamahotsava*)." Then he comments on the expression "the great festival" (*mahotsava*):

> With the word "great festival" he hints (*dhvanati*) at the utmost (*atyantam*) goal (*upādeyatām*) of the Self (*ātman*) by connection (*śakti*)[98] with it (*tad*), the fullness of intense joy (*pramodanirbharatāṁ*).[99]

"Meditation," "seeing," and "touching" are characterized as "the great festival." What is this festival? Kṣemarāja explains it to be that which is to be ultimately (*atyantam*) reached (*upādeyatām*) by the Self (*ātman*) — the connection, the union. What is this union? It consists in the "fullness of the highest joy." In this way it becomes clear why Utpaladeva has chosen the expression "the great festival": a festival is characterized by a joyful gathering, a joyful community. The *ātman* — the inner core of everything, the innermost reality of human beings — is identified as the fullness of the highest joy and bliss. The connection (*śakti*), or the touch of this *ātman*, is, therefore, the experience of this highest joy, the opening of this core — a festival of joy. The statement in the commentary reminds us

---

98. *Sakti*: "close connection," "clinging," etc., from *sañj*, "to cling or stick or adhere to" (cf. MW, p. 1132).

99. *ŚSĀ*, p. 197. — *Pramoda:* "excessive joy, delight, gladness" (MW, p. 686), with the intensifying prefix *pra*, "excessively, very, much" (MW, p. 652) and derived from the root *mud*, 'to be merry or glad or happy" (MW, p. 822).

of a verse in the *Spanda Kārikās*,[100] which will be examined in detail later:

> The will (*icchā*) of the limited individual alone is not able to vitiate the impulse of the will. But by the touch (*sparśa*) of the power (*bala*) of the Self (*ātmā*), man (*puruṣa*) becomes equal (*sama*) with that (*tat*). — *Spanda Kārikās* 1.8

Prabha Devi, the disciple of Swami Lakshman Joo, comments on the verse *Śivastotrāvalī* 13.6 in this way: *Sparśa* means immediate, inner and external experience. The "great festival" occurs when the inhalation and the exhalation are dissolved and *kuṇḍalinī* wakes.[101] In this way she — belonging to a line of transmission of esoteric teaching — puts into our hands a key to understand the encoded expression "the great festival of worship" (*pūjana-mahotsava*), which is used many times in the *Śivastotrāvalī* in the context of Śaiva Kuṇḍalinī Yoga.

The important conclusion that *sparśa* denotes the highest stage of spiritual experience, even above "vision," is confirmed by two further verses of the *Śivastotrāvalī*:

> O Lord (*prabho*)! For some (*keṣāmapi*) arises the thirst (*tṛṣi*) for your meditation (*dhyāna*), for the vision (*darśana*) and touch (*sparśana*) of the great lake of your worship, which has a cool taste (*śītalasvādu*). — *Śivastotrāvalī* 17.28

> The festival of your touch (*sparśanotsavaḥ*) [belongs to] the perfect one (*siddha*) who has given up (*tiraskāra*) the effort of meditation (*dhyānāyāsa*) — precisely this is the rule of worship (*pūjāvidhi*) [followed by] those who love you; may it always be so for me. — *Śivastotrāvalī* 17.4

---

100. *Spandakārikās of Vasugupta with the Nirṇaya by Kṣemarāja*, ed. Madhusudan Kaul (KSTS; 42) Srinagar 1925, p. 21.

101. Private communication (Srinagar, 16 September 2003).

Again it becomes clear that the experience of *sparśa* denotes the highest stage, the aim of the spiritual practices in this tradition. It cannot be reached by willpower or external means (like concentration on the breath, etc.) or through any other deliberate effort. Rather, it happens to oneself at a level of the spiritual process where one's own initial effort has ceased. Using the categories of the "ways" (*upāyas*) in non-dualistic Śaivism of Kashmir, one could say that it occurs when the "individual way" (*āṇavopāya*) has been left behind and turns into the two higher ways, the "way of power" (*śāktopāya*) and finally the "way of Śambhu" (*śāmbhavopāya*). It resonances with criticism for Haṭha-Yoga and other forms of *yoga* which stress the effort of the practitioner — a criticism which will be more explicit in Abhinavagupta and Kṣemarāja.

The experience that the essence of all things consists in intense joy, the purest light and subtle sonic vibrations (cf. *TĀ* 29.159cd-160) is the basis for a deeply positive view of phenomenal reality for the authors of non-dualistic Śaivism of Kashmir, in contrast to those of Advaita Vedānta. It seems that the dimension of Śakti in Kashmir Śaivism allows a form of non-dualism which is philosophically developed at the price neither of the reality of phenomenal world (by separating the Highest and the world) nor of the "transcendence" of the Highest (by identifying the Highest and the world). Rather, Śakti integrates the Divine (from which it is inseparable, cf. *Vijñāna-Bhairava*, verses 18 and 19) and the World (as its core and source).

This positive attitude towards the cosmos and its beauty is expressed in the following verse:[102]

---

102. *ŚSĀ*, p. 204. — For this topic see Bettina Bäumer, "Beauty as Ānandaśakti in Kashmir Śaivism," in: Harsha V. Dehejia/ Makarand Paranjape (eds.), *Saundarya: The Perception and Practice* →

> What (*yat*) [arouses] joyful astonishment (*camatkṛtim*) in all beautiful things (*subhaga-artha-vastuṣu*) by means (*vidhinā*) of a mere touch (*sparśa-mātra*) — that (*tāṁ*) is offered (*samarpayati*) to you; through it the one filled with unshakable love (*acala-bhakti-śālinaḥ*) adores you in your beautiful body (*vapu*).
> — *Śivastotrāvalī* 13.14

Swami Lakshman Joo translates and comments on this verse in Hindi in the following way:

> (O Sadāśiva!) That, which elicits (by the connection with the highest reality, *pāramārthika-yukti*) through all beautiful objects of the senses (since they are not separated from your spiritual form) an extraordinary astonishment by means of a mere touch (by the first appearance, *prāthamika ālocana* [in consciousness]), through this adore the one marked by your unshakable love, your worshipper, your spiritual form (*cinmaya svarūpa*).[103]

In this way he provides an important explanation as to what is the meaning of *sparśa* in this context: it is the first instant (*prathamā tuṭiḥ*) in which a sensation arises in one's awareness, yet before any thought (*vikalpa*) forms, before an integration of this sensation in the patterns of perceiving and interpreting sensory information could happen. In this "pure moment" one is able to touch the "beauty" itself, the essence of the beautiful thing, which connects one to its source, the highest reality, or the highest beauty. In contrast to the yogic practice of sensory withdrawal (*pratyāhāra*) as the prevention of contact between the senses and their objects (cf. *YS* II.54 and 55), this practice consists in the "catching" of the first moment when the senses

---

→ *of Beauty in India*, New Delhi: Samvad India Foundation, 2003, pp. 35-43.

103. *ŚSĀ*, pp. 204f. — I would like to thank Dr. Bäumer for the translation of this passage from Hindi.

come in contact with an object, where the pure reality of a thing can be touched. In this way Swami Lakshman Joo follows the commentary of Kṣemarāja, who explains "by means of a mere touch" (*sparśa-mātra-vidhinā*) in the following way:

> By the imagination (*vikalpena*) of contact (*samparka*) with *saṁvit* by means of permeation (*vyāpāreṇa*)[104] with *saṁvit*.[105]

Within the immediate "touch" of the pure nature of an object, of the essence of a sensory impression which is evoked by *śakti-kuṇḍalinī*,[106] happens a touch of an "absolute nature":

> The first impression (*saṁvedana*) of the first consciousness (*prathama-saṁvit*) of happiness (*sukha*), of the sound *sīt* (*sītkāra*), of a being (*sat*) and of sameness (*sāmya*) is the touch (*sparśa*) of *anuttara-saṁvit*. — *Tantrāloka* 5.142[107]

What is the reason for this? Swami Lakshman Joo says that the objects of the senses are "in truth" not separated from the highest reality. Kṣemarāja expresses it in this way:

> Although objects, due to the power of *māyā-śakti*, are to be accepted (*heya*) or abandoned (*upādeya*) — in truth they are beautiful, since they consist of *cinmaya*. All things have alone the purpose (*prayojana*) of beauty (*subhaga*). If these things become objects of sensual experience, then that which is cognized in the manner of senses (*indriya-pathagataṁ*) are form (*rūpa*), tactile quality (*sparśa*), and so on.[108]

---

104. Derived from the root *āp*, "to permeate," "pervade," "fill," "spread," etc. (cf. MW, p. 1037).

105. *ŚSĀ*, p. 205.

106. Cf. Swami Lakshman Joo, "The Secret of Understanding the Primal Power of Śiva," in: Kaul "Kamal" (ed.), *Awakening of Supreme Consciousness*, op. cit., pp. 87-97, here: pp. 88f.

107. This verse has been analysed under the heading "The Touch of Anuttara-Saṁvit", p. 154ff.

108. *ŚSĀ*, p. 205.

Kṣemarāja states an important qualification: objects of the senses are not to be simply accepted to be one with the Highest, since they are normally experienced in the realm of duality, in the realm of the power of *māyā-śakti* which hides their real nature, which is also Śakti, non-dual with regard to the Highest (*anuttara*). But "in truth," in reality they are "beautiful," since they consist of the nature of *cit*.

Important in this verse with regard to this Tāntric "theology of the senses" is the word "is offered" (*samarpayati*): "What [arouses] joyful astonishment in all beautiful things by the means of mere touch — that is offered to you." It reminds us of Abhinavagupta's "Hymn to the Wheel of Deities within the Body" (*Dehasthadevatācakra-Stotra),* in which he exclaims:[109]

> I praise Bhairava full of bliss (*ānanda-bhairava*),
> Of the nature of *cit* (*cinmaya*),
> Who is always worshipped by the deities of senses (*indriyadevyaḥ*)
> In the lotus of the heart
> With the [offerings of the] joy (*bhoga*) [of the senses]
> On their own objects. — Verse 3

And about the sense of touch, which is in his view as divine as all the other senses, as well as concerning the organ of touch, the skin, he says:[110]

> I adore Vārāhī in form of the skin,
> Who rests on the western petal of the flower
> And delights Bhairava

---

109. Sanskrit text: Pandey, *Abhinavagupta*, op. cit., pp. 952f. German translation by Bettina Bäumer (*Abhinavagupta. Wege ins Licht. Texte des tantrischen Śivaismus aus Kaschmir*, Zürich: Benziger, 1992, pp. 212-15, here, p. 213).

110. Ibid.

With the flowers of touch,
Which stir the heart. — Verse 10

With every touch of the skin the highest Deity (here called "Bhairava") is adored; each sensual joy is a form of worship of the Highest. This experience of the world represents the exact opposite of the world-view of certain forms of Advaita Vedānta, which propound an attitude of *asparśa*,[111] of "not-touching" — an attitude of distance, even of disgust for the sensually experienced world, not least of which for women, as being the realm of *māyā* and thus a hindrance to the experience of the Real. This positive view of *sparśa*, of the contact with the sensory world in Tāntric Kashmir Śaivism has, in my opinion, a metaphysical basis: in contrast to the description of the nature of the Absolute (*Brahman*) as the non-relative, as untouched by change and relations in Advaita Vedānta, the Kashmiri Śaivites developed a complex model of the transcendent-immanent Highest (*anuttara*) which is dynamically related with the world of change through his power (*Śakti*), and at the same time remains transcendent.

Abhinavagupta : Tantrāloka
With Commentary (Viveka) By Jayaratha

Introduction

The *Tantrāloka* (= *TĀ*) is the main work of Abhinavagupta (c. 975–1025) and therefore of the Trika school of non-dualistic

111. The term *asparśa-yoga* occurs twice in the *Gauḍapādīya-kārikā* (GK III.39 and IV.2). On the term *asparśa* in early Advaita philosophy see Richard King, "Asparśa-Yoga: Meditation and Epistemology in the Gauḍapādīya-Kārikā": *Journal of Indian Philosophy* 20 (1992) pp. 89-131.

Śaivism of Kashmir. With its 5858 verses, divided into 37 chapters (*āhnika*, literally "work of a day") of varying length it is the most extensive text of Abhinavagupta. The verses are mainly in a simple metre, *anuṣṭubh*;[112] also the metres *āryā* and *vasantatilakā* are found.[113] Abhinavagupta composed the *Tantrāloka* as one of his last works — the fruit of his lifelong occupation with the Tāntric traditions, especially the Kaula tradition, Sanskrit grammar, logic, literature, poetics, aesthetics, dramaturgy, philosophy, Buddhism, etc. from which many books emerged.[114] As Ingalls shows,[115] the *Tantrāloka* is not a text from the first phase of his life, as Pandey maintained.[116] He connects the Tāntric texts of Abhinavagupta

---

112. Cf. Teun Goudriaan, "Hindu Tantric Literature in Sanskrit," in: id./ Sanjukta Gupta, *Hindu Tāntric and Śākta Literature* (A History of Indian Literature; II/2) Wiesbaden: Harrassowitz, 1981, pp. 1-172; here p. 163 (= *HTSL*).

113. Cf. Navjivan Rastogi, *Introduction to the Tantrāloka: A Study in Structure*, Delhi: Motilal Banarsidass, 1987, pp. 167f.

114. Pandey gives a list with the names of 44 known works, which don't comprise his whole corpus: Kanti Chandra Pandey, *Abhinavagupta: An Historical and Philosophical Study* (1936) (The Chaukhamba Sanskrit Studies; 1) Varanasi: Chaukhamba Amarabharati Prakashan, Reprint 2000, pp. 27ff. Among them are such voluminous texts like the *TĀ* or the commentary to *Dhvanyāloka* (*Dhvanyāloka Locana*) or the commentary to *Nāṭyaśāstra* (*Abhinavabhāratī*). See V. Raghavan, *Abhinavagupta and His Works* (Chaukhambha Oriental Research Studies; 20) Varanasi/Delhi: Chaukhambha Orientalia, 1981.

115. Daniel H.H. Ingalls, "Introduction," in: *The Dhvanyāloka of Ānandavardhana with the Locana of Abhinavagupta*, ed. Daniel H. H. Ingalls. Translated by Daniel H.H. Ingalls, Jeffrey Moussaieff Masson, and M.V. Patwardhan (Harvard Oriental Series; 49) Cambridge, Mass./London: Harvard University Press, 1990, pp. 1-39; here p. 32.

116. Cf. Pandey, *Abhinavagupta*, op. cit., p. 41.

with his youth, before he started with literature and the *pratyabhijñā*-philosophy. To present the Tāntric phase as a kind of folly of one's youth is, in my opinion, an element of a particular strategy of Pandey to safeguard the honour of Abhinavagupta as a philosopher and brāhmaṇa and to create a distance between Abhinavagupta and the morally and religiously indecent Kaula Tantrism.

In *TĀ* 1.278-284 — at the end of the general introduction to the whole text — Abhinavagupta gives a list of the themes of all 37 chapters and their correlations; this detail already shows his systematic way of presentation. In my opinion, one could characterize the *TĀ* as a scholastic *summa* of non-dualistic Śaivism of Kashmir, in the best sense of scholasticism.[117]

---

117. José Ignacio Cabézon defines the term "scholasticism" by means of eight criteria by which it seems to be very much fitting for the *TĀ*:

    1. *Tradition:* a strong sense for tradition, its definition, maintenance and defence against its erosion;
    2. *Language*: an interest in language and especially in scripture and expressibility (even of the inexpressible);
    3. *Abundance*: a comprehensive approach to texts, categories and disputations;
    4. *Completeness*: a sense for the wholeness of the system, which disregards nothing;
    5. *Accessibility*: the epistemological approach to reality (by means of revelations, insight, examination);
    6. *Systematic representation*: a repetition of the order of the world;
    7. *Rationalism*: rational argumentation and analysis, avoidance of contradictions; and
    8. *Self-reflexivity*: use of the instruments of examination also for the practice of examining itself, including the meta-levels of the discourse like logic and hermeneutics.

→

Already in the twelfth century Śivānanda chooses the term *Trika-śāstra* (authoritative doctrinal text of the Trika school) to denote the *Tantrāloka*, which expresses the high position of this text,[118] and the commentator Jayaratha also underlines its didactic character.[119]

The title means "light on Tantra" or "light of the Tantras." In this way the primary intention of the work is expressed: to present a compendium (*saṁgraha-grantha*) of the available Tāntric literature of this time and a systematic interpretation and illumination of its content.[120] At the same time, Abhinavagupta wanted to create a theological and ritual manual (*prakriyā*) for his *Anuttara-Trika*-system (*anuttaraṣaḍardhārthakrama*), as he himself says in his introduction to the *Tantrāloka* (1.14-15). He declares the main basis of his text to be the *Mālinīvijayottaratantra*,[121] which he denotes as the essence of the Trika revelation (cf. *TĀ* 1.17-18).

The commentary (*viveka*) by Jayaratha (second half of twelfth century), the only preserved commentary on the *Tantrāloka*, is today an integral part of the work and represents an invaluable key to the understanding of the text, for the decoding of its code language, which is at times used by Abhinavagupta.[122]

→ Cf. José Ignacio Cabézon (ed.), *Scholasticism: Cross-Cultural and Comparative Perspectives*, Albany: State University of New York Press, 1998.

118. Cf. Rastogi, *Introduction to the Tantrāloka*, op. cit., p. 1.

119. Ibid., p. 10.

120. Ibid., p. 4.

121. *Mālinīvijayottaratantram*, ed. Pt. Madhusudan Kaul (KSTS; 37) Bombay 1922 (=*MVT*). — For *MVT* see Vasudeva, *The Yoga of the Mālinīvijayottaratantra*, op. cit.

122. For the *viveka* see Rastogi, *Introduction to the Tantrāloka*, op. cit., pp. 87-153.

The *Tantrāloka* was printed for the first time between 1918 and 1938 in Srinagar and Bombay, and was published in the "Kashmir Series of Texts and Studies" (= KSTS), edited by the Kashmirian Paṇḍits Mukund Ram (vol. 1) and Madhusudhan Kaul (vols. 2-12).[123] This edition is presumably based on four manuscripts.[124] A critical edition of the text does not exist. An edition which is available nowadays, is the reprint of the KSTS-edition, extended by an introduction (vol. 1) and appendix (vol. 8, list of sources used by Abhinavagupta, etc).[125] Since the main text is a mere reprint, the mistakes in the KSTS edition are not corrected.

The first and only complete translation into a European language is the Italian translation by Raniero Gnoli in 1972,[126] based on the KSTS-edition. But this translation does not include the commentary by Jayaratha, which is necessary for understanding Abhinavagupta's text. Teun Goudriaan has indicated the merits of this pioneering work while pointing out the shortcomings, that Gnoli sometimes translates too freely and includes the commentary of Jayaratha into the translation of the verses of the *Tantrāloka* as paraphrases, without making clear these additions.[127] A French translation

---

123. *Tantrāloka of Abhinavagupta with Rājānaka Jayaratha's Commentary*, 12 vols. (KSTS; 3, 28, 30, 36, 35, 29, 41, 47, 59, 57), ed. Pt. Mukund Ram and Madhusudan Kaul, Srinagar and Bombay, 1918-1938.

124. Cf. Rastogi, *Introduction to the Tantrāloka*, op. cit., p. 160.

125. *The Tantrāloka of Abhinavagupta with the Commentary of Jayaratha*, ed. R. C. Dwivedi and Navjivan Rastogi, 8 vols., Delhi: Motilal Banarsidass, 1987. — The *TĀ* is quoted from this edition.

126. Raniero Gnoli, *Luce delle Sacre Scritture di Abhinavagupta* (Classici delle Religioni: Le religioni orientali), Torino: Unione Tipografico-Editrice Torinese, 1972; 2nd edn. (Biblioteca Orientale; 4) Milano 1999.

127. Goudriaan, "Hindu Tantric Literature," in: *HTSL*, op. cit., p. 162, fn. 2.

of chapters 1 to 5 by André Padoux and Lilian Silburn was published in 1998, which gives summaries and extracts of the commentary for some verses.[128] Padoux legitimates this selection of the first five chapters — hardly a fifth part of the whole text — by arguing that the spiritual doctrine, which represents the goal of all the spiritual ways presented in the *Tantrāloka*, is contained in the first five chapters, while the remaining chapters only explain the different rituals to reach this goal. In my view this opinion does no justice to the *Tantrāloka*, which is extraordinarily composed as a holistic text, where passages at any distance from each other can refer to and illuminate each other. The text can only be understood as an integral, complex texture (Skr. *tantra*). In my view it is also a typically Western — and reductive — approach to hold the philosophical and spiritual part in higher esteem while neglecting the ritual aspects. How important these ritual aspects are is demonstrated by the fact of their voluminous description, especially the description of initiatory rituals (*dīkṣā*) in chapters 14 to 26.

The word *sparśa* occurs in the *Tantrāloka* at different places with different meanings. In a text like *Tantrāloka* no verse is negligible or less important. It will turn out that each use of *sparśa* — even if the word is used to mean a consonant or the subtle elements — will lead into the centre of the vision of reality which Abhinavagupta unfolds in this text. However, I will concentrate on selected passages in which the word appears as important for our topic, *śaktisparśa*.

---

128. Abhinavagupta, *La Lumiére sur les Tantras. Chapitres 1 à 5 du Tantrāloka*. Traduits et commentés par Lilian Silburn et André Padoux (Collège de France. Publications de l'Institut de Civilisation Indienne, Série in-7⁰, Fasc. 66) Paris: Édition-Diffusion de Boccard, 1998.

The Sensual Touch: Tantrāloka 3.328-329

Sparśa is one of the five "subtle elements" (*tanmātras*, literally "that alone" or "only that"):[129] *śabda* (sound), *sparśa* (touch), *rūpa* (form), *gandha* (smell), *rasa* (taste). In the view of the Indian philosophies, starting with Sāṁkhya, the five elements (*mahābhūtas*) arise from the "subtle elements."[130] The elements — earth, water, fire, air, ether — are nothing other than aggregates of the *tanmātras*. Abhinavagupta here follows the classical position (cf. *TĀ* 9.289), in that the elements have no self-supporting existence independent from the essential "qualities" of which they are composed (cf. *ĪPK* III.1.10-11 *v*).[131] From the subtle elements *sparśa* and *śabda* the element "air" (*vāyu*) arises (cf. *TĀ* 9.285ab); from the connection of *sparśa*, *śabda* and *rūpa* arises the element "fire" (*tejas*) (cf. 9.287ab); from the connection of these three essential qualities with *rasa* arises the element "water" (*jala*); and the final aggregate of all the *tanmātras* is "earth" (*pṛthvī*, cf. 9.287ab-288). *Sparśa* is the essential quality and is at the same time that which it qualifies, i.e. the tactile quality of the elements which are felt with the sense-organ skin; they are not distinct realities (cf. the discussion in *TĀ* 9.920-294ab).

---

129. On *tanmātra* in classical Sāṁkhya (which represents the general basis of the notion in later schools) see: *Encyclopedia of Indian Philosophies*. Vol. IV: *Sāṁkhya. A Dualist Tradition in Indian Philosophy*, ed. Gerald James Larson and Ram Shankar Bhattacharya, Delhi: Motilal Banarsidass, 1987, pp. 50-53; 264f; 281f; Gerald James Larson, *Classical Sāṁkhya: An Interpretation of its History and Meaning*, Delhi: Motilal Banarsidass, 1969, 2nd rev. edn. 1979, rpt. 2001, pp. 187f; in Yoga see: Swāmi Hariharānanda Āraṇya, *Yoga Philosophy of Patañjali with Bhāsvatī* (1963), Calcutta: University of Calcutta, 3rd rev. edn. 1981, 3rd enl. edn. 2000, pp. 173f.; 324.

130. Cf. *Sāṁkhyakārikā* XXII and XXVIII.

131. See Torella, *ĪPK*, p. 196, fn. 20.

Abhinavagupta adopts the definition of classical Sāṁkhya when he says that the *tanmātras* result from the "I-sense" (*ahaṁkāra*),[132] in which the quality (*guṇa*) *tamas* is dominating, which is connected with darkness, matter, heaviness, limitation:

> The *tamas-ahaṁkāra* veils the subjective aspect (*bhoktraṁśa*). It is called the first of the gross elements (*bhūtādi*).[133] From it originate the "subtle elements" (*tanmātra*), which are the cause (*kāraṇa*) of the five [gross] elements (*bhūta*).
>
> — *Tantrāloka* 9.271cd-272ab

That is to say, the *tanmātras* spring from the original, essential nature of the perfect Self (*pūrṇahantā*) and give rise to the perception of reality as separated from it. With the *tanmātras* "the objective perceptible reality (*grāhya*) starts" (*TĀ* 9.280ab). The *tanmātras* are in this way part of the necessary explanation: if there is, in truth, only the one non-dualistic reality (the perfect Self), why do I obviously perceive an objective, dualistic world of "I" and "other," of objective matter (things, plants, soil, . . .) separated and differentiated from me?

According to Abhinavagupta's definition (cf. *TĀ* 9.280cd), *sparśa tanmātra* is, as a *tattva*, the general principle (*sparśatva*), which is included in all forms of touch — of the sensation of touch, touching, touchability and the tactile quality of something. From a different perspective one could say that *sparśa tanmātra* is the "energy," the innate power of the tactile quality of an entity, of an element (*bhūta*) as well as the "touch"

---

132. Literally, *aham* (I), *kāra* (to make, do, work) — that process, which creates the wrong impression of an independent, substantial "I," the fictitious I.

133. Abhinavagupta refers here to *Sāṁkhyakārikā* XXV; cf. Larson, *Classical Sāṁkhya*, op. cit., p. 185.

of this energy, which operates through the sense organ of touch, the skin (*tvak*).[134]

In the non-dualistic perspective of the Trika school, *sparśa* is, like all the 36 *tattva*s or dimensions of reality, at the same time the cosmic expansion of Śiva, the highest of the 36 dimensions of reality, which pervades every *tattva*. It is a mode of the one reality, an internal modification of this one Real:

> *śivatattvam eva ekaṁ vastu sat*
> Indeed, the *tattva* Śiva is the one real.
> — *Īśvarapratyabhijñāvivṛttivimarśinī* III. 263[135]

In his commentary on the *Svacchandatantra*, Kṣemarāja defines *tattva* as that which "spreads" (*tananāt tattvam*), that which brings forth the manifestation.[136] Abhinavagupta writes in the third chapter about the power of emission (*visargaśakti*), the creative power of Śiva, the Goddess Parāparā, which is the cause (*kāraṇa*) of the universe (cf. 3.226):

> (228) The highest power (*param vīryam*)[137] is the energy (*kalā*) of the five elements (*pañcabhūta*); as the object of enjoyment

---

134. Jaideva Singh says in his introduction to *PHṛ*: "The *indriyas* are not sense-organs but powers which operate through the sense-organs." (*PHṛ*, intro., p. 16).

135. Quoted from Torella, *ĪPK*, p. 189, fn.2.

136. Cf. *Uddyota* zu *SvT* 4.241f; quoted from *Vāc* 365.

137. *Vīrya* is translated with "manliness, valour, strength, power, energy, virility, semen virile, vigour, efficacy" (MW, p. 1006). Jaideva Singh translates *vīrya* in *PTV* generally as "seminal energy" (e.g. *PTV*, p. 42). This expresses in my view a male perspective of the translator — because it would mean, that the spiritual process connected with it is reserved only for men. Silburn on the contrary translates as "efficacy" or "efficience (the exercise of efficient power)" (*K*, p. 219). But she underlines: "Even a rare word cannot convey the exceptional significance of *vīrya* in those ancient texts." →

(*bhogya*), it is food and the nature of sound (*śabda*), of touch (*sparśa*) and of taste (*rasa*).

(229) Even a sweet sound intensifies the power (*vīrya*), and so this power is seen as pure (*śuddham*) and ultimate (*param*), whose nature is the desire to emit.

(230ab) It is strength (*bala*), vitality (*ojas*), life (*prāṇa*), beauty (*kāntatā*). — *TĀ* 3.228-330ab[138]

The divine power is the innate, vibrating, luminous nature of *sparśa* with regard to every dimension of manifestation: of the elements, the subtle elements, the senses, etc. According to Kṣemarāja, the highest power of *cit* (*citśakti*, Citi, Kuṇḍalinī, Vāmeśvarī, "who emits the universe") displays herself wholly in the limited individual. When she begins to veil her nature, she takes the form of *khecarī* (who moves in void); then, concealing her undifferentiated nature, she takes the form of *gocarī* (who moves in the rays [of cognition]), i.e. the inner organ (the intellect, "I"-sense, etc.). When she further veils her nature, she takes the form of *dikcarī* (who moves in the spatial directions), i.e. the exteriorized sense-organs; finally she takes the form of *bhūcarī* (who moves upon the earth), i.e. differentiated objective existence.[139]

Here we meet the "metaphysical" basis of the Tāntric ways in which the senses and the sensual experience — especially in its most intense form, sexuality — are not devaluated, opposed

→ (ibid., p. 176, fn.). She explains *vīrya* as "the essence of semen," on which the *guru* acts in the case of a man, to bring it up to *brahmarandhra*; in the case of a woman he acts on her *prāṇa* (ibid., p. 175).

138. On this passage see Bettina Bäumer, "Beauty as Ānandaśakti," op. cit. (fn. 102).

139. Cf. *PHṛ*, p. 81 (commentary *sūtra* 12); cf. *K*, p. 8.

or combated, but are seen rather as a means to realize the Self, since they are nothing other than the veiled forms of the Self, the highest reality.

The body is not to be ascetically subjugated, but on the contrary it is the irreplaceable organ for the touch of the Highest (*anuttara*).[140] By means of the one-pointed awareness of the power of the senses, one can become one with that, whose nature is bliss. Through the thought-free awareness of beautiful music, or the beauty of a landscape or of a person or any other thing one can enter the source of its beauty, "pure beauty itself." One becomes one with the inner core of the beauty of music, etc. which is pure joy.

Jayaratha quotes in his commentary on 3.229 the following verse from the *Vijñāna-Bhairava Tantra*, which deals also with the sensual experience of sound, here vocal music (*gīta*):[141]

> When the mind of a *yogī* is one with the unparalleled joy of music and other [aesthetic delights], then he is identified with it due to the expansion of his mind which has merged in it.
> — *Vijñāna-Bhairava* 73

Some verses before, in *TĀ* 3.208-210, in the context of the "power of emission" (*visargaśakti*), Abhinavagupta also writes about the sensual experience of music, but also speaks of touch:

> (208cd) The power of emission (*visargaśakti*) of Śambhu[142] is present everywhere (*sarvatra*).

140. Cf. Bernard Faure, *The Red Thread: Buddhist Approaches to Sexuality*, Princeton: Princeton University Press, 1998, p. 61. Quoted from David Gordon White, "Introduction" to: id. (ed.), *Tantra in Practice* (Princeton Readings in Religion; 8) Delhi: Motilal Banarsidass, 2001, pp. 3-38; here: p. 10.

141. *Vijñāna-Bhairava: Commentary by Swami Lakshman Joo*, op. cit., p. 82.

142. "The Benevolent," name of Śiva.

> (209ab) This is the reason for the movement (*vibhrama*) [of everything in the direction] towards the essence of joy (*ānandarasa*).
>
> (209cd-210) A proof (*mānatā*) is therefore the vibration (*spanda*) in the heart (*hṛdaya*), for example, during sweet (*madhura*) singing (*gīta*), a touch (*sparśa*) or [the smell of] sandalwood (*candana*), etc. when the state of indifference (*mādhyastha*) has vanished (*vigama*), and which is called the power of joy (*ānandaśakti*). By this a person is [called] "with heart" (*sahṛdaya*). — *TĀ* 3.208cd-210

Jayaratha states in his commentary that the power of emission belongs to Śiva, who is in the realm (*dhāman*) of *akula*. *Akula* is the negation of *kula*, literally "family, herd, swarm, body," etc., in metaphoric sense "multitude, number" (cf. MW 294). The word is used here in a technical sense for the cosmic manifestation as the condensation of the pure spirit.[143] Jayaratha refers here to Abhinavagupta's central statement in chapter 3 of the *Tantrāloka*:

> The highest power (*parā śakti*) of the deity (*deva*), *akula*, is called *kaulikī*, through which *kula* expands, and from which the lord (*prabhu*) cannot be separated. — *TĀ* 3.67

---

143. Abhinavagupta comments on the word *kula* in *PTV* (Sanskrit: pp. 11ff, English translation: pp. 31ff) starting from the adjective *kaulika*, which is used in *PT* verse 1. He quotes here at the beginning (*PTV*, Sanskrit p. 11) *Siddhānta Kaumudī* p. 362: "*Kula* is used in the sense of thickening and family (*kula saṁstyāne bandhuṣu ca*)." *Kula* denotes in this technical sense the condensation, compression, consolidation (*ghanatā*) of the pure *cit* in the form of the manifest reality (see *PTV*, notes of J. Singh, p. 35; Pandey, *Abhinavagupta*, op. cit., pp. 594ff — Pandey also gives here other meanings). In a general sense ("family") *kula* is also used for a Tāntric group (cf. Mark S.G. Dyczkowski, *A Journey in the World of the Tantras*, Varanasi: Indica, 2004, p. 193, fn. 2).

In this way he underlines that all the dimensions of the Real are in a dynamic unity: *akula*, the sphere of resting in pure light (*prakāśa*), the fullness of unity of the Whole without any tendency to manifest the universe out of it, without differentiation of Śiva and Śakti;[144] *kula*, the dimension of "the fullness of the reality of the highest *saṁvit*"[145] from which Śiva emanates, and the dimension of the Goddess "Parā, the nature of the fullness of the universe" (*viśvapūrṇasvabhāvā*), the "body of *kula*" (*kula-śarīra*),[146] which is denoted as *kaulikī* or *kuṇḍalinī*. Since these dimensions are differentiated but essentially one, each of them represents absolute "fullness" and not a diminution of the absolute fullness.

Abhinavagupta continues:

> (68) The form of the pair (*yāmala rūpa*), the pulsating unification (*saṁghaṭṭa*) is called "power of bliss" (*ānandaśakti*), from which the universe emanates (*visṛjyate*). (69) a reality (*tattva*) higher (*para*) than the Highest (*parā*) and the not-highest (*aparā*), called the Goddess (*devī*), essence (*sāra*), heart (*hṛdaya*), the emission (*visarga*) of the highest Lord (*prabhu*). — *TĀ* 3.68-69

The Goddess embraces even the non-duality of *kula*, *akula*, and universe. The sensual experience of music or touch, etc. is in this perspective a contact with the essence of the phenomenal reality, the power of "Śiva," the "power of joy." One could object: Is it really so? The typical situation is that in everyday life we perceive only the gross, condensed form of manifestation with our contracted state of the power of senses and our scattered awareness. The precondition to experience

144. Cf. *TĀV*, vol. 2, p. 827.

145. Ibid.

146. *TĀV*, vol. 2, p. 828.

the vibrating, sparkling *essence* of sound, touch, fragrance, etc. is, as Abhinavagupta clarifies, that the state of indifference (*mādhyastha*) has vanished. Jayaratha explains in his commentary how this is defined: it is the state of a "not-participating observer, a witness" (*taṭasthyaparihāreṇa*), literally "standing at the bank of a river" and watching something indifferently. The point is to overcome this attitude and, as Jayaratha says, "to tune oneself equally" (*tadekatānatā*), to attain literally "the state of union with the tone" — to tune one's own perception and awareness like an instrument, corresponding to the "frequency" of the Power which is the essence of everything. It means, in my understanding, a refinement of the senses, for example, by meditation, contact with nature, etc. The subtle vibration and movement (*spanda*), which is felt in the heart, is in fact the pulsation of the Power (*śakti*) itself — and, one has to mention, at the same time she is not completely tangible or comprehensible (like an objective "thing"), but transcends Her perceptible dimension. Abhinavagupta explains this subtle vibration with the loving union of God (*deva*) and His Power (*kaulikī*), the rubbing friction and movement (*saṁghaṭṭa*) of this union, from which — continuously — the power of bliss and the emission of the universe arises. It is this background which explains the eminent role within the Tāntric paths of the sexual experience, the most intensive form of touch: sexual joy can lead to the highest bliss, the state of *cidānanda* — a joy which arises from the union of "Śiva" and "Śakti" (*rudra-yāmala*).[147] Silburn expresses this connection in this way: the union of *siddha* and

147. *Vijñāna-Bhairava: Commentary by Swami Lakshman Joo,* op. cit., p. 71 (on VBh 68).

yoginī "reveals" the state of the "unifying friction of Śiva and the energy whence cosmic bliss surges."[148]

Afterwards Jayaratha quotes a verse of Utpaladeva, to characterize the nature of Śakti:[149]

> She [*citi*] is the luminous vibrating (*sphurattā*), the absolute being (*mahāsattā*) unmodified by space and time; it is that which is said to be the heart (*hṛdayam*) of the supreme Lord, insofar as it is his essence. — *ĪPK* I. 5.14

The sensual experience is the contact with Śakti, the essence of reality. But what does "contact" mean in the view of a non-dualistic system? Where there is contact, there is also differentiation. However, only at the level of consciousness in everyday life, of the limited individual (*māyāpramātā*) is found the contact between subject and object. In the non-dualistic perspective, the multitude of the powers of sensual touch (*sparśa*), of the tactile quality of an entity, and of the power which is the source of every sensation of touch, is in fact a unity, possibly being different modes of the one power. They are dimensions of the luminous vibrating "power,"

---

148. *K*, p. 151. — Let us ask: Why this intensive reflection on *ānanda* (bliss, intense joy)? In my understanding, it is not a mere *topos* of Hindu spirituality, which identifies *Brahman* with *ānanda* (e.g. *Taittirīya Upaniṣad* III. 6: "*Brahman* is *ānanda*"; *Chāndogya Upaniṣad* IV. 10.4: "*Brahman* is joy" [*ka*]), or later in Advaita Vedānta with *sat-cit-ānanda*, in Trika as "dense mass of *cit* and *ānanda*" (*cidānandaghana*, e.g. *maṅgalaśloka* of *Pratyabhijñāhṛdaya*; cf. *PHṛ*, trans. J. Singh, op. cit., p. 45). Rather, it could be seen as an attempt to explain the concrete experience of *ānanda* by people, the momentary opening of the heart and the sudden visibility of the "Self" as *ānanda*, and to try to draw their conclusions of this experience in the form of a "theology of *ānanda*."

149. Quoted in *TĀV*, vol. 2, p. 553. As source it is wrongly given *ĪPK* I 5.18.

"vitality" or "beauty" which is the core of everything and is adored as a Goddess by the Śaivites.

Abhinavagupta quotes the following verse from *Triśirośāstra*:

> This [17th "energy," *kalā*], the light (*prakāśa*) of all things, is [successively] free from emission (*visargarahita*), *śaktikuṇḍalika*, [then] *prāṇakuṇḍalika*, and, at the highest point of the emission, *parākuṇḍalinī*. — *TĀ* 3.138-139

The Touch of the Mirror: Tantrāloka 3.6

At the beginning of chapter three, Abhinavagupta uses an interesting simile where we again meet our term "touch" (*sparśa*). It is not an important passage in regard to our topic of *śaktisparśa*, but it provides an opportunity to present Trika's understanding of the nature of reality as such. The context is his explanation in chapter three about how to reach the plane of the Highest (*anuttara*) by the "highest means" (cf. *TĀ* 3.1ab). First he expounds upon the nature of phenomenal reality in relation to the Highest or the "Light" (*prakāśa*), "pure light" (*prakāśamātra*). The phenomenal world is not separated from the Light. The appearance of the manifest universe occurs as the free play of emission and withdrawal within the "sky" of the nature of the supreme Lord. Everything that exists arises from this "pure light" or "pure sky" and dissolves back into it. With "light" and "sky" — or void (*kha*)[150] — Abhinavagupta uses two central characterizations of the Highest (*anuttara*).

---

150. We meet the term "sky" (*kha*) in relation with the "Highest" (*anuttara*) also in the first verse of *PT*, which talks about the "sameness with that which moves in *kha*" (*khecarī-samatāṁ*). *PTLv* defines *khecarī-samatā* as "the power of *saṁvit* (*saṁvit-śakti*) that moves on the plane of "knowing" (*bodha*)," characterized as free of thought constructs (*avikalpa*) and full (*pūrṇa*), undivided. *Bodha* →

He explains this relation with the metaphor of a mirror: the manifold universe is like a reflection in the mirror of this light. He had already used this metaphor in his early work *Paramārthasāra*:[151]

> Within me the universe shines, as pots, etc. [appear] in a pure mirror; everything flows out (*prasarati*) of me, like the multiplicity (*vicitratvam*) of dreams in a sleeping person.
>
> I myself am of the form (*rūpa*) of the universe (*viśva*), [which is like] a body (*deha*) with hands and feet. I myself shine (*sphurāmi*)[152] in things like light in its [different] forms (*bhāsvarūpa*). — *Paramārthasāra* 48-49

This exclamation of an awakened one (*buddha*) reminds us of similar passages in the Upaniṣads (*Taittirīya Upaniṣad* 1.10; *Chāndogya Upaniṣad* 7.25, etc). Just as dreams are manifold in the one consciousness of the sleeper, in the same way the Light of *cit*, the nature of the "Supreme Lord" in which the universe emerges, remains undivided, one, full, despite the plurality

---

→ means "knowing, understanding, waking" (MW, p. 734); from *budh*, "wake, wake up, be awake" (cf. MW, p. 733). Jaideva Singh renders *bodha* with "universal Divine Consciousness" (*PTV*, p. 7), an interpretative rendering.

151. *The Paramārtha-Sāra by Abhinavagupta with the Commentary of Yogarāja*, ed. Jagadisha Chandra Chatterji (KSTS; 7), Srinagar: Research Department of the Kashmir State, 1916.

152. *Sphurattā*: dynamic, pulsating, shining, luminous, vibrating (contrary to *bhāti*), one of the names and aspects of śakti (cf. *ĪPK* I. 5.13), closely related with *spanda*, a "vibration without movement," since movement belongs to the realm of time and space; it is the ecstasy of the self-reflective awareness (*vimarśa*) of the Light itself, the essential nature of the highest Reality; cf. *Spanda-Kārikās: The Divine Creative Pulsation — The Kārikās and the Spanda-nirṇaya*, trans. Jaideva Singh, Delhi: Motilal Banarsidass, 1980. Reprint 1994, p. xvii (intro.).

of the phenomenal world appearing within it. And this *cit* or *saṁvit*, this Light of the supreme Lord is "within me," this is me, it is not separated from me. It is me from which everything emerges, flows out — this is the Advaitic experience, the experience of the universal, unlimited "I" (*aham*), expressed in this exclamation.

We meet this simile again in two other verses of Abhinavagupta's *Paramārthasāra*:

> Just as the image of a city or a village, etc. appears (*bhāti*) as different in a mirror (*darpaṇa-bimbe*), though non-different from each other and from the mirror, in the same way the world (*jagat*), though unseparated from the absolute pure "knowing" (*bodha*) of the highest (*parama*) Bhairava, appears as separated from it and from each other. — *Paramārthasāra* 12-13

Abhinavagupta also uses this simile in the *Īśvarapratyabhijñāvimarśinī* I. 6.3 and refers to it in several passages of the *Tantrāloka* (3.44; 3.268, etc).[153] The simile could be wrongly understood to be saying that the phenomenal reality is a mere illusory appearance. In my view, it is saying that the reflected image and the face of the mirror cannot be separated, as they form a unity — but they can be differentiated. We are never separated from the Real which is pure, vibrating light and bliss, we are very close — one need only to slightly "tilt" the mirror to move from the "reflection" to the primary, pure face.

However, Jaideva Singh is right to underline the limits of this simile:[154] the mirror is unaware of the reflection, while

153. See also beginning of Kṣemarāja's *Spandanirṇaya* (ibid., pp. 1f).

154. Jaideva Singh, *Vedānta and Advaita Śaivāgama of Kashmir: A Comparative Study*, Calcutta: Ramakrishna Mission Institute of Culture, 1985, reprint 2000, p. 18.

the universe *consists* of the awareness of the Light, the "Supreme Lord." Secondly, in the case of the Highest, there is no outer, external object which is reflected in the mirror. Rather, the phenomenal world which arises from the Light (*prakāśa*) is the reflective awareness (*vimarśa*) of the Light itself. Abhinavagupta himself clarifies in chapter three of his *Tantrasāra* that there is no image (*bimba*) which is reflected. But what is the cause of the reflection (*pratibimba*) if there is nothing? Abhinavagupta replies:

> The cause is only the power of the Supreme Lord, which is in other words called "freedom" (*svātantrya*). In the last analysis it is the Lord which contains all reflected reality within himself and whose self is the universe, because the universe is of the nature of *saṁvit*; it is the place of the revelation of *caitanya*.[155]

After expounding on the relation of the Highest, the One and the manifold world with the doctrine of reflection, Abhinavagupta then underlines the difference between *bodha*, undivided, unlimited consciousness, and *abodha*, empirical consciousness. A mirror, the eye, the surface of water — they can reflect only what is similar to it, i.e. form; they cannot reflect touch or smell (cf. *TĀ* 3.5). Abhinavagupta illustrates this with a simile:

> She who is in love (*rāgiṇī*) yet keeps it hidden sees the beautiful reflection (*pratibimba*) of her beloved in the mirror (*darpaṇam*); then, even though she touches it to her two jug-like breasts, she is not satisfied. — *TĀ* 3.6

In opposition to this, *bodha* can reflect all sensations — touch, smell, taste, etc. — at once.[156] This explains the phenomenon

---

155. *Tantrasāra of Abhinavagupta* (KSTS; 17) Bombay 1918.

156. Cf. Lakshman Joo, *Kashmir Śaivism*, op. cit.

of synaesthetic experiences reported by mystics. Abhinavagupta explains it with the perfect purity of *bodha* (*cit* or *saṁvit*):

> Therefore, the universe, reflecting itself in the mirror of *saṁvitti*, expresses (*vadati*) the purity (*vimala*) of the cosmic form (*viśvarūpatā*) of the lord (*nātha*). — *TĀ* 3.44

Swami Lakshman Joo identifies this state of *bodha* or *saṁvit*, which he calls "God-consciousness," with *śāmbhava*, the "divine way", in contrast with the limited intellect (*buddhi*).[157]

The simile could also imply the meaning that one remains unsatisfied so long as one touches only the "image," the reflection of the Light, in the form of the phenomenal world despite its beauty. One remains unsatisfied until one touches the source of the reflection, this Light, directly and finally recognizes one's identity with that Light.

In the Krama school of non-dualistic Kashmir Śaivism this pure *saṁvit*, from which the phenomenal world appears and into which it is dissolved again, is identified with the goddess Kālī. The word is derived from the root *kal*, which is traditionally connected with five meanings, among them *kṣepe*, "to throw." The meaning is that *saṁvit* — revered as the goddess Kālī — "throws out" or emanates the phenomenal world within her own nature, without establishing a difference between "world" and herself as the source of the emanation:

> Kālī is the supreme goddess Saṁvit, who, joyously radiant, sprays out (*ullasayatīti*) the universe (*viśva*) in the form of the subject (*pramātṛ*), cognition (*pramāṇa*), and object

157. Cf. *Vijñāna-Bhairava: The Practice of Centring Awareness*, op. cit., p. 161 (commentary to *VBh* 135).

> (*prameya*), consisting in non-difference (*abheda*) from Her own self in external things — that is called *kalayati*.[158]

Though the world appears to be separate, it exists in the mirror of the Self of the Goddess who establishes the world in the form of Her own nature:

> The supreme Kālasaṁkarṣiṇī,[159] the goddess Kālī establishes (*avasthāpayati*) differentiation among the subject, cognition, and object, which have arisen (*ārohita*) in her own nature (*svarūpa*), non-different in the mirror (*makura*) of her own *saṁvit* — that is called *kalayati*.[160]

Any appearance (*ābhāsa*) of anything which exists originates from this *saṁvit*, revered as the Goddess, the Womb or the Heart (*hṛdaya*) from which everything emerges. Any appearance is the free play of this *saṁvit*. It seems that Advaitic Śaivism represents a different answer to the question which every non-dual system must face: what is the status of the "many," of the manifold phenomenal world which we experience, in relation to the "One"? Advaita Vedānta answers with the illusionary nature of the phenomenal world: the world is "false" (*mithyā*). Non-dualistic Kashmir Śaivism affirms the existence of the phenomenal world in the most positive attitude ever posited, in saying that the world is the

---

158. Quoted in Rājānaka Lakshmana [= Swami Lakshman Joo]: *Śrīkramanayapradīpikā*, ed. Prabhā Devī, Srinagar: Guptagaṅga, Iśvara Ashram, 1959, p. 3.

159. *Kālasaṁkarṣiṇī*: "the one who draws together Time (*kāla*)," from *kṛṣ*, "to draw" (MW, p. 306); Silburn renders it as "the one who squeezes time" (*K*, p. 83, fn. 5). She says in relation with the highest stage in the rising of *kuṇḍalinī*, the stage of *unmanā*: "This is Kālasaṁkarṣiṇī who, in an instant, swallows up time." (*K*, p. 83)

160. Rājānaka Lakshmana, *Śrīkramanayapradīpikā*, op. cit., p. 4.

own nature of Śakti, the Goddess, the dynamic, creative, flashing-pulsating essence of the Supreme (*anuttara*), unseparated from it. To explain why we usually do not perceive this true nature of reality, Trika establishes a doctrine of a gradually subtler awareness which develops during the spiritual process, beginning from the lowest level of awareness (at the *sakala* state), the conventional perception of the limited individual wherein we perceive a thing purely as an object, seemingly independent from our perception.

The Touch of Anuttara-Saṁvit: Tantrāloka 5.142

Swami Lakshman Joo says that sensual experiences are sexual.[161] This is his interpretation of one verse from the *Vātūlanāthasūtrāṇi*:[162]

> The rising (*udaya*) of the great festival of union (*mahāmelāpa*) [takes place by] the pulsating touch (*saṁghaṭṭa*) of *siddha* and *yoginī*. — *Vātūlanāthasūtrāṇi* 4

One level of meaning is the sexual ritual (*mahāmelāpa*), in which male and female *yogīs* — the *siddha* and the *yoginī* — unite in a ritual context. *Saṁghaṭṭa* — the "rubbing together, embracing each other, touching, clasping" — is a graphic expression for the sexual act. Another level of meaning is the union of the power of seeing with a form, the power of touching with something touched, the power of hearing with sound, etc. Swami Lakshman Joo describes the core of the sexual ritual when he says:

> The Kaula (Śiva) *yogī* also realizes Śakti-Kuṇḍalinī as "the essence of Desire" (*kāmatattva*) through contemplation of

---

161. Cf. Lakshman Joo, "Secret Understanding of the Primal Power of Śiva," op. cit., p. 90.

162. *Vātūlanāthasūtra with Anantaśaktipāda's Vṛtti* (KSTS; 29) Bombay, 1923.

> the power of desire (*kāma-kalā*) during the observance of the secret religious rite (*caryākrama*) at the moment of absorption (*samāveśa*), i.e. the compenetration (*saṁghaṭṭa*) of *siddha* and *yoginī*.[163]

What does "contemplation" mean here, exactly? As Swami Lakshman Joo specifies, it refers to a technique called *kāma-kalā*. He says with coded words: when the *yogī* touches *kāma-kalā* during the sexual act and enters into the "reality of poison" (*viṣa-tattva*), he experiences the state of *Śaktikuṇḍalinī*. What does this mean? Concerning *kāma-kalā*, the point is to catch the first moment (*prathamā tuṭi*), in which the powers of the senses and its objects unite.

Abhinavagupta deals with it in a verse in the fifth chapter of the *Tantrāloka*. Here we meet the word *sparśa* again in a marked context:

> The first impression (*saṁvedana*)[164] of the first awareness (*prathama-saṁvit*) of happiness (*sukha*), of the sound *sīt* (*sītkāra*),[165] of being (*sat*) and sameness (*sāmya*) is the touch of *anuttara-saṁvit* (*sparśa-anuttara-saṁvit*).
>
> — *Tantrāloka* 5.142[166]

---

163. Lakshman Joo, "Secret Understanding of the Primal Power of Śiva," op. cit., p. 89.

164. Literally: *sam* expresses intensity, completeness, union; *vedana*: knowledge.

165. Cry of a woman out of lust in the sexual act; cf. *TĀ* 3.146-148; 29.158-159. See *Vāc*, pp. 301f, 421. Abhinavagupta's and Jayaratha's male-biased perspective of the sexual ritual is visible in these details.

166. See also *TĀ* 3.166cd-167.

A Note on Anuttara

The keyword in this verse which is important for our topic is *anuttara*. Literally, it means "without a Higher."[167] Throughout his Italian translation, Gnoli uses the literal meaning, *senza superiore* or *la natura senza superiore*.[168] Padoux translates it as "the Absolute," but admits that he hasn't found a satisfying translation of the word.[169] Jaideva Singh translates the word as "the Supreme, the unsurpassable, the Absolute Consciousness,"[170] the latter already a marked interpretation of the word. Silburn and Padoux use in their French translation of the *Tantrāloka* "Sans-Égale,[171] ou Incomparable"[172] as well as "l' Absolu."[173] Muller-Ortega translates *anuttara* as "Ultimate" or "Supreme."[174] Sanderson uses also the English term "the ultimate."[175]

---

167. The word consists of the prefix *an-* (negation) — like in *anupāya* — and *uttara*, "upper, higher, superior" and so on (cf. MW, p. 178).

168. Gnoli, *Luce delle Sacre Scritture*, op. cit., pp. 68; 101 *passim*.

169. Cf. *Vāc*, p. 235, fn. 25.

170. PTV, p. 5.

171. *Lumière*, pp. 303, 307.

172. *Lumière*, pp. 78, fn. 7; 248 274, 307; cf. Padoux, *anuttara: Tantrikābhidhānakośa*, pp. 1, 121.

173. *Lumière*, p. 307.

174. Cf. Paul Eduardo Muller-Ortega, *The Triadic Heart of Śiva: Kaula Tantricism of Abhinavagupta in the Non-Dual Shaivism of Kashmir*, Delhi: Sri Satguru Publications 1989, pp. 8; 63 *passim*.

175. For example in the translation of verse 1 of Abhinavagupta's *Tantrasāra* (= *TS*); cf. Alexis Sanderson: "A Commentary on the Opening Verses of the Tantrasāra of Abhinavagupta," in: Sadananda Das/Ernst Fürlinger (eds.), *Sāmarasya: Studies in Indian Arts, Philosophy and Interreligious Dialogue*, New Delhi: D.K. Printworld, 2005, pp. 89-148.

Sometimes the expression "transcendent" is used in connection with *anuttara*.[176] Padoux is right to underline that something like "transcendence" in the true sense does not exist in a non-dualistic system.[177] Already Woodroffe pointed at the risk of an erroneous use of the term "transcendence" for the Tāntric view of Reality, because — like in Vedānta — an unbridgeable distance between "the Divine" and "the world" would resonate with it, a non-relation within the "Absolute":

> Both "Absolute" and "Transcendental" mean "beyond relation". But the term "beyond" may be used in two senses: (a) exceeding or wider than relation; (b) having no relation at all. The first does not deny or exclude relation, but says that the Absolute, though involving all relations within itself, is not their sum-total; is not exhausted by them; has Being transcending them. The latter denies every trace of relation to the Absolute; and says that the Absolute must have no intrinsic or extrinsic relation; that relation, therefore, has no place in the Being of the Absolute.[178]

Rather, Trika represents a complex ontology in which the opposition of transcendence and immanence is transcended, as Jaideva Singh puts it, formulating a kind of "Kaula-ontology":

> The union of the *dūtī* and the person performing the *yāga* is referred to as *kaula* which means that it is neither

176. For example Bäumer, *Abhinavagupta*, op. cit., p. 78 (opening verse of *TS*).

177. *Vāc*, p. 235, fn. 25.

178. John Woodroffe/Pramatha Nātha Mukhopādhyāya, "Power As Consciousness — Cit-śakti" (1929), in: id., *The World as Power*, Madras: Ganesh & Co., reprint 2001, p. 305.

transcendent, nor immanent but is the origin of both.[179]

The importance of the term *anuttara* for Abhinavagupta becomes clear when he denotes the stream within Tāntric Śaivism for which the *Tantrāloka* should serve as the ritual and theological manual (*prakriyā*) of the "doctrine of Anuttara-Trika" (*anuttara-ṣaḍardhārthakrama, TĀ* 1.14).[180] He calls the *Parātriśikāvivaraṇa* (*PTV*) *anuttaraprakriyā* (cf. *TĀ* 9.313), offering therein a sixteenfold interpretation for the word *anuttara*.[181] He dedicates an important hymn to the theme of *anuttara*: the *Anuttarāṣṭikā*, "Eight Verses about the Highest."[182] *Anuttara* is one keyword in the first *maṅgala-śloka* (opening verse) of the *Tantrāloka* as well as the *Tantrasāra*, *Parātriśikāvivaraṇa* and *Mālinīślokavārttika*. Jayaratha says that this benedictory verse embodies the whole doctrine of Trika.[183]

---

179. Jaideva Singh, *Mahamahopadhyaya Gopinath Kaviraj Memorial Lectures 1979*, University of Calcutta, Estates and Trust Office, 1981, p. 39.

180. The word *Anuttaratrikakula*, which is quoted by Dyczkowski together with the source *TĀ* 1.14, is not found there (cf. Dyczkowski, *Doctrine of Vibration*, op. cit., p. 12).

181. *PTV*, Sanskrit text: pp. 7-11; English translation: pp. 20-27. — The short commentary on *Parātriśikātantra*, the *Parātriśikālaghuvṛtti* (*PTlv*), is denoted as *Anuttara-tattva-vimarśini* as well (cf. Muller-Ortega: *Triadic Heart*, op. cit., p. 47). Alexis Sanderson has argued that this text is not a work by Abhinavagupta (see Sanderson, "Commentary on the Opening Verses of the Tantrasāra," op. cit., p. 142, fn. 124).

182. Sanskrit text in Pandey, *Abhinavagupta*, op. cit., pp. 943-44. English translation: see part II, fn. 64.

183. Cf. *TĀV*, vol. 2, 3. See the translation of the verse in chapter II (Hermeneutical Reflections), footnote 73. — On the interpretation of this verse see Sanderson, "Commentary on the Opening Verses of the Tantrasāra," op. cit.

In the fifth *maṅgala-śloka*, Abhinavagupta explains *anuttara* immediately after the invocation of the three goddesses of Trika — Parā, Parāparā and Aparā (cf. *TĀ* 1.2-4):

> The power of freedom (*svātantryaśakti*), that which longs for the succession (*krama*) [in the form of time] to emanate, and that which is the succession itself (*kramatva*) — these [three] are the manifestations of the magnificence (*vibhūti*) of the omnipresent Lord (*vibhu*). May these three Goddesses reveal their inner nature to me, [i.e.] *anuttara*. — *Tantrāloka* 1.5

In the context of the three "ways" (*upāya*) Abhinavagupta first of all connects *anuttara* with the highest, the "non-way" (*anupāya*):

> Higher than these is the knowledge without means (*upāyādivivarjitam*), which rests in the power of bliss (*ānandaśakti*), called *anuttara*. — *Tantrāloka* 1.242

Also at the beginning of chapter two of the *Tantrāloka*, in which Abhinavagupta describes the entering into the Highest "without means" (*anupāya*) — the spontaneous, unmediated, direct realization (cf. *TĀ* 2.3) — he uses the word *anuttara* in the sense of the "highest plane" (*pada*, *TĀ* 2.1, cf. the final verse 2.50). In chapter three he describes the entry into the realm of *anuttara* (*pada anuttara*) by the "highest means" (*para upāya*), i.e. "the way of Śambhu" (*śāmbhavopāya*). In effect, the aim of every spiritual path in Trika is always to attain *anuttara*.[184] (related with *śāktopāya* see 4.278, with *āṇavopāya* 5.159).

Important for an attempt to understand what is the meaning of *anuttara* is the commentary of Jayaratha to *Tantrāloka* 3.67:

184. *Anuttara* in relation to *śāktopāya* see *TĀ* 4.278, with *āṇavopāya TĀ* 5.159.

> The highest reality (*param tattvam*) is the unnameable (*anākhya*), of the nature of highest self-awareness (*paraparāmarśātmā*), the Highest (*anuttara*), the light itself (*prakāśa eva*) (. . .).[185]

Anuttara is used in the context of a negative theology — the "inexpressible" (*anākhya*)[186] as a name for the highest Reality — which we also find in a similar way ("nameless," *nirnāma*) in Abhinavagupta's *Mālinīślokavārttika* 1.20ab. "Nameless" (*nirnāma*) is here a name for Śakti:

> When Maheśvara unites even there with the power that is always part of his self and attains to supreme perfection, then his highest face [appears], which is the abode from which emission flows, which is beautified through its universal bliss rising from the unfolding of the highest reality. Since [this face] is established as the seed of the universe without differentiation into further faces (*bhāvi*), it is called the heart, vibration, knowledge (*dṛk*), the highest (*parā*), essence, nameless (*nirnāma*), wave, etc.
>
> — *Mālinīślokavārttika* 1.17-20ab[187]

In chapter four Abhinavagupta says: as one sees one's own face in the mirror and knows it to be one's own face, in the same way one becomes "that" (*tanmaya*) if one holds up Bhairava to the mirror of meditation (*dhyāna*), worship (*pūjā*) and adoration (*arcana*, cf. *TĀ* 4.207-208). And he concludes: "The realization of identity (*tanmayībhāvana*) is attained within *anuttara* (*anuttarātman*)." (4.209)

At the end of chapter five, Abhinavagupta mentions that *dhyāna*, *uccāra* and *karaṇa* are the means to reach "the realm of

---

185. *TĀV*, vol. 2, p. 427.

186. See A. Padoux, *anākhya*: *Tāntrikābhidhānakośa* I, p. 115 (especially referring to the Krama school).

187. Hanneder, *Abhinavagupta's Philosophy of Revelation*, op. cit., p. 61.

the Highest" (*anuttara-pada*). Also, sexual practices (e.g. *TĀ* 29.140) form part of the *karaṇas* (cf. *TĀ* 5.128cd-131ab), as Jayaratha reveals in his commentary.[188] This fact becomes also visible in 5.112cd-113ab when Abhinavagupta talks about the "non-manifest (*avyakta*) *liṅga*" and identifies it with the "heart of the *yoginī*," which is — along with other layers of meaning — a coded symbol for the female sexual organ, the vagina:

> This *liṅga* is the heart of the *yoginī* (*yoginīhṛdaya*), beautiful (*sundaram*) with the bliss (*ānanda*) of the union (*samāpatti*) of "semen" (*bīja*) and "womb" (*yoni*),[189] which brings forth the indescribable (*kāmapi*) *saṁvit*. — *TĀ* 5.121

In this "heart of the *yoginī*" the *yogī* shall find rest (*viśrānti*, cf. 5.120cd). In verse 124 Abhinavagupta talks about the union (*samāpatti*) with this *liṅga*; Jayaratha clarifies the connection with the sexual act in the state of absorption (*caryākrama*): "Certainly (*atha*) the entry (*āveśa*) into *saṁvit* is possible within *caryākrama*."[190] Afterwards he quotes the verse: "The *maṇḍala* in the form of a triangle (*trikoṇa*) associated with the three powers (*śaktitraya*) shall be worshipped (*pūjyam*)"[191] as well as: "It [*yoginīhṛdaya*] is praised as the cause (*kāraṇa*) of the bringing forth (*prasava*) of everything (*sarva*) and gives birth (*syandi*) to bliss (*ānanda*). It is denoted as the sexual organ (*upastha*) and as the realm of *sauṣumna*."[192] He says at the

---

188. Cf. *TĀV*, vol. 3, pp. 1058f.

189. The two code words *bīja* and *yoni* can represent vowel/consonant, man/woman, Śiva/Śakti.

190. Cf. *TĀV*, vol. 3, p. 1046.

191. Ibid. — The triangle, with the vertex directed downwards, is the symbol for the Goddess (Śakti) and the female sexual organ (*yoni*). The three energies are *icchā* (Vāmā), *jñāna* (Jyeṣṭhā) and *kriyā* (Raudrī); see *Vāc* pp. 166-218.

192. *TĀV*, vol. 3, p. 1046.

beginning of the commentary: "In this [*liṅga*] of the nature of the highest realm of *anuttara* (*anuttaradhāmātmani*), which is excellent 'Union with the *liṅga*' — the oneness (*ekātmyam*) with the emission (*visarga*)."

Despite the coded language, it becomes clear that:

— the sexual union is viewed as a means for the attainment of *anuttara*, i.e. the state of identity with the "highest reality," the "light itself" (cf. *TĀV*, vol. 2, 247); and

— *anuttara* is identified with *yoginīhṛdaya*.

Jayaratha's interpretation is confirmed by Abhinavagupta, when after this reflection about the non-manifest *liṅga* he says: "This means to realize *anuttara* was described here because it is the same as what it [*anuttara*] is." (*TĀ* 5.125ab). In this way we find a non-duality of means (*anuttara*) and end (*anuttara*): The means to attain *anuttara* — in the sense of the highest state of identification with the highest reality, "the one highest *saṁvit*" (*TĀV*, vol. 2, 2) — is *anuttara*, in the sense of the vagina (*yoginīhṛdaya*). This may seem to be a surprising conclusion. Here it is important to see that both words, as in other cases, have several dimensions of meaning which permeate each other.[193] But like in the case of the metaphor "heart," the sexual dimension of *anuttara* and its relation with the Tāntric sexual ritual is evident, and it must be included in the understanding of the term, which is nothing less than one of the main theological terms of Trika Śaivism. Concerning the relation between the different dimensions of *anuttara*, the

193. For *hṛdaya* see Paul Eduardo Muller-Ortega, *The Triadic Heart of Śiva. Kaula Tantricism of Abhinavagupta in the non-dual Shaivism of Kashmir* (SUNY Series in the Shaiva traditions of Kashmir) Albany: State University of New York Press, 1989.

"metaphysical" level and the level of human sexuality, Abhinavagupta himself says in *Parātriśikāvivaraṇa*:

> This [*anuttara*] is the great secret (*mahāguhya*), the origin of the emergence of the universe (*jagat*). Through the bliss (*ānanda*) which emerges from the union (*samāpatti*) of the two [sexual partners][194] it is clearly manifest (*aguhya*), inasmuch as it is the joy of everybody (*sarvacamatkāramayam*).[195]

The sexual background of *anuttara* in my opinion is also confirmed by its use in Buddhist Tāntric traditions: the highest of the four categories of Tantras is called *anuttarayoga-tantra* (Tib. *rnal 'byor bla med*); in this category the four main "consecrations" (*abhiṣeka*) consist of sexual rituals. To this category belong the *Kālacakratantra*, *Guhyasamāja* and *Hevajratantra*, with its full name *Hevajraḍākinījālasaṁvara*.[196] This

---

194. Cf. the note: *PTV*, p. 60, Fn. 9.

195. *PTV*, Sanskrit text: p. 19; English translation: p. 55.

196. *Guhyasamāja Tantra*, ed. Yukei Matsunaga, Osaka: Toho Shuppan 1978; *Guhyasamāja Tantra*, ed. [Sanskrit text] together with Tibetan version and English translation by Franscesca Freemantle (dissertation, University of London, 1971); David Snellgrove, *The Hevajra Tantra: A Critical Study* (London Oriental Series; 6.2) London: Oxford University Press, 1959. On the *anuttara-yoga*-class see David Snellgrove, *Indo-Tibetan Buddhism: Indian Buddhists and Their Tibetan Successors*, vol. 1, Boston: Shambala, 1987, p. 121; Daniel Cozort, *Highest Yoga Tantra*, Ithaca, New York: Snow Lion Publications 1986. — Sanderson is of the opinion, based on comparisons of texts, that the last phase of Vajrayāna, represented by the Yoginītantras, is dependent on the Śivaite Tantras (Alexis Sanderson, "Vajrayāna: Origin and Function," in: *Buddhism into the Year 2000. International Conference Proceedings*, Bangkok/Los Angeles: Dhammakaya Foundation, 1994, pp. 87-102). Davidson views this dependency as not historically evident (Davidson, *Indian Esoteric Buddhism*, op. cit., p. 113). Wayman explains the →

background is also evident in verse 5.142, our starting point, where the "touch of the *anuttara-saṁvit*" occurs in a sexual context. In his study of the metaphor "heart" in the texts of non-dualistic Śaivism of Kashmir, Muller-Ortega obviously fails to notice this connection of *anuttara* and *yoginīhṛdaya*; he does not cite the commentary of Jayaratha on *Tantrāloka* 5.124. The identification of *anuttara* — the word for the "highest reality" in Trika — and the female sexual organ clearly shows how deeply the interpenetration of the theological yogic dimension and the dimension of the sexual ritual can extend in the Kaula Tantrism of the *Tantrāloka*. In my opinion, this identification is the hidden centre of the "doctrine of Anuttara-Trika" (*TĀ* 1.14), which extends through the whole text, beginning with the first of the opening verses. It is again a confirmation for my conviction that no part of the *Tantrāloka* can be separated or isolated if one strives towards an integral understanding, as it is the case in the French translation by Padoux and Silburn. A similar case is the German translation of *Tantrasāra* by Bettina Bäumer (only six selected chapters), which omits the later chapters on rituals, including the sexual rituals.[197] In his

→ existing parallels in a different way and talks about a syncretism of Tāntric Buddhism and Tāntric Śaivism of Kashmir, from which the most important Tantras of the *anuttarayoga-tantra* emerged (Alex Wayman, "An Historical Review of Buddhist Tantras," in: *International Symposium on Indo-Tibetan Tantric Buddhism:* Central Institute of Higher Tibetan Studies, Rare Buddhist Texts Research Project, Sarnath, 27-29 March, 1995, papers). On the relation of Tāntric Buddhism and Śaivism see Michel Strickmann, *Mantras et mandarins: Le bouddhisme tantrique en Chine*, Paris: Gallimard, 1996, pp. 24-41.

197. Bäumer, Bettina, *Abhinavagupta. Wege ins Licht. Texte des tantrischen Śivaismus aus Kaschmir* (Klassiker der östlichen Meditation. Spiritualität Indiens) Zürich: Benziger, 1992.

criticism of the study *The Triadic Heart of Śiva* by Muller-Ortega, Alexis Sanderson has underlined the problem of a one-sided, "spiritual" presentation which reflects characteristic Western interests, but neglects the important role of ritual in these systems.[198]

I have analysed the use of *anuttara* in Trika more carefully, since it is an important example for the hermeneutical pitfalls encountered when Western readers meet, understand (misunderstand), interpret or translate Trika texts, especially the later works of Abhinavagupta with its Kaula Tantrism. Together with *cit, saṁvit, vimarśa* and the like, *anuttara* represents a special case of operative keywords of this tradition which form the central knots in the whole net of convictions. In this case, similar to the case of the cultural and religious keywords like *dao, wu wei* and *ziran* in Daoism,[199] we meet in an especially intense fashion the problem of the transfer to other languages,[200] which is always a "Translation of Cultures" (C. Geertz), a translation of meaning-systems.

***

198. Cf. Alexis Sanderson, "Review of Muller-Ortega, Paul Eduardo: The Triadic Heart of Śiva," Bulletin of the School of Oriental and African Studies 53, Part 1 (1990), pp. 354-57; here: p. 356.

199. See for example Günter Wohlfahrt, "Truth lies in Translation. Philosophische Bemerkungen zu Wahrheit und Lüge von Übersetzungen am Beispiel einer Passage aus dem Laozi," in: Rolf Elberfeld/Johann Kreuzer/John Minford/Günter Wohlfahrt (eds.), *Translation und Interpretation* (Schriften der Akadémie du Midi; 5) München: Fink 1999, pp. 233-47.

200. See Susanne Feldmann, "Kulturelle Schlüsselbegriffe in pragma-semiotioscher Perspektive," in: Doris Bachmann-Medick (ed.), *Übersetzung als Repräsentation fremder Kulturen* (Göttinger Beiträge zur Internationalen Übersetzungsforschung; 12) Berlin: E. Schmidt, 1997, pp. 275-80; Shingo Shimada, "Schlüsselbegriffe im

→

Let us go back to our verse from the *Tantrāloka* (5.142):

> The first impression (*saṁvedana*) of the first awareness (*prathama-saṁvit*) of happiness (*sukha*), of the sound *sīt* (*sītkāra*), of being (*sat*) and sameness (*sāmya*), is the touch of *anuttara-saṁvit* (*sparśa-anuttara-saṁvit*).

In the commentary, Jayaratha decodes the words with the first letter *S*, which Abhinavagupta uses in the context of his reflection on the phoneme *Sa*, the first letter of the *mantra SAUḤ*. Jayaratha says: "*sat* — something pleasing (*ramaṇīyam*), external (*bāhyam*), like women (*strī*) and the like."[201] The word *sāmya* he explains with: "avoiding (*parihāra*), attachment (*rāga*), as well as disgust (*dveṣa*)."[202] *Sparśa* he explains with: "the direct perception (*sākṣātkāra*) of the supreme *saṁvit*. This is the meaning (*iti artha*)."[203] Like in the context of the *Śivastotrāvalī*, we meet again the meaning of *sparśa* as immediate contact, direct perception.

The crucial question is now: immediate contact — with what? How can we understand the expression *anuttara-saṁvit*, which we let pass untranslated? If we take *saṁvit* to be a synonym of *cit* and try to understand *cit* as the most subtle

---

→ westlichen und japanischen Selbstverständigungsdiskurs: 'Gemeinschaft' und 'Gesellschaft'," in: Hammerschmid/ Krapoth (Hg.), *Übersetzung als kultureller Proze ß*, op. cit., pp. 228-54; Birgit Röttger-Rössler, "Die Malaiische Chronik in deutscher Übertragung. Zum Problem des Transfers kulturspezifischer Bedeutungsstrukturen," in: ibid., pp. 255-315; id., "Die Wortlosigkeit des Ethnologen. Zum Problem der Übersetzung zwischen den Kulturen am Beispiel indonesischer Gefühlstermini," in: Bachmann-Medick (ed.), *Übersetzung als Repräsentation fremder Kulturen*, op. cit., pp. 199-213.

201. *TĀV*, vol. 3, p. 1073.

202. Ibid.

203. Ibid.

state of pure "light," the "highest reality" (cf. Jayaratha: *Tantrālokaviveka*, vol. 2, 427), the basis of all conscious life — not simply "consciousness" — then we could interpret this passage in this way: to catch the first moment of a perception, be it inner (an emotion) or outer (a sensation), yet before the processes of discursive thinking, before the beginning of the contraction (*saṁkoca*) of the pure *cit* is the chance to touch the ultimate, undifferentiated, pure light (*prakāśa*) beyond time and space,[204] also called *pratibhā* by Abhinavagupta.[205] This "catching" denotes one's awareness of *cit* — the pure, blissful, non-dualistic Light, which arises simultaneously with each moment of experience — in the experience of seeing, touching, eating, running and everything else. Normally, people live unaware of it. The aim of spiritual practice according to Trika is to reach this state of unlimited *saṁvit* and to remain within it throughout one's life: while walking, eating, conversing, shopping, and so forth.

The specifically "Tāntric" context of this experience — the sudden bursting open of *anuttara-saṁvit*, not by means of prolonged asceticism and meditation, but by catching the "first moment" within the sexual experience — becomes clear in the commentary. A hint to the background of the sexual ritual (*kulayāga*) could be the notion of "sameness," the call for an attitude of equanimity, because the ritual could be a cause of attachment or passion (*rāga*) as well as for disgust if one considers, for example, the ritual contact with a mixture of semen and menstrual blood (*kuṇḍagolaka*),[206] the quintessence

---

204. Cf. Kṣemarāja, *PHṛ*, commentary *sūtra* 1, 50.

205. Cf. *PTV* (ed. J. Singh), English translation, p. 93.

206. Cf. *TĀV* on 29.14-16. 22ab. 128ab. pp. 170-73.

of impurity in the view of the orthodoxy of the brāhmaṇas.[207]

The key-word "poison" (*viṣa*), which is mentioned by Swami Lakshman Joo in connection with the practice of *kāmakalā*, occurs in *Vijñāna-Bhairava* 68:[208]

> One should place one's bliss-filled mind between "fire" (*vahni*) and "poison" (*viṣa*), or filled with breath; then, one will be united with the blissful union [of Śiva and Śakti].
>
> — *Vijñāna Bhairava* 68

Already, the code language has given us a hint that the means for realization (*dhāraṇā*) of *anuttara-saṁvit* consists of a sexual practice. Swami Lakshman Joo confirms this in his commentary.[209] He gives a pointer as to what is this catching of the first moment of a sensual or an emotional experience: like in many *dhāraṇā*s, the main point is the entering into the "centre" (*madhya*). One meaning is that it is this moment when thought ceases, as Swami Lakshman Joo expounds, and where you have a chance to touch the ground and source of consciousness, *anuttara-saṁvit*: "The first movement is *nirvikalpa*, and then *savikalpa* comes. The moment in between is *nirvikalpa* (. . .)."[210] *Nirvikalpa* means "devoid of thought-constructs," "devoid of dualistic thought." This first, initial moment of perception is the *śāmbhava*-state or, in the

207. Cf. Alexis Sanderson, "Purity and power among the Brahmans of Kashmir," in: Michael Carrithers/Steven Collins, Stevens/ Stevens Lukers (eds.), *The Category of the Person: Anthropology, Philosophy, History*, Cambridge: Cambridge University Press, 1985, pp. 190-215; here: p. 201.

208. *Vijñāna-Bhairava: The Practice of Centring Awareness*, op. cit., p. 75 (the translation is slightly changed).

209. Ibid., p. 77.

210. Ibid.

framework of the stages of the "word" (*vāc*), it is *parāvāc*;[211] as Jayaratha said, it is the direct perception (*pratyakṣa*) of *anuttara-saṁvit*. In his *Parātriśikāvivaraṇa*, Abhinavagupta describes with precision that the state of *anuttara* (or *saṁvit, pratibhā, nirvikalpa saṁvit, parāvāk,* or *unmeṣa*) occurs or unfolds in the centre between two thoughts, two breaths, two steps, two things, etc.[212] In regard to the sexual act, it is the awareness in the first moment in which the orgasm starts to rise up and during the first instant when begins the relaxation after the orgasm. In the Tāntric code language, the first state is called "fire" (*vahni*), the latter "poison" (*viṣa*).[213]

In *Tantrāloka* 3.170 Abhinavagupta refers to the meaning of *viṣa* as "omnipenetration," as a poison that can penetrate the whole body. One could interpret the double meaning of *viṣa* in this way, that the sexual energy which under usual (mundane) conditions functions as a poison can lead to the highest state, the "omnipenetration" (*mahāvyāpti*, cf. *TĀ* 5.49), if this energy is transformed in the form of the rising *kuṇḍalinī*.[214] Jayaratha comments 3.170-171 in this way:

---

211. Cf. *Vāc* p. 180.

212. "That indeterminate consciousness (*nirvikalpa saṁvid*), however, which does not pervade undivided the various incompatible percepts like blue, yellow, etc. cannot be (considered to be) prior also to the endless determinate percepts such as blue, yellow, etc. brought about by its own efficacy, as for instance, a perception pinned totally to the blue. But, known by different names such as *unmeṣa, pratibhā,* etc. it does occur in the interval between two different determinate ideas or percepts, one that has just terminated and the other that is about to arise (*astamitodeṣyat*)." (*PTV*, ed. J. Singh, English translation, p. 93).

213. Cf. *K*, p. 140, fn. 8. — Silburn mentions here another meaning of the technical terms "fire" and "poison": the contraction and expansion of energy during the ascent of *kuṇḍalinī*.

214. This interpretation is indicated by Silburn, cf. *K*, p. 15.

> *Viṣa* is manifested in its reality when the fullness (*pūrṇa*) is revealed at the moment in which the distinction between the subject and object vanishes. Then, through the unifying friction (*saṁghaṭṭa*) appears the reality of the nectar (*amṛta*), the starting point of the unfolding (*vikāsadaśāmaya*).[215]

Kṣemarāja indicates in his *Pratyabhijñāhṛdaya* (commentary to *sūtra* 18) as to which practice is meant to induce *vahni* and *viṣa* without directly mentioning the sexual context.[216] It consists in a twofold movement of contraction (*saṁkoca*) and expansion (*vikāsa*) of the "power" (*śaktisaṁkocavikāsa*). The contraction is called *vahni* (fire). It is the conscious contraction of all the powers of breath, speech, thought and sense into one point. For this process, Kṣemarāja uses the metaphor of "the withdrawal of the legs of a tortoise into the interior" [of the armour plating].[217] Silburn mentions that this "withdrawal" of these powers sometimes also occurs spontaneously during everyday life. Some *dhāraṇā*s of the *Vijñāna-Bhairava* talk about it: one experiences something so intense — be it extreme rage or extreme fear, extreme effort (cf. *VBh* 118; 101) or extreme joy (cf. *VBh* 69-73) — that one is automatically within it with one's full awareness. All powers of the senses are directed to this one point, and thoughts cease (*nirvikalpa*). The breath stops automatically and rushes into the flow of the "median way" (*madhya-nāḍī* or *suṣumnā*),[218] and one attains, in the case of *vahni*, a state of deep absorption (*samādhi*) with closed eyes. *Viṣa* is the countermovement, the unfolding of these powers by the sudden opening of all sense-organs: all powers of the

215. *TĀV*, vol. 2, p. 522.

216. *PHṛ*, pp. 94-103; see the explanation in *K*, pp. 50-52.

217. Cf. *PHṛ*, commentary to *sūtra* 18 (*PHṛ*, p. 97).

218. On *suṣumnā* see *K*, pp. 31f.

senses — of touching, seeing, smelling, tasting, hearing — are simultaneously directed towards touch, fragrance, sound, etc. One does not lose the contact with the inner reality — one experiences *samādhi* with open eyes. Kṣemarāja explains that this practice of inner absorption during the outer expansion of the senses is called *bhairavī-mudrā*.[219] *Viṣa* is connected with the higher, rising *kuṇḍalinī* (*ūrdhva kuṇḍalinī*), while *vahni* is connected with "the lower *kuṇḍalinī*." When *kuṇḍalinī* rises to the uppermost *cakra* called the *brahmarandhra* and touches it, one experiences "omnipenetration."

Abhinavagupta says in his hymn "The Gift of Experience" (*Anubhavanivedana*) about *bhairavī-mudrā*:[220]

> If a *yogī* has dissolved thought and breath within the inner object and directs his look unchanged outwards — seeing and yet not seeing — this attitude is the seal of Śiva (*śāmbhavī-mudrā*). — *Anubhavanivedana* Vers 1ab

In chapter five of the *Tantrāloka* Abhinavagupta seems to describe the core of *bhairavī-mudrā* — the integration of the outer, sensual experience and the absorption into one's own Self. We can recognize in these two verses the two movements of the gradual closing of the senses through "immersion" (because of the rising power of breath, cf. *VBh* 67) and the full activity of all senses, without losing this state of immersion:

---

219. *PHṛ*, p. 98. — Swami Lakshman Joo connects in his commentary of *VBh*, p. 77 *bhairavī-mudrā* with the "festival of union of *siddha* and *yoginī*" (*yoginī-melāpa*). He expounds: "*Bhairavī-mudrā* is to keep the eyes wide open without blinking. (. . .) Just keep the eyes wide open and the breath within fixed. (. . .) *Bhairavī-mudrā* is the ending point of *yoginī-melāpa*. When *melāpa* is over then he enters in *bhairavī-mudrā*." (*Vijñāna-Bhairava: The Practice of Centring Awareness*, op. cit., pp. 89f).

220. Sanskrit text: Pandey, *Abhinavagupta*, op. cit., p. 953.

(126) Those who undergo the practice of enjoyment (*bhogavidhi*) of objects [of the senses], [undergo] sorrow (*duḥkha*) and happiness (*sukha*) which result from them yet don't become involved in them (*anāviśanta*), those from whom doubts (*śaṅkā*) have vanished (*galita*) and whose mind (*citta*)[221] is immersed (*nimagna*), they know the inner joy (*saukhyam-anta*) of the gradual ceasing (*kṣaya*) of the activity (*vṛtti*) [of the mind].

(127) The Self (*ātman*), i.e. one's own nature (*svabhāva*), which is *cit*, the inner senses, the outer group of senses, whose functioning is dependent on these, the objects of the senses, pleasant (*sukha*) or otherwise — when all that is engaged, the *yogī* experiences the most evident appearance [of the reality] free from duality (*bheda*) and rests in it, wonderful with the rays, in fullness (*pūrṇa*). Gather this reality (*tattva*) in yourself! — *TĀ* 5.126-127

After paraphrasing this verse, Jayaratha cites the following in his commentary:

That one whose [mind] is constantly fixed inwardly (*antar*) and whose vision (*dṛṣṭi*) is [simultaneously] fixed outwardly, [he] attains (*aśnute*) the highest level (*paraṁ padam*).[222]

And he continues with a remarkable statement:

---

221. *Citta:* "limited, empirical consciousness." The word is defined by Jaideva Singh in the following way: "the individual mind, the limitation of *citi* or Universal Consciousness manifested in the individual mind, consisting mainly of *sattva*, the mind of the *māyā-pramātā*." (*PHṛ*, Glossary of Technical Terms, p. 163) He follows the definition of *citta* by Kṣemarāja in his *Bodhavilāsa* 4: "*Citta* is the contraction of *citi*." (Cf. Padoux, "*Cit*": *Tāntrikābhidhānakośa* II, p. 243).

222. *TĀV*, vol. 3, p. 1051. Rastogi and Dwivedi give as source of this verse *Yogavāsiṣṭa*.

> According to that which was said before, though [engaged] in outer activity (*vyavahāra*), [actually] one is nothing other than (*mātra*) in repose (*viśrānti*) within one's own [self] (*svātma*), the highest (*parama*). One experiences the eminent (*atiśaya*) joyous astonishment (*camatkāra*).[223] This is the meaning. Therefore, consisting of duality (*bheda*) [of the pair, of "inwardly" and "outwardly"], it has the characteristics of non-duality. [. . .] Truly, this is the highest form of the complete expansion (*visphurjitam*) of the *yogīs*, the state of stability (*avasthānam*), in that they remain in the realm of difference (*bheda*) with the nature of non-difference (*abhedarūpatayā*).[224]

In this way, the sexual act becomes an interiorized form of sexuality (*caryākrama*)[225] which can result in the experience of one's own Self: the sexual touch can lead to "the touch (*sparśa*) of *anuttara-saṁvit*."

Dyczkowski comments on the expression *sparśa* in a passage in Bhāskara's commentary of *ŚS* 2.7 in the following way, in brackets: "a subtle tactile sensation (*sparśa*) (which corresponds to the direct vision of supreme consciousness)."[226] Here we

---

223. Abhinavagupta presents in the *ĪPVV* the following definition: "*Camatkṛti* means the act of a person savouring (*bhuñjānasya*), that is, the bliss constituted by the full achievement of fruition" (*ĪPVV* II, p. 177; quoted from Torella, *ĪPK*, pp. 118f, fn. 23). It is the exceedingly great astonished enjoyment of the highest joy (*ānanda*), which is, together with *cit*, the nature of the innermost Self, one's true nature. In the aesthetic context, in his *Abhinavabharatī*, Abhinavagupta defines *camatkāra* as the peak of aesthetic experience, the complete absorption into joy, unlimited and free of any dissatisfaction (cf. *Vāc*, p. 174, fn. 21).

224. *TĀV*, vol. 3, pp. 1051f.

225. Cf. *K*, p. 157; *Lumière*, p. 291 ("pratique sexuelle interiorise").

226. Dyczkowski, *Stanzas on Vibration*, op. cit., p. 262.

are not interested in the particular context in which the word *sparśa* occurs, but rather in the way in which Dyczkowski comments on this word. It is instructive that even in a passage where "touch" is expressedly used, he falls back on the sense of sight (vision) to denote the highest state. Almost uniformly in the Western history of thought was the sense of sight held to be the highest among the senses, and therefore was seen as more apt to describe the highest experience: the *visio Dei*, a glimpse of God, the mystical vision. But, in fact, the authors of Trika talk about touch in connection with the highest spiritual experience. While sight implies a distance and therefore a duality, the sense of touch is pervasive. Touching and being touched fall into one another. Through the organ of touch, the skin, two persons merge into one another, duality is overcome, at least for a few moments. The sense of touch is therefore especially fitting to characterize the state of "all-pervasion" (*mahāvyāpti*): if they are touched by the light of *cit*, of the Self, the innermost nature of everything, then *siddha* and *yoginī* touch the whole universe, the whole universe touches them, as in an unutterable embrace, which they experience within their embrace. At this point it should be clarified that according to Abhinavagupta the experience of *mahāvyāpti* is not limited to the interiorized sexual act (*caryākrama*), but can also be attained in other ways, alone.[227]

The "Touch of Ants" (Pipīlikāsparśa): Tantrāloka 11.29-32 and Commentary

To understand the passage 11.29-32, we have to delve deeply to glean its context. In chapter eleven, Abhinavagupta discusses the topic of *kalādhvan*, the highest and most subtle

227. Cf. *TĀ* 29.7, where Abhinavagupta distinguishes between six types of the "*kula* sacrifice" (*kulayāga*), whether based on "external reality, *śakti*, couple, the body, vital breath, mind."

of the three "ways" (*adhvan*), of which the universe consists, unlike the "gross way" (*bhuvanādhvan*) — the way of the 108 worlds — and the "subtle way" (*tattvādhvan*) — the way of the 36 levels of reality (*tattvas*). Each of the three "ways" has for its part a gross, subtle and highest form (cf. *TĀ* 6.36). It is important to realize that it is not simply a conceptualization of reality. Abhinavagupta explicitly criticizes the interpretation that the "sixfold way" (*ṣaḍadhvan*)[228] is simply a term for groups in which *tattvas* are pooled so that one is able to complete the initiation within a shortened version. Rather, it is "absolutely real" (*TĀ* 11.6-7). Here the spiritual role of the *ṣaḍadhvan* is mentioned: the master uses it during initiation (*dīkṣā*) in order to lead the disciple from the earth-*tattva* to Śiva (cf. *TĀ* 15; *Svacchandatantra* 4).[229]

Kalādhvan consists of five *kalās*, "bounds," "divisions," "the boundaries" of the 36 *tattvas*. How can we understand this term? Abhinavagupta offers a key to understand *kalādhvan* in *Tantrāloka* 6.37: "*Kalādhvan* is clearly grounded on *prāṇa* (breath, the power of life, life)." In this way, the connection between *kalādhvan* and yogic practices (breathing practices), including its cosmological dimension, is evident (cf. 6.53ff).

In *Tantrāloka* 11.8 Abhinavagupta specifies five *kalās*:

— *nivṛtti*: the outermost bound, which contains the *pṛthvī tattva* (earth-*tattva*);[230]

228. The sixfold way divides into the three ways on the objective side (*kalās*, *tattvas*, and *bhuvanas*) and into the ways of *varṇas*, *mantras* and *padas*; cf. *Vāc*, pp. 330-71 (ch. 6).

229. Cf. *Vāc*, p. 331.

230. Abhinavagupta defines *pṛthvī tattva* at the beginning of *TĀ* 9, in which he explains the *tattvas*: *Pṛthvī tattva* is to be understood as the highest universal nature of the manifold phenomena which are characterized by the properties of durability (*dhṛti*), of solidity →

— *pratiṣṭhā*: contains 23 *tattvas*, from *jala* (water) up to *prakṛti*;

— *vidyā*: contains seven *tattvas*, from *puruṣa* up to *māyā*;

— *śānta*: contains four *tattvas*, from *śuddhavidyā* up to *śakti*;

— *śāntātīta*: contains the highest level of reality, *śiva tattva*.

Abhinavagupta explains that the four lower *kalās* correspond with the four cosmic spheres, which are denoted as "eggs" (*aṇḍa*). He defines *aṇḍa* as "cover" or "sheath" (*āvaraṇa*, *TĀ* 11.12b). *Āvaraṇa* is the term for the retinue which surrounds a deity in seven concentric circles.[231] From the context it becomes clear that Abhinavagupta means the "coverings" of the true, real nature of reality, i.e. "Śiva" or that *tattva* which is beyond the cosmic, universal "coverings" (as distinguished from the individual coverings, the *kañcukas*) and at the same time the essential nature of reality, that is, of all *tattvas* (cf. *TĀ* 6.1). At this point Abhinavagupta distinguishes between the 36th *tattva* (*anāśritaśiva*), which is traditionally seen as the highest, and a 37th and even 38th dimension of reality, which he newly introduces, without any Āgamic support. "*Śivatattva* is the void beyond void (*śūnyātiśūnya*), Anāśrita[Śiva]" (*TĀ* 11.21ab). It is the absolute

→ (*kāṭhinya*) and of weight (*garimā*) and in this way belong to this level of the manifestation of Śiva (cf. *TĀ* 9.2-4). Accordingly all fluid "worlds" belong to the *tattva* of "water" in which the highest principle "water" is manifested (cf. *TĀ* 9.1). *Kalās* are very subtle powers which work respectively in different *tattvas* and belong together through them (cf. *TĀ* 11).

231. Cf. *Nandīśvarāvatāra* — *Recension* of *Niḥśvāsāgama*, which was followed in Kashmir (cf. Sanderson, *Meaning in Tantric Ritual*, op. cit., p. 19, fn. 11).

void in which — as Kṣemarāja defines it — Śiva in the form of Anāśritaśiva does not perceive the absolute unity of *cit*.[232] At this point it should be clarified that this is not simply an abstract theological term or category, but rather that Abhinavagupta seems to be talking about a specific concrete level of spiritual experience. This becomes tangible through the characterization of the next stage: a higher dimension is the 37th *tattva*, denoted as "the highest Śiva" (*paraśiva*), "absolutely free" (*svatantram*), the "beautiful awakening" (*bodha-sundaram, TĀ* 11.21cd). If it is imagined as an object of experience, then the last reality, which never can become an object of perception, is represented by the 38th *tattva*. After these words, Abhinavagupta talks about *sparśa*:

> Smell (*gandha*), taste (*rasa*) and form (*rūpa*),[233] put in order according to their subtlety, have their support (*dhāra*) at the end of *guṇa-tattva* and at the end of *māyā-tattva*. Touch (*sparśa*), which always (*sadā*) participates in the subtle

232. *Cidaikhyākhyātimayānāśritaśivaparyāyaśūnyātiśūnyātmā;* quoted from *Vāc* 311. — Anāśritaśiva means literally "Śiva not related"/ "unrelated." In the *PTV* (commentary on *PT*, verse 1) he is characterized as the 36th *tattva* (*PTV*, Sanskrit text: p. 7, translation: p. 20). Abhinavagupta expounds the difference between "Anāśritaśiva" and "the Highest Śiva" in the last of the sixteenth interpretations of *anuttara* very clearly: "Śiva" means the accepting (*svīkṛta*) of the highest state, "Anāśritaśiva" is to witness the state with hesitation (*śaṅkyamāna;* cf. *PTV*, Sanskrit text: p. 10, translation: p. 25). Anāśritaśiva is only a part (*bhāga*) of the "Goddess" (*devī;* in the sense of *citi;* cf. *PTV*, commentary on *PT*, verse 3, Sanskrit text: p. 23, translation: p. 66), *anāśrita tattva* is the "seat" of the Highest Goddess, Parā (Sanskrit text: p. 43, translation: p. 108).

233. Silburn translates with "les organes, de la vision, de l'ouie du goût et de l'odorat" (Lilian Silburn, *La Kuṇḍalinī ou L'Energie des Profondeurs*, Paris 1983, p. 165), while the text does not mention sense-organs (*jñānendriyas*), but rather *tanmātras*.

> (*saukṣmyabhāk*), remains in principle (*naya*) at the end of *śakti-tattva* and is desired (*spṛhayālavaḥ*) by the *yogī*.[234] But at the end of touch is *saṁvitti*, pure (*śuddha*), of the nature of the firmament (*vyomarūpiṇī*). Arisen (*rūḍha*) [there], one reaches the Highest (*param*) whose nature is the light [that is] its own [source] (*svaprakāśātmikām*).[235]
>
> — *TĀ* 11.29-31

First Abhinavagupta talks about the "subtle elements" (*tanmātra*). He states an interesting order of precedence: *gandha, rasa* and *rūpa* belong to the "lower," grosser dimensions of reality; even the highest of them still is found within the realm of *māyā-tattva*. *Sparśa*, on the other hand, already belongs to the subtler dimension, to the "pure principles" (*śuddha tattva*) of reality, above *māyā*, i.e. the level of Śakti (*śakti tattva*).

Abhinavagupta clarifies that *sparśa* denotes an experience for which *yogīs* yearn. What is this experience? From the whole context of chapter eleven we can see that it concerns the gradual dissolution (*grasana*) of the gross, contracted forms of the cosmic expansion of Śiva — starting with the *tattva* "earth" (*pṛthvī*) — in ever-subtler forms of his power, back to "Śiva." The experience of *sparśa* seems to be a moment within the

---

234. Flood translates this passage differently: "By this the *yogī* is eternally cut off from desire." (Gavin D. Flood, *Body and Cosmology in Kashmir Śaivism*, San Francisco: Mellen Research University Press, 1993, p. 285). Flood states that his translations are often based on Silburn's translations. However, she translates here in a different way: "à laquelle aspire sans cesse le yogin" (Silburn, *La Kuṇḍalinī*, op. cit., pp. 165f), in the English translation: "ceaselessly yearned for by the yogin" (*K*, p. 139). In the text Flood talks about "the following passage from chapter 29 of the *TA*" (Flood, *Body and Cosmology*, op. cit., p. 285), while it is in fact chapter 11.

235. Or: self-emitting light.

process of a withdrawal of the more and more gross manifestation of "Śiva." On this level of Śiva, one recognizes everything as His expansion. Abhinavagupta describes these processes in both directions in detail in his *PTV*.[236] From the context we can also see that this process happens within the *kalādhvan*, which is, according to Abhinavagupta, grounded in *prāṇa*. In this way we can conclude that — from the perspective of the individual — *sparśa* is part of a spiritual process which is based on the innermost power of the breath (*prāṇa*).

Jayaratha expounds upon the manner of "touch" in the following way: "*Sparśa* — like (*prāya*) the touch (*sparśa*) of crawling (*saṁcarat*) ants (*pipīlikā*)."[237] And he quotes the *Svacchandatantra*:[238]

> As has been said: "After having crossed Śakti, then, O Goddess, she manifests herself as Vyāpinī (omnipenetrating) at the end of this (*taccheṣe*). The experience (*anubhava*) which appears here is the touch (*sparśa*) like that of ants."
>
> — *Svacchandatantra* 4.384

The edition of the *Tantrālokaviveka* by Rastogi and Dwivedi gives the variant reading *tvakśeṣe*, "at the end of the skin" (*tvak*). One could understand this reading to mean that the sensation of *sparśa* would occur at the highest of the five *cakras* in Trika, i.e. at *brahmarandhra*, "*Brahman*'s opening" at the

---

236. Cf. *PTV*, Sanskrit text: pp. 46f (starting with *svarūpasatattvam ca asyāḥ paripūrṇaprasara* . . .), translation: pp. 114f.

237. *TĀV*, vol. V, p. 2120.

238. In *TĀV* the source is given as *SvT* 4.382. In fact, according to the edition of *SvT* by V. Dwivedi it is the verse 4.384: *The Svacchandatantram with Commentary Uddyota by Kṣemarājācārya*, ed. Pt. Vraj Vallabh Dwivedi (Parimal Sanskrit Series; 16) Delhi: Parimal Publications, 1985, p. 241.

uppermost part of the skull. This would be in contradiction to the description of Swami Lakshman Joo that this crawling sensation occurs at the lowest *cakra, mūlādhāra,* and from there wanders up the body. It may happen that different people have this experience in different ways. In any event the commentary of Kṣemarāja on *Svacchandatantra* 3.384 confirms a different reading, which gives a different meaning:

> The component of the *mantra* (*mantrāvayava*) which still remains after the piercing of *śakti* (*śaktibheda*) is Vyāpinī. It is the limb of the *mantra* which is denoted by the term Vyāpinī (omnipenetrating) because it penetrates every *tattva* up to the end of Śakti. So this component of the *mantra* is called Vyāpinī. *Tacchеṣe vyāpinī bhavet* (it is Vyāpinī at the end of that) is the clear reading. Because sound (*śabda*) has calmed the emergence of the experience, the appearance of touch (*sparśaprathārūpa*) is like the movement of ants (*pipīlikāketi*). From *pipīlikānām* (ants), [however] the word (*śabda*) *nām* is absent. This was the doing of Īśvara.

That means that the plural "ants" is the correct reading; he bases this argument on the authority of the Lord (*īśvara*). What is the meaning of this highly technical passage? When Kṣemarāja talks about the "components of the *mantra*," he refers to the twelve main "energies" (*kalā*) of the *praṇava mantra oṁ,* as described in *Svacchandatantra, Netratantra* and other texts. These twelve "energies" can be understood as twelve "movements" of *kuṇḍalinī,*[239] or stages in the rising of *kuṇḍalinī.* Within the framework of the term *uccāra* (from *uccār,* "to rise, emit, utter") in reference to the *mantra oṁ,* the Tantras reflect the rising of the power of breath accompanied by a sonic vibration.[240] These twelve stages are in ascending order:

---

239. Cf. *K,* p. 49.

240. Cf. *K,* p. 96, fn. 15.

1. *akāra* (A)
2. *ukāra* (U)
3. *makāra* (Ṁ)
4. *bindu* (point)
5. *ardhacandra* (half-moon)
6. *nirodhikā* (the hindering)
7. *nāda* (sound)
8. *nādānta* (the end of sound)
9. *śakti*
10. *vyāpinī* (the penetrating)
11. *samanā* ("with thoughts," the mental)
12. *unmanā* ("without thoughts," the transmental)

They denote stages of the cosmic emanation — movements of the "highest *kuṇḍalinī*" (*parakuṇḍalinī*) — and, at the same time, stages of the resorption of this cosmic manifestation of Śiva, in the form of the spiritual, yogic process, the rising of *kuṇḍalinī*.[241] From our passage *Tantrāloka* 11.29-31 and its commentary, we can see that the experience of *sparśa* occurs during the rise of *kuṇḍalinī* at the stage of Śakti. Afterwards, "at the end of touch," there is *saṁvit* or *cit*, of the nature of light (*prakāśa*) without any outer source, here described as *vyoman* (firmament), as void.

After the word *sparśa*, Jayaratha explains the next word of the verse (*TĀ* 11.30):

> "Participator in the subtle" (*saukṣmyabhāk*) — it is perceptible neither as gross (*sthūla*) nor as subtle (*sūkṣma*), as somebody says (*ko 'pītyuktam*). Therefore, it is the highest means (*paramupāya*).[242]

241. See Padoux, *Vāc*.

242. *TĀV*, vol. V, p. 2120.

Afterwards Abhinavagupta quotes the following verse from the *Spandakārikās* (3.10):

> From that the point (*bindu*) arises, from that sound (*nāda*), from that form (*rūpa*), from that taste (*rasa*). These stir up (*kṣobha*), but not touch (*sparśa*). — *TĀ* 11.32

Jayaratha comments:

> The *yogīs* — having already uprooted the sense of identification of the "I" with the body and having aimed towards the highest principle (*paratattva*) — experience without any delay (*acirāt*) the "perfections" (*siddhis*)[243] as manifestations (*abhivyakti*) of *bindu*, *nāda*, etc. as well as forms, if they are [born] out of hindrances (*āsādana*). However, they occur through a state of agitation (*kṣobhakatvena*), but touch (*sparśa*) does not. [. . .] Form (*rūpa*) one sees even in darkness, i.e. the vision (*darśana*) of the visible reality. One experiences something like taste (*rasa*) even in the absence of a substance, like the taste of nectar (*amṛta*), which one enjoys. What then is the proof (*pramāṇa*) that one experiences these elements, and that it is not a mistake to long for this touch (*sparśasya spṛhaṇīyatvam*)? To this doubt he answers: [the next verse of *TĀ* follows]

> As the highest Lord has already said in Śrīpūrva (=*Mālinīvijayottara*): "The supportive (*dhārikā*) [power], the nourishing (*āpyāyinī*), the awakening (*boddhrī*), the sanctifying (*pavitrī*), the granting of space (*avakāśadā*)" — with these words the essential own nature is denoted, which consists in the "cessation" (*nivṛtti*) and others. — *TĀ* 11.33-34ab

Obviously, with the quotation of *Spandakārikās* 3.10 Abhinavagupta underlines the special rank of *sparśa* in this

243. The eight "yogic powers."

spiritual process. What does it mean? It deals with subtle sensations which occur during this process (during meditation) as hindrances on the way to the pure state of *saṁvit*, whose nature is void. Silburn describes it in this way: ". . . strange luminous dots, smells, savours and sounds arising unexpectedly as a result of deep absorption."[244] Swami Lakshman Joo explains that these experiences of the subtle elements occur at the beginning of the spiritual way, at the stage of exercise with breath, *prāṇāyāma*. But he also includes *sparśa* in this list:

> He [the *yogī*] sees divine figures and wonderful scenes where celestial beings of wonderful beauty move about. He tastes divine juice and smells divine smell. He has very wonderful experiences of all these. But his breath continues going in and coming out. He hears very beautiful and melodious tunes. . . . He also experiences tender and soft touch. Similarly, divine tastes and divine smells pass his way. But all these things are nothing but obstacles in the path of *yoga*. These divine experiences of sense objects distract his attention from the path.[245]

Patañjali describes these phenomena in his *Yogasūtras*:[246]

> From that [knowledge of the *puruṣa*] arise prescience (*pratibhā*), supernatural hearing (*śravaṇa*), feeling (*vedana*), seeing (*ādarśa*), tasting (*āsvāda*) and smelling (*vārtā*).
>
> — *Yogasūtras* III.36

---

244. *K*, p. 139.

245. Kaul "Kamal" (ed.), *Awakening of Supreme Consciousness*, op. cit., pp. 27f.

246. Cf. the translation in Swāmi Hariharānanda Āraṇya, *Yoga Philosophy*, op. cit., p. 312.

Vyāsa says in his commentary: "From *vedana*, the divine sense of touch is felt."[247] In *Yogasūtras* III.37 Patañjali characterizes these phenomena as "impediments to absorption (*samādhi*)."[248]

Unlike this *yoga*-tradition, *Spandakārikās* 3.10 does not count *sparśa* among the hindrances on the way to the highest state. The reason is that the appearance of *sparśa* is not connected with "agitation" like the subtle (Silburn: "strange") sensations of sounds, smells, etc. which occur at this stage of meditation.

Interesting is the clear characterization of this *sparśa* as a bodily sensation "like crawling ants." As we have seen in the introduction, we already find this description in the Tantras:

> Closing all the apertures of the senses, by the slow upward rise of the Energy of Breath one feels a touch like the movement of ants (*pipīla-sparśa-velāyām*). At that time the supreme joy is revealed. — *Vijñāna-Bhairava*, verse 67[249]

As we have seen in *Tantrāloka* 11.30f, *sparśa* occurs in the moment before the attainment of the highest state, the "supreme joy" (*paramam sukham*) — or, as Abhinavagupta says, the pure state of *saṁvit*, of the nature of light. From this equivalence we learn that *saṁvit*, the Self, the essential nature of everything, is supreme joy and light, a condensed mass of *cit* and *ānanda* (*cidānanda-ghana*; cf. *maṅgala-śloka* of the *Pratyabhijñāhṛdaya*).[250]

On the basis of *Vijñāna-Bhairava* 67 we can see the concrete process which leads to the experience of *sparśa* and this state

247. Ibid.

248. Ibid., p. 313.

249. *Vijñāna-Bhairava: The Practice of Centring Awareness*, op. cit., p. 73. Here *sparśa* is translated with "sensation."

250. PHṛ, p. 45.

of *saṁvit*. It is clarified with the help of the commentary by an experienced *yogī*, Swami Lakshman Joo. It consists in the following steps:

1. The outflow of the power of the senses is gradually calmed; that is, the fivefold flow of the power or the "light" of the senses in the form of the *tanmātras* — the power of hearing (*śabda*), of touching (*sparśa*), of seeing (*rūpa*), of tasting (*rasa*) and smelling (*gandha*) — are stilled.[251]

2. The gradual calming takes place by the "rising power of the breath," the so-called "vertical breath" (*udāna*). Swami Lakshman Joo defines it as "elevated energy of *prāṇa-śakti*", i.e. "[. . .] one-pointed *prāṇa-śakti*. When *prāṇa-śakti* is without thought, without movement of thought [. . .]. It is real breath, but breath without any movement of breath."[252] Here it is important to see that he distinguishes this stage from *prāṇa-kuṇḍalinī*. The condition necessary for *prāṇa-kuṇḍalinī* to begin to rise is: "when *madhya-dhāman* is everywhere, then *kuṇḍalinī* rises."[253] *Madhya-dhāman*, the "realm of the centre," is a synonym for *suṣumnā*. By way of the dissolution of thoughts brought about by one-pointedness, e.g. by the awareness on the one point between the ingoing and outgoing breaths, "the centre unfolds" (*madhye vikāsite*, *VBh* 26). It unfolds until one realizes that it is "all," the universal centre, "the light (*prakāśa*) between being and non-being" (*bhāvābhāva*, *TĀ* 1.84).

---

251. Cf. Lakshman Joo, *Vijñāna-Bhairava*, op. cit., p. 73 (commentary on *VBh*, p. 67).

252. Ibid.

253. Ibid., p. 74.

3. When *kuṇḍalinī* begins slowly to rise, the "touch of ants" (*pipīlikāsparśa*) occurs.[254] Swami Lakshman Joo describes the sensation in this way: "You feel the sensation of the movement of ants, moving from bottom to top in your body . . ..."[255]
4. One experiences the highest joy.

Now it becomes clearer why the sensation of the "touch of ants" is longed for by a *yogī*: it is the sign that *kuṇḍalinī* rises.

Let us have a look at the particular stages: *udāna* is one of the five forms of *prāṇa*: *prāṇa* (outgoing breath), *apāna* (ingoing breath), *samāna* (equal breath), *udāna* (rising breath) and *vyāna* (omnipenetrating breath). Utpaladeva briefly describes the functioning of these five forms of *prāṇa* in *Īśvarapratyabhijñākārikā* III. 2.19-20 and commentary (*vṛtti*):

— The individual, the limited Self who identifies itself with *prāṇa* in the form of inhalation and exhalation corresponds with the wakeful state (*jāgrat*) and sleep (*svapna*). It is the common, dualistic form of breathing and perception.

— When inhalation, denoted as the "moon" (*candra*) and exhalation, denoted as the "sun" (*sūrya*) become equal (*sāmye*) as day and night in the equinox (*viṣuvatīva*), then the *prāṇa* is called *samāna*.

— After the union of inhalation and exhalation, when the breath flows up the "median way" (*madhya-mārga*), it is called *udāna*. This corresponds with the fourth state (*turīya*).

---

254. Ibid.

255. Ibid.

— The highest breath is *vyāna,* whose essence is "all." It corresponds with the state "beyond the fourth" (*turīyātīta*), without spatio-temporal limitations. In this state the power of breath stops to flow and enters the state of absolute fullness (*pūrṇa*). In both states the power of breath (*prāṇa-śakti*) appears as "similar to the supreme Lord." (*Īśvarapratyabhijñākārikā* III. 2.20 *v*)

Despite the technical language, it becomes clear that the different states of *prāṇa* result in different states of the person. With the help of the description from Silburn, also both scholar and practitioner, this transformation of the breath becomes more clear:[256] in meditation one concentrates upon the point where exhalation arises and inhalation ends — the void in which both rest.[257] Thereby the breath becomes interiorized and loaded with power, and it rushes into the "median way" (*suṣumnā*). There, inhalation and exhalation neutralize each other, vanish and make way for the "equal breath" (*samāna*). In it the power is accumulated and rises as "vertical breath" (*udāna*), then as *ūrdhva kuṇḍalinī* or *prāṇa-śakti.* Its rising from *cakra*[258] to *cakra* in the *suṣumnā* (median

256. Cf. *K*, pp. 39f.

257. Cf. *VBh*, p. 25: "O Bhairavī, by focusing one's awareness on the two voids [at the end] of the internal and external breath, thereby the glorious form of Bhairava is revealed through Bhairavī." (*Vijñāna-Bhairava: The Practice of Centring Awareness*, op. cit., p. 22). Bhairavī is a name of the Goddess (or Śakti), the consort of Bhairava.

258. Silburn explains *cakra* (wheel) as part of the "subtle physiology" (cf. *K*, pp. 25-33). It is a vibratory centre, located along the central axis. "The *cakra*s appear to be centres of power where the entire energy first concentrates and then radiates." (*K*, p. 31). Trika acknowledges five main wheels: (1) root support (*mūlādhāra*), (2) navel centre (*nābhi-cakra*), (3) heart centre (*hṛdaya-cakra*), (4) *kaṇṭha*

→

way)[259] "[. . .] brings forth the melting of all duality."[260] When the power of breath spontaneously rises from the heart to the highest centre, *brahmarandhra*, then it becomes the "all-pervasive breath" (*vyāna*).

In a private lecture on *kuṇḍalinī* in 1972, Swami Lakshman Joo describes in detail what are the conditions for the experience of the "touch of ants" (*pipīlikāsparśa*). There are the following steps:

1. One concentrates without pause on the centre between two thoughts or inhalation and exhalation, or on the point between sleeping and being awake.
2. The breath revolves only around this one point, moves only at one point, and goes neither in nor out for 30 seconds.
3. If the awareness on the centre is maintained, then the already transformed breath rushes down in *suṣumnā* on the right side. It rushes down to the lowest *cakra*, *mūlādhāra*, close to the rectum, at the right side.
4. At the *mūlādhāra*, one feels a crawling sensation for only two seconds.

→ (at the back of the throat) and (5) the point between the eyebrows (*bhrūmadhya*). Finally the rising energies expand to *brahmarandhra* at the crown of the skull.

259. Silburn underlines that the (unavoidable) expression '"way" — like "channel" (*nāḍī*) — should not give the image of a static conduit of the energy; rather, it denotes the flow of the energy within the void (cf. *K*, p. 26, fn. 2): ". . . being empty, it does not offer any obstruction, for it is only in the void that the breath vibrates and becomes conscious again, thus recovering its universal essence." (*K*, p. 26)

260. Abhinavagupta, *ĪPV* on *ĪPK* III. 2.20.

Swami Lakshman Joo explains:

> Crawling means ecstasy. It is blissful crawling. It is just the crawling when union of man and woman is to take place, I mean the flow of seminal fluid, the climax is to take place. In that moment is the crawling, the beginning of intense pleasure takes place there. But there, that crawling is strengthening [. . .]. So it is why sexuality is put just to divert your attention from *cit kuṇḍalinī*, so that you can maintain without *cit kuṇḍalinī* in this world, you can maintain to live . . .. While losing that sexuality, *cit kuṇḍalinī* rises at the same time. [. . .] This sensation takes place only for a few seconds, not more. Then it rises. *Cit kuṇḍalinī* rises in one flash. When it rises, one gets absolutely blissful existence. It can't be described. The happiness is like sexual happiness, but when you compare the sexual happiness with that happiness, it will be one million parts less. So he gets intensity of that bliss, *ānanda*, ecstasy, more than ecstasy, more than bliss. And at the same time he realizes the reality of Self, his nature: "I am, really I am, I am only bliss, *ānanda*, *cit*."[261]

This important description makes it clear:

— Swami Lakshman Joo emphasizes both the close connection between this experience and that of orgasm, as well as how they remain distinct. He identifies the "crawling sensation" with the start of the orgasm. It is a very short sensation. It appears at

---

261. Lakshman Joo, *Kashmir Śaivism*, op. cit. (Audio Study Set, Chapter 17 "Kuṇḍalinī and Its Purposes," disk 12). The book version is extensively edited and not reliable as a document of the oral teaching (cf. Swami Lakshman Joo, *Kashmir Śaivism: The Secret Supreme*, ed. John Hughes, Culver City, Kashmir Shaivism Fellowship, 3rd rev. edn., 2000, pp. 118f).

the lowest cakra, *mūlādhāra*, at the base of the spine or of the sexual organs (*kulamūla*).[262] In the traditional conception, *kuṇḍalinī* rests there, coiled up in three and a half coils. The sensation spreads, rising up through the body.

— The process is distinguished from that described in *VBh* 67: There *kuṇḍalinī* rises very slowly in the form of *prāṇa kuṇḍalinī*; here in the form of *cit kuṇḍalinī* it rises in a flash from the lowest to the uppermost *cakra*. This becomes evident when Swami Lakshman Joo describes the rise of *prāṇa kuṇḍalinī*: "*Prāṇa kuṇḍalinī* takes place in the same way like *cit kuṇḍalinī*: slipping, rushing down in central vein (*suṣumnā*), and reaching the *mūlādhāra cakra* and causing the crawling sensation there, for one or two seconds. Sensation is over, finished, that crawling sensation at the state of rectum."[263] He describes afterwards how by the slow rise of *prāṇa kuṇḍalinī* one *cakra* after another is set rotating with high speed, beginning with *mūlādhāra* up to the *bhrūmadhya* between the eyebrows.

What is the cause for this sensation of "the touch of ants"? Silburn explains it with the vibration of the *cakras*, which are put into movement by the rising energy.[264] But the description of her teacher, Swami Lakshman Joo, makes clear that the sensation of *sparśa* occurs first, at the beginning of the rise of *kuṇḍalinī*, and only then the *cakras* are set rotating and

262. Cf. *K*, p. 27. — Jayaratha uses the expression *kulamūla*, e.g. in his commentary on *TĀ* 5.94-95 (*TĀV*, vol. III, p. 1022).

263. Lakshman Joo, *Kashmir Ṣaivism*, op. cit.

264. Cf. *K*, p. 66.

vibrating. At the same time it becomes obvious that the sensation of *sparśa* is connected with the beginning of the rise of the power, as well as with the sexual experience during the beginning of the rising motion towards orgasm.

The "Touch of Fullness" (Pūrṇatāsparśa): Tantrāloka 5.100-108

In chapter 5 of the *Tantrāloka* Abhinavagupta uses the expression *sparśa* within an important context: the proceeding to the "highest state of pervasion (*vyāpti*)" which is reserved for the "great *yogī*" (*mahāyogī,* cf. *TĀ* 5.99). The "great pervasion" (*mahāvyāpti*) occurs when the identification with a self (*ātmā*) which is not the Self disappears and one attains one's own true nature (cf. *TĀ* 5.106ab-107cd). This state is connected with certain spiritual phenomena. In the next verse (107ab-108cd) Abhinavagupta quotes the *MVT* 11.35,[265] which gives a list of "the Five" (*pañcamī*): *ānanda* (bliss), *udbhava* (jumping), *kampa* (trembling), *nidrā* (spiritual sleep), and *ghūrṇi* (vibrant whirling). One could denote them as five "signs of immersion" (*āveśa*).[266] In *Tantrāloka* 5.111 Abhinavagupta connects each state with a certain part of the subtle body: *ānanda* with the lower triangle (*trikoṇa*) in *mūlādhāra; udbhava* with *kanda,* a place five fingers below the navel; *kampa* with the heart-*cakra* (*hṛd*); *nidrā* with *tālu,* also called *lambikā,* at the back of the vault of the palate;[267] and *ghūrṇi* with the inner *dvādaśānta,* called *brahmarandhra,* at the crown of the skull. Silburn states about this connection:

> Mystical experiences and significant phenomena occur in rapid succession as the corresponding centres are affected

---

265. *MTV,* p. 77.
266. Cf. *Lumière,* p. 309 (glossary).
267. Cf. *K,* p. 28.

> and the *kuṇḍalinī* energy begins to spread through the entire being of the *yogin*. When she saturates the whole body, absolute bliss prevails, but as long as she remains confined to one centre, the way is not clear and certain phenomena occur. [. . .] As Abhinavagupta further explains, these experiences are nothing but the reactions of a *yogin* in contact with plenitude (*pūrṇatāsparśa*). The reactions [. . .] cease as soon as one becomes identified with Reality.[268]

From Silburn's description it becomes very clear that *sparśa* denotes the highest experience possible, before one is identical with "Reality," as she says, or *anuttara*, the "Highest," as Abhinavagupta would say, where the differences between experiencer, experience and experienced vanish.

Abhinavagupta uses the term *sparśa* in connection with the first sign, *ānanda*:

> [He/she] who wants to enter (*vivikṣoḥ*) the highest way (*pare pathi*) through meditation, through means which reside in the body (*dehagata*), experiences bliss (*ānanda*) by a touch of fullness (*pūrṇatāsparśa*). — *TĀ* 5.100cd-101ab

A Note on "Fullness" (*pūrṇatā*)

In the texts of the non-dualistic Śaivism of Kashmir, the term "fullness" (*pūrṇatā, pūrṇa*) plays an important role. It is one of the prime characteristics attributed to the "Highest" (*anuttara*). Abhinavagupta says in *Tantrāloka* 1.108ab: "Such is Śiva, the highest (*paramaḥ Śiva*), whose nature is fullness (*pūrṇa*)." Already in *Vijñāna-Bhairava,* Absolute Reality is characterized by fullness: "[. . .] the one who knows that *Brahman* is always full (*paripūrṇa*) remains happy" (*VBh* 125).[269] In the same Tantra

268. *K*, p. 71f.

269. *Vijñāna-Bhairava: The Practice of Centring Awareness,* op. cit., p. 148.

the state of fullness is characterized in the following way:[270]

(14) This state of Bhairava is free from the limitations of space, time and form. It is not particularized by a specific place or designation. In reality, it is inexpressible, because it cannot be described.

(15) It is filled with the bliss of one's own experience, and it is beyond the realm of thought. This state which is always full is the state of Bhairavī who is Bhairava himself.

(16) His body of glory should be known as immaculate, all-inclusive fullness. In this supreme reality, who can be the object of worship and who is there to be pleased?

— *VBh* 14–16

This state of fullness is identified with the "highest goddess" (*parā devī*, cf. *VBh* 17). From this perspective "the touch of fullness" can be understood as the touch of Śakti (*śaktisparśa*). *Anuttara* is fullness, denoted by the phoneme "A," the unity of all powers, the non-differentiation of all forms of emanation. Abhinavagupta says in the fifteenth interpretation of the word *anuttara* in the *Parātriśikāvivaraṇa*:

> A is the energy (*kalā*) who is above the range of *māyā* (*amāyīya*), beyond hearing (*aśrauta*),[271] uncreated (*naisargika*), of the form of joyful astonishment (*camatkārarūpa*) regarding its own waveless ocean of *cit*, resting in the great light (*mahāprakāśaviśrānti*). It spreads from the first to the last level (*bhūmi*) [of emanation], the state of fullness (*paripūrṇa*) of the I (*aham*) in a single perfect reflection (*āmarśa*) of the universe (*viśva*), the shining and vibrating expansion (*ullāsa*) of its power (*śakti*).[272]

---

270. Ibid., pp. 13f.

271. Jaideva Singh translates *aśrauta* with "not found in Śrutiśāstra (i.e. in the Vedic tradition)." (*PTV*, p. 24).

272. *PTV*, commentary on *PT* śl. 1. Sanskrit text: p. 9, translation: p. 24.

In a non-dualistic experience of reality, "fullness" is not only the nature of the Highest, separated and far from oneself, but is a state which is always present and whose experience is to be reached. It is the state of *anuttara*, the "highest fullness," as it is expressed in *Vijñāna-Bhairava* 148:

> If anyone is established in any of the ways [described here], what he experiences is fulfilled day by day, until his spiritual satisfaction reaches its utmost fullness (*atyanta-pūrṇatā*).[273]

Then every situation, whatever one experiences, is pervaded by this fullness, by "Bhairava."[274] One of these situations is the sexual experience, as Abhinavagupta states, in the context of his reflection about the esoteric meaning of the phoneme "S":

> Fullness (*pūrṇatā*), the principle (*tattva*) of passion (*kāma*), is experienced during the union (*saṁghaṭṭa*). — *TĀ* 3.170ab

Where is this "touch of fullness" experienced? It is the contact of a *cakra* with the vibrating power of the rising *kuṇḍalinī*, as Jayaratha states:

> In whichever best (*vara*) *cakra* one experiences the joy (*āhlāda*) of the touch (*sparśa*) of the unsheathed (*nirvṛtti*) [state].[275]

---

273. *Vijñāna-Bhairava: The Practice of Centring Awareness*, op. cit., p. 173.

274. Commentary of Swami Lakshman Joo on *VBh*, p. 148, ibid.

275. *TĀV*, vol. III, p. 826. — The five "sheaths" (*kañcukas*) of the true nature, the Self, the *aham*, are understood as (1) time (*kāla*) or limitation of the eternity of the Self, (2) fragmentation ((*kalā*) or limitation of the efficacy of the Self, (3) destiny, fate (*nyati*) or limitation of the freedom of the Self, (4) passion, attachment (*rāga*) or limitation of the fullness and all-satisfaction of the Self and (5) ignorance (*avidyā*) or limitation of the omniscience of the Self. Cf. Abhinavagupta, *Paramārthasāra*, verse 15 (*The Paramārthasāra by Abhinavagupta with the Commentary of Yogarāja*, ed. Jagadisha

→

In this way Silburn expounds upon the experience of joy through the "touch of fullness": it appears when the "lower triangle" (*trikoṇa*) in the lowest *cakra* (*mūlādhāra*) is touched by the "fullness."[276] The lower triangle in the root centre, called the *trikoṇa*, is distinguished from the inner *dvādaśānta* (*ūrdhva-dvādaśānta*) or *brahmarandhra*, in which a triangle, called *triśūla*, is also imagined.[277] *Gorakṣa* locates the lower triangle "between the anus and the sexual organ";[278] in its centre rests the *kuṇḍalinī* energy, "the coiled one."[279]

Silburn clarifies that this experience of joy, connected with the lowest *cakra*, represents a lower stage. It is experienced by somebody who:

> [. . .] despite his earnest desire to do so, fails to penetrate into the way of the Supreme Reality. He has already discovered the interiority of the Self, he dwells in the fourth state, but the bliss flooding through him should not be mistaken for the bliss of the fully-unfolded *kuṇḍalinī*, since it is still related to the lower centre — *trikoṇa*, or *mūlādhāra*. At this stage, there is only a peaceful state, a self-awareness filled with wonder (*camatkāra*) free of dualizing thought (*vikalpa*).[280]

Here it is important to see the distinction between the experience of the Self (*turīya*, the "fourth state" of absorption)

→ Chandra Chatterji (KSTS; 7), Srinagar: Research Department of the Kashmir State, 1916). On the *kañcuka*s see Jaideva Singh, *Mahamahopadhyaya Gopinath Kaviraj Memorial Lectures 1979*, University of Calcutta, Estates and Trust Office, 1981, pp. 24f.

276. Cf. *K*, p. 72.

277. Cf. *K*, p. 31.

278. Gorakṣanātha, *Amaraughaśāsana*, quoted from *K*, p. 125.

279. Cf. *K*, p. 27.

280. *K*, p. 72.

and of Śiva in the universe, associated with the fully-unfolded *kuṇḍalinī* (*turīyātīta*, "beyond the fourth state")[281] — or, in other words, the states of the merger of everything into the Self (*ātmavyāpti*)[282] and the turning of this Self-pervasion into "divine pervasion" (*śivavyāpti*), where all things fuse into Paramaśiva, "[. . .] where the divine essence is perceived as all-pervading."[283]

Silburn's description is confirmed by the commentary of Jayaratha on *Tantrāloka* 5.100cd-104ab. He clarifies that the experience of *ānanda* is a lower, preliminary stage of the spiritual experiences connected with the unfolding of *kuṇḍalinī*, before the other "signs" occur (*udbhava, kampa, nidrā, ghūrṇi*). He comments on the expression *pūrṇatā-sparśa* in the verse as follows: "[. . .] in the beginning (*prathamam*) on the grounds of mere eagerness (*aunmukhya-mātrāt*) but not with immersion into that (*na tu tadāveśāt*)."[284] One could perhaps interpret his statement in this way: the experience of "the touch of fullness" occurs at the beginning of the process when there is the proper intention, but without any deep or complete absorption. Therefore, *sparśa* here seems to be used in a relative way, in the sense of "only a touch" of fullness, expressing the

---

281. Cf. *K*, p. 30.

282. "All the categories of the universe (from the material elements up to the highest levels) have merged into the Self, which is called *ātmavyāpti*, so that the entire universe abides within the Self of the *yogin* who himself rests in his own Essence." (*K*, p. 59) There begins the process of equalization, identification with the Real, the final stage, called "divine pervasion" (*śivavyāpti*). — On the difference between *ātmavyāpti* and *śivavyāpti* see Kṣemarāja, *ŚSV* 3.7.

283. *K*, p. 167.

284. *TĀV*, vol. III, p. 1028.

preliminary character of this experience, before the complete equalization with the "fullness" occurs at the highest stage.

Contrary to Silburn, who connects the experience of the "touch of fullness" with the state of the "fourth" (*turīya*), Swami Lakshman Joo connects it with "deep sleep" (*suṣupti*), a stage of absorption before *turīya*, when he talks about the five states (*jāgrat, svapna, suṣupti, turīya, turīyātīta*) of the "individual subjective body of Śiva":[285] "The touch of one's self was found in sound sleep."[286] According to Swami Lakshman Joo, *yogīs* call this state *rūpastha*, "grounded in one's own self."[287] Only the state "beyond the fourth" (*turīyātīta*) is the state of absolute fullness.[288]

But, is it legitimate to connect these states during the rise of *kuṇḍalinī* with the five states of "waking," "sleep," "deep sleep," "the fourth" and "beyond the fourth"? The tradition[289] distinguishes the meaning of these five states for "worldly" people, *yogīs* and "enlightened ones" (*jñānins*). In this way *suṣupti* is, for a "worldly" person, deep sleep, a state of consciousness without knowledge of any object. With regard to the yogic experience, *suṣupti* represents a phase in deep absorption (*samādhi*) where the difference between subject and object is dissolved and one touches one's own non-dual nature. At this stage, *jñānins* are in the state of the "great pervasion"

---

285. It is distinguished from the universal subjective body of Śiva, the 36 *tattvas* (cf. Lakshman Joo, *Kashmir Śaivism*, op. cit., p. 71). On the doctrine of the "four feet" (*catuṣpād*) in Advaita Vedānta see Andrew O. Fort, *The Self and Its States: A State of Consciousness Doctrine in Advaita Vedānta*, Delhi: Motilal Banarsidass, 1990.

286. Lakshman Joo, *Kashmir Śaivism*, op. cit. (Audio Study Set).

287. Ibid.

288. Ibid.

289. Lakshman Joo, *Kashmir Śaivism*, op. cit. (Audio Study Set, CD 7).

(*mahāvyāpti*), in which one experiences everything as penetrated by the Self. Swami Lakshman Joo attributes the different states to the different dimensions of the divine power, *kuṇḍalinī*:

— *jāgrat* and *svapna* to the realm of the "lower power" (*aparāśakti*),

— *suṣupti* to the realm of the "transcendent-immanent power" (*parāparāśakti*),

— *turīya* to the realm of the "highest power" (*parāśakti*).[290]

We already find the connection between the process of the rise of *kuṇḍalinī* and the five states with Utpaladeva. With regard to the transformation of breath, he attributes the state of "deep sleep" (*suṣupti*) to "the equal breath" (*samāna*, cf. *ĪPK* III. 2.19-20), the phase in the *kuṇḍalinī* process before the "fourth" (*turīya*) state, that is, before the rise of the vertical breath (*udāna*) in the *suṣumnā* and the rise of *kuṇḍalinī*. This fits the statement of Silburn that the experience of *ānanda*, as a result of the "touch of fullness" (*pūrṇatā-sparśa*), should not be confused with the impact of the fully-unfolded *kuṇḍalinī*. However, it does not fit her statement in the same passage that one is already in the state of *turīya*.

To summarize: the term *pūrṇatā-sparśa* denotes a preliminary experience. One only verges on the "fullness" which is the nature of the Highest; one is only grazed by fullness in this state. Only in the next state does one not lose one's awareness of one's own true nature — fullness, unlimitedness, joy, light, which is the "Goddess" (Śakti) Herself:

> The Bhairava-state, the experience (*anubhava*) of the bliss (*ānanda*) of [one's] non-difference from the universe

290. Ibid.

(*bharitākārā*) alone is Bhairavī, the self of Bhairava.

— *VBh* 15.[291]

Sparśa as Consonant

The word *sparśa* denotes the 25 consonants of the Sanskrit alphabet, comprising the greatest group of the 50 phonemes (*varṇas*). They are denoted by "touch" because the particular organ (*karaṇa*) — the tongue, the lip — has to touch the place of articulation to form the sound.[292] The consonants are divided into five classes according to the place where the organs of articulation (the palate, tongue, upper lip, lower lip or teeth) touch each other: gutturals (*ka-varga*), palatals (*ca-varga*), cerebrals (*ṭa-varga*), dentals (*ta-varga*) and labials (*pa-varga*).

The consonants form part of a complex Tāntric philosophy of phonemes, which are denoted as "the little mothers" (*mātṛkā*) from whom the world emerges. This doctrine is revealed by Abhinavagupta in the *Tantrāloka* and *PTV* under the name *varṇa-parāmarśa*[293] and is traditionally denoted as *mātṛkā cakra* (the wheel of the mothers). In this doctrine, the 36 *tattvas* are represented by the 50 letters of the Sanskrit alphabet. The 36th

---

291. I partly follow here the translation of Jaideva Singh, *Vijñānabhairava or Divine Consciousness: A Treasury of 112 Types of Yoga*, Delhi: Motilal Banarsidass, 1979, reprint 2003, p. 14.

292. Cf. K. V. Abhyankar, *A Dictionary of Sanskrit Grammar* (Gaekwad's Oriental Series; 134), Baroda: Oriental Institute 1961; see *Vāc*, p. 309, fn. 244.

293. Padoux translates *varṇaparāmarśa* with "phonematic awareness" (*Vāc*, p. 228). *Parāmarśa* is the act of awareness, of self-recognition. Jayaratha uses the word *parāmarśa* for the recognition of the "I" (*aham*), the full recognition of one's true nature (*pūrṇāhantā*), "in the form of the pure radiance of the Self" (Jayaratha, commentary on *TĀ* 3.203-204).

tattva, Śiva, is represented by the 16 vowels from *A* to *Ḥ*. The *śakti-tattva*, the universe of the 35 *tattva*s which is a "reflection" (*pratibimba*) of *śiva-tattva*, is represented by the other phonemes, especially the consonants. The doctrine of *mātṛkā cakra* aims at the fundamental assertion that Śiva and Śakti are in permanent union. The Highest rests in its own light, in the unity and non-differentiation of the whole reality, in fullness (the Śiva-aspect), and at the same time manifests itself in the plurality of the universe (the Śakti-aspect), *within* its own unity and without diminishing its fullness.

The emanation of the phonemes (*parāmarśodaya-krama*) is described by Abhinavagupta in *Tantrāloka* 3.67-200ab. Jayaratha summarizes it in a long commentary on *Tantrāloka* 3.67, where Abhinavagupta talks about *kuṇḍalinī*: *anuttara*, the highest reality (*para tattva*), light (*prakāśa*), the unnameable (*anākhya*) which cannot be denoted by any definite designation like "Śiva" or "Śakti," is called *akula* or *avarṇa* (without phonemes). When *anuttara* longs for the emanation of the universe, it emanates in itself Śiva and Śakti as *parā* or *kaulikī*. From the union (*sāmarasya*) of Śiva and Śakti, from their form as a pair (*yāmala*), from their intensive pulsating touch or embrace (*saṁghaṭṭa*)[294] the emission of the universe arises: the powers of will (*icchāśakti*), of knowledge (*jñānaśakti*) and of action (*kriyāśakti*). From these three powers, together with

294. From *saṁghaṭṭ*, "to strike or clasp or rub together, knead, bruise, to strike against, touch" (cf. MW, p. 1130). The root *ghaṭṭ* means: "to rub, touch, shake, cause to move, stir around" (cf. MW, p. 375). The expression of Jayaratha in his commentary on 3.68 therefore literally means: "the unified frictional movement of the nature of vibration" (*spandarūpatā svātmocchalattā ityarthaḥ*, *TĀV*, vol. II, p. 433). Jayaratha connects the union of Śiva and Śakti with the sexual act (*caryākrama*) of man and woman, in which emission (*visarga*) appears through joy (*ānanda*) in the pulsating union (*saṁghaṭṭa*) (ibid.).

citśakti and *ānandaśakti*, the phonemes of the emanation emerge. In short, it is the movement of the supreme *kuṇḍalinī* (*parakuṇḍalinī*) which brings the universe into existence, in the form of the emanation of the universal phonic energy.[295] Kṣemarāja clarifies this connection between Śakti and the inner nature and power of the phonemes by saying that "[. . .] the nature of the energy of the phonemes (*mātṛkā*) is none other than that of the supreme word (*parāvākśakti*) of the supreme Bhairava (. . .)."[296]

In *Tantrāloka* 3.148cd-162ab Abhinavagupta describes in what way the consonants appear in this process of the "phonematic" emanation of reality.

According to the doctrine of *mātṛkā cakra*, as summarized by Swami Lakshman Joo, the lowest *tattvas* — the five elements (*mahābhūtas*) — appear with the gutturals from *ka* to *ṅa*, created by *citśakti* and *ānandaśakti*. The five subtle elements (*tanmātras*) appear with the palatals *ca* to *ña*, created by *icchāśakti*. The *tattvas* of the five organs of action (*karmendriya*) — of procreation, excretion, motion, grasping and speech — appear with the cerebrals from *ṭa* to *ṇa*, created by Anāśritaśiva. The five sense-organs (*jñānendriyas*) — the nose, tongue, eye, skin and ear — appear with the dentals from *ta* to *na*. The five *tattvas* of the cogito-emotional organ (*manas*), the intellect (*buddhi*), the I-sense (*ahaṁkāra*), "nature" (*prakṛti*)[297] and "ego

295. See *Vāc*, p. 126. — Padoux underlines that this universal movement of *kuṇḍalinī* is analogous to the movement of *kuṇḍalinī* in the yogic process, which has therefore also a cosmic aspect (ibid.).

296. *ŚSV* 2.3, quoted from *Vāc*, p. 130.

297. *Prakṛti*: "making or placing before or at first; the original or natural form or condition of anything; original or primary substance; origin; nature, character; nature (distinguished from *puruṣa*)," etc. (cf. MW, p. 654).

connected with subjectivity" (*puruṣa*)[298] appear with the labials from *pa* to *ma*. With the labials, the emanation of the universe ends (cf. *TĀ* 3.150ab). The 25 consonants in this way represent the Highest in its manifest expansion in the form of the phenomenal world which is recognizable with the senses and organs of cognition:

> This recognizable (*jñeya rūpa*) in fact does not extend beyond the twenty-five. Therefore, it is clearly said that the recognizable is of the nature of the consonants (*sparśa*).
>
> — *TĀ* 3.153

Jayaratha elucidates that "this" (*idam*) means the universe (*viśvam*) which reaches from the *tattva* "earth" (*pṛthvī*) up to the *puruṣa tattva*. He explains the word *sparśa* in the verse: "'touch' — they are touched (*spṛśyante*) by the senses (*indriyaiḥ*)." Afterwards he quotes a grammatical definition of the consonants: "*Sparśa* starts with *ka* and ends with *ma* (*kādayo māvasānāḥ sparśaḥ*)." And he continues: "It is said that they are of the nature of the "denoter" (*vācaka*)." The nature of the consonants consists in denotation of objects. That which is the "denoted" (*vācya*) — the objects of cognition — can be touched by the senses. In other words, the 25 consonants (*sparśa*), from which arise the *tattvas* from "earth" up to *puruṣa* (the whole phenomenal world), form the touchable dimension of the "letter-less" (*avarṇa*), un-denotable (*anākhya*) Reality, or the *vimarśa*-aspect (from the root *mṛś*, "to touch") of the highest light (*prakāśa*).

---

298. *Puruṣa*: "a man, male, human being, a person, the animating principle (soul or spirit) in men and other beings, the Soul of the universe, the primeval man as the soul of the universe" (cf. MW p. 637).

"Śakti, of the Nature of Touch": Tantrāloka 29.159cd-160ab

In chapter 29 of the *Tantrāloka* we find a synonym for *sparśa*, i.e. *samīra*, "air," in an important context. *Sparśa* is traditionally related with the element "air" (*vāyu*).[299] Jayaratha elucidates that *samīra* stands here for "touch" (*sparśa*).

Abhinavagupta says:

> The highest Bhairava (*bhairava parama*),[300] here residing as sound (*nāda*), with eight aspects (*aṣṭavidha*), of the nature of

---

299. See Bettina Bäumer, "Vāyu," in *KTK* III, pp. 143-87.

300. Bhairava, "frightful, terrible, horrible" (cf. MW, p. 767), one of the names and forms of Śiva (like Sadāśiva, Maheśvara, Kāmeśvara, Mahākāla, . . .), here in his terrible aspect; the Buddhist counterpart of Bhairava is Heruka. The name Bhairava is unattested in the early Śaiva literature, e.g. in the *Pāśupatasūtras* (cf. Davidson, *Indian Esoteric Buddhism*, op. cit., p. 211). Silburn renders the name with "undifferentiated Śiva" (*K*, p. 218). In *Yogasaṁcāratantra*, quoted in *TĀ* 4.130-146, it is said: "As soon as [the *yogin*] knows this supreme light — his own Self — then he knows *Bhairava*, the universal cause, perfect light of Consciousness or supreme Subject. Such is the Knowledge of the ultimate reality." (quoted from *K*, p. 145) — *VBh*, p. 130 gives a "spiritual etymology" of the word: "Bhairava is one who with fear (*bhaya*) makes everything resound (*ravayati*), and who pervades the entire universe. He who utters this word "Bhairava" unceasingly becomes Śiva." (*Vijñāna-Bhairava: The Practice of Centring Awareness*, op. cit., p. 154). In *TĀ* 1.96 Abhinavagupta gives a different beautiful and surprising etymology of the name "Bhairava": "He who carries the whole universe, who nourishes and supports it, and who is carried by it (*bha*), he is the sound (*rava*) who by his power of awareness protects who are frightened by the world of transmigration (*bhīru*)." (Quoted from ibid., p. xiii). — On "Bhairava" see Heinrich von Stietencron, *'Bhairava': Zeitschrift der Deutschen Morgenländischen Gesellschaft*, Supplement I, Teil 3 (1969), pp. 863-71; Elizabeth Chalier-Visuvalingam, "Śiva und seine Manifestationen als Bhairava," in: Cornelia Mallebrein →

> light (*jyoti*), resonance (*dhvani*) and touch (*samīra*), is known as the supreme pervasion (*vyāptirucyate paramā*) of Māntrī.
> — *TĀ* 29.159cd-160ab

The meaning of the verse can only be derived from the whole context, the chapter 29 of the *Tantrāloka*, in which Abhinavagupta describes the "secret ritual" (*rahasyacarcāvidhi*, *TĀ* 29.1) and which is therefore the most coded part of the text.[301] It gives a very subtle spiritual analysis of the sexual act, in the context of the whole "theology of the senses" in this system. At the same time we can understand the verse, in my opinion, only in the context of the theme "*uccāra* of *oṁ*." Therefore, for the interpretation of the verse we must again delve deeply, and at the same time try not to lose our thread in this labyrinth of intertextuality.

At the beginning of chapter 29, in verse 2, Abhinavagupta states that according to the Kaula practice (*kulaprakriyā*) the ritual is suitable only for masters and disciples who are in the thought-free state (*nirvikalpa*). The ritual can be performed in a sixfold way: in outer activities (*bahiḥ*), with a Śakti,[302] as a pair (*yāmala*),[303] in the body (*deha*), in the breath (*prāṇa*),[304] or

→ (Hg.), *Die anderen Götter. Volks- und Stammesbronzen aus Indien*, Köln: Edition Braus, 1993, pp. 70-89; id.: *Terreur et Protection: Mythes, rites et fêtes à Bénarés et à Kathmandou*, Bruxelles et al., Peter Lang, 2003.

301. My summary of chapter 29 is based on the Abhinavagupta's text with commentary and *K* (ch. 5) as well as John R. Dupuche: *Abhinavagupta: The Kula Ritual As Elaborated in Chapter 29 of the Tantrāloka*, Delhi: Motilal Banarsidass, 2003.

302. Silburn explains: through the mere view of a woman (cf. *K*, p. 178).

303. Jayaratha explains *yāmala*: "through the sexual union (*mithuna*) in the form of the "original sacrifice" (*ādi-yāga*)." (*TĀV*, vol. VII, p. 3295).

304. Jayaratha comments: "median way (*madhyanāḍī*)" (ibid.) = *suṣumnā*.

within thoughts.[305] Afterwards, in verses 96 to 168, Abhinavagupta describes the "secret ritual" (*rahasya vidhi*), i.e. the "original sacrifice" (*ādiyāga*) of the pair (*yāmala*). This is the direct context of our verse.

First he mentions that it includes the "three M" (cf. *TĀ* 29.28). Jayaratha explains the three Ms as wine (*madya*), meat (*māṁsa*) and sexual intercourse (*maithuna*).[306] Later, Abhinavagupta states that the only quality which is necessary for the female partner (*dūtī*) in the ritual to possess is the tendency towards "non-difference" or "non-duality" (*avibheditā*) — caste, youth, beauty or any other such quality play no part (cf. *TĀ* 29.100cd and commentary). When the *dūtī* is present and the man and woman have venerated each other, then ". . . they venerate the 'main wheel' (*mukhya cakra*) by a process (*krama*) with the 'inner organ' (*antaraṅga*). The 'inner organ' of *saṁvit* is that from which bliss (*ānanda*) flows." (*TĀ* 29.105)[307]

Here we meet again a highly coded language. How can we understand the "main wheel"? Here we have to distinguish this type of "energy-centres" from the five main *cakras* (*mūlādhāra, nābhicakra, hṛdayacakra, kaṇṭha, bhrūmadhya*). Silburn (*K* 172-174) describes the *mukhya cakra* in the following way: It is the main "wheel" (*cakra*) in relation to the secondary centres of energy (*anucakra*), i.e. the sense-organs. It is also denoted as "the central wheel" (*madhya cakra*). Silburn identifies it with the "median way" (cf. *K* 139) without using the word *suṣumnā*. When the *yogī* rests in the "centre" (*madhya*), while he undergoes the outer sensual experience of touch, the energy

305. Jayaratha: "in the intellect (*buddhi*)" (ibid.).

306. *TĀV*, vol. VII, p. 3355.

307. Silburn expounds that the "inner organ" is related to the "heart" or to the sexual organ (cf. *K*, p. 182).

centres of the senses then become connected with the "centre." The "inner" and the "outer" melt into each other, and the "centre" (*madhya*) unfolds. Different layers of meaning overlap here, sometimes in a perplexing way: the *mukhya cakra* or *madhya cakra* is also called "the heart of the *yoginī*" (*yoginīhṛdaya*) or "the mouth of the *yoginī*" (*yoginīvaktra*, *TĀ* 29.124). Both expressions also denote in the same breath the female sexual organ, because this *cakra* is connected with the sexual openings. In which way? Silburn expresses the connection between *mukhya cakra* and the sexual organ (*mukha*) like this: *mukha* arises from the main *cakra* (cf. *K* 173). She underlines at the same time the differentiation between sexual organ and *madhya vaktra* (cf. *K* 190).

Abhinavagupta continues: "And, externally, the sacrifice (*yāga*) is satisfaction (*tarpaṇa*) and is denoted as expansion (*vikāsa*)." (*TĀ* 29.107) The partners shall satisfy "the secondary *cakras*" (*anucakra*, the sense-organs), with the corresponding means,[308] to attain unity (*ekatā*) with the principal wheel (*mukhya cakra*, cf. *TĀ* 29.109cd-111ab). It seems that Abhinavagupta plays here with the different layers of meaning of "principal wheel": the mystic "centre" which is void, the opening to infinity, and the female sexual organ. Afterwards the "deities of the senses" (*aṇucakra-devya*) one after another enter into the *saṁviccakra*, into the "centre" (*madhya*, cf. *TĀ* 29.112ab), into the "resting place of the overall *saṁvit* (*sarva-saṁvid-viśrāntisthāna*)," as Jayaratha comments.[309] The energies of the senses become one with the "centre" which opens and unfolds.

---

308. Jayaratha explains: "Embracing, passionate kissing, etc." (*TĀV*, vol. VII, p. 3369). Silburn expounds that from it intensive heat and passion spread (*ucchalana*), and from it the intensely vibrating, rising *kuṇḍalinī* (cf. *K*, p. 184).

309. *TĀV*, vol. VII, p. 3370.

Abhinavagupta continues:

> This union (*yāmala*), in which each dualistic consciousness gradually disappears (*galitabhidā*), is *saṁvit* itself [. . .], *anuttara* of the essence of universal bliss (*jagadudārasānanda*), of which both consist. — *TĀ* 29.115cd-116

At this stage follows that part of the ritual in which the sexual fluids (*kuṇḍagolaka*) which had been produced during orgasm are exchanged "from mouth to mouth": from the "mouth of the *yoginī*" (*yoginī vaktra*), the vagina, to the mouth of the male partner and vice versa, then again back to the man, who finally spits the fluid in a bowl (*arghapātra*, cf. *TĀ* 29.127cd-129ab and commentary).[310]

A Note on the Touch of the Sexual Fluids (*TĀ* 29.173-174)

In a later passage of *Tantrāloka* 29, Abhinavagupta again describes a ritual with sexual fluids. First he gives an important statement about the Tāntric "theology" of the body, the senses, sexuality, obviously to legitimize the rite involving contact with sexual fluids:

(170) Where everyone always enjoys themselves and which is presided over by the god and goddess, there is the

---

310. Dupuche is not sure if there are two fluids, of both man and woman (cf. Dupuche, *Kula Ritual*, op. cit., p. 270, fn. 148). But it is foregone that, during orgasm, the sexual emissions of both man and woman mix together somewhat in the vagina. Therefore, it is clear why this mixture has to go first from the "mouth of the *yoginī*" to the mouth of the man. — Silburn characterizes this process of an exchange from "mouth to mouth" as *saṁpuṭīkaraṇa* (cf. *K*, p. 192). She refers to a customary practice in Kashmirian marriage: "The couple stands inside a circle and the bridegroom's mother puts in her son's mouth a morsel of food which he cuts into two; one piece he introduces into the bride's mouth and she in turn puts a morsel in the mouth of the bridegroom." (*K*, p. 191)

supreme *cakra* (*cakra param*) which manifests in the "sacrifice of the goddess" (*devīyāga*).

(171) The body (*deha*) itself is the highest *liṅga* (*param liṅgam*),[311] Śiva of the nature of all *tattvas*. Surrounded by the wheel of the deities (*devatā cakra*) [of the senses], it is the best abode (*dhāma*) for worship (*pūjā*).

(172) It is, truly, the main (*mukhya*) *maṇḍala*, consisting of the threefold trident (*tritriśūla*),[312] the lotus (*abja*), wheel (*cakra*) and void (*kha*). Here, the wheel of the deities is always venerated externally and internally (*bahiranta*).

(173) Then let them, in full awareness (*parāmarśa*) of the own *mantra*, in a process (*vidhinā*) of emission (*sṛṣṭi*) and resorption (*saṁhāra*), touch (*spṛśet*) the manifold (*bahula*) juice (*rasaiḥ*) of joy (*ānanda*) which was produced beforehand (*pūrva*).

(174) By this touch (*sparśa*) the wheel of *saṁvit* (*saṁvit cakra*) awakens (*buddha*). The Lord (*īśvara*) [over the wheel]

---

311. *Liṅga*: "a mark, spot, sign, emblem; the sign of gender or sex; the male organ or phallus" (MW, p. 901); the abstract symbol of Śiva, ". . . a symbol (*pratīka*) of that fathomless light of Śiva" (Diana L. Eck, "Banaras," in: *EncRel* [Eliade] II, pp. 57-59; here: p. 58). It is worshipped in the form of a stone or marble column which generally rises out of a vagina or womb (*yoni*) as the symbol of divine procreative energy (cf. MW, p. 858).

312. The triangles in the three *cakras* (cf. *K*, p. 33): in *mūlādhāra* (*trikoṇa*, the "triangular sanctuary," *K*, p. 27), in *bhrūmadhya* (*triveṇī*, ". . . at the confluence of the whole triplicity, fire, sun and moon: *udāna*, *prāṇa*, and *apāna*" *K*, p. 29) and inside *brahmarandhra* (*triśūla*, a triangle "of dazzling light" representing the triple energy of will, knowledge, and activity, cf. *K*, p. 31).

attains the highest abode (*para dhāma*) due to having satisfied all the deities [of the senses].[313]

The central statement in this passage is the identification of the human body with the sacred symbols, *liṅga* and *maṇḍala*: like the *liṅga*, the body itself represents Śiva, like the *maṇḍala*, the body itself is a sacred space.

From the commentary of Jayaratha we can see that the characterization "threefold trident, lotus, *cakra*, void" is not related to the word "body" of verse 171 — as Silburn translates[314] — but to the "supreme *cakra*" of verse 170. Thereby we get the hint that the expressions "supreme *cakra*" and the "main *maṇḍala*" in fact denote the sexual act. Already in *Tantrāloka* 3.95cd-96ab Abhinavagupta terms the union of the two triangles of man and woman as the *maṇḍala*, literally "the six-spoked" (*ṣaḍavasthiti*). This is confirmed by the code words which are used in this passage: "lotus" is the Tāntric codeword for the female sexual organ. The term "empty space" (*kha*) in *TĀ* 5.93-95 was already connected with the female sexual organ (*kulamūla*). If this interpretation is correct, than we can conclude that *tritriśūla* and *cakra* are the corresponding code words for the male sexual organ. Evidence could be the "etymology" of *cakra* given in *Tantrāloka* 29.106cd: "The word

313. On this passage see André Padoux, "Maṇḍalas in Abhinavagupta's Tantrāloka," in: Gudrun Bühnemann et al., *Maṇḍalas and Yantras in the Hindu Traditions*, New Delhi: D.K. Printworld, 2007, pp. 225-38.

314. Cf. *K*, p. 203: "The body itself is the supreme wheel, the eminent, beneficent *liṅga*, the chosen [place] of the divinized energies and the realm of the highest worship (*pūjā*). It is indeed the chief *maṇḍala* composed of the triple trident, the lotuses, the centres, and the etheric void (*kha*). There, all the [divinized] energies are ceaselessly worshipped, both externally and internally." (*TĀ 29.171-172)*

cakra is derived from the root *kṣa* (to expand), *cak* (to be satisfied), *kṛt* (to cut) and *kṛ* (to act)." Abhinavagupta continues with a kind of Tāntric "theology" of sexuality, for which he gives a different meaning to central elements and symbols of theology and ritual like *maṇḍala, pūjā, triśūla* or *liṅga*, before the background of the spirituality of the sexual ritual.[315] Then one can possibly translate his code language like this: The *maṇḍala* — the interiorized sexual union — is the best realm (*dhāman*), filled with light, a place for the worship (*pūjā*) of all "deities of the senses." In the context of the Brāhmanical orthodoxy at this time, this over-coding must have been extremely provocative, so the code-language works also as a protection.

Jayaratha explains that "juice" is the sexual fluid that emerges from the main *cakra*.[316] Here again we see the identification of "the main wheel" (*mukhya cakra*) with the female sexual organ (*yoni*). As we have said, this contact with sexual fluids forms the quintessence of impurity in the view of most brāhmaṇas. What is the deeper meaning or purpose of this transgressive ritual? Jayaratha quotes the following verse of the *Tantrāloka* (26.44): "Whatever leads the mind to an opening, that same means one should venerate. This is

---

315. Cf. *TĀ* 5.121: "This *liṅga*, the "heart of the *yoginī*" (*yoginīhṛdaya*), beautiful with bliss, brings forth an extraordinary form of consciousness due to the union of seed and womb." See for the different layers of meaning of this passage — among others *yoginīhṛdaya* in the sense of vagina — Paul Eduardo Muller-Ortega, *The Triadic Heart of Śiva. Kaula Tantricism of Abhinavagupta in the non-dual Shaivism of Kashmir* (SUNY Series in the Shaiva traditions of Kashmir) Albany: State University of New York Press, 1989; Delhi: Sri Satguru Publications, 1997, pp. 111ff.

316. Cf. *TĀV*, vol. VII, p. 3407.

Śambhu's instruction."[317] The extreme situation to break a taboo reminds us of methods described in the *Vijñāna-Bhairava*: through the unexpected, sudden experience of extreme fear, of extreme pain, or extreme joy, the "absolute reality" (*brahmasattā*, cf. *VBh* 118)[318] suddenly opens due to the intensive one-pointedness of this state and the immediate cessation of thoughts (*vikalpa*). What happens in these moments? Bettina Bäumer says about them: "In these moments one touches the core of one's own being and consciousness, which is pure, pulsating, intensive energy (*spanda*)."[319]

***

After orgasm, the "appeased" (*śānta*) state occurs. Abhinavagupta uses for it the metaphor of the "waveless ocean" (*TĀ* 29.134ab). All "deities" (*devatā*, divine powers) of the main *cakra* and the secondary *cakra*s cease to work within this emptiness (*śūnya*). Jayaratha comments: all things have completely vanished.[320] One loses consciousness of one's own surroundings.[321] One is in "complete joy" (*nirānanda*, cf. *TĀ*

---

317. Ibid., p. 3408.

318. "At the beginning and end of a sneeze, in a state of fear or sorrow, [standing] on top of an abyss or while fleeing from a battlefield, at the moment of intense curiosity, at the beginning or end of hunger — such a state comes close to the experience of *Brahman*." (*Vijñāna-Bhairava: The Practice of Centring Awareness*, op. cit., p. 139)

319. "In solchen Momenten berührt man den Kern des eigenen Seins und Bewusstseins, der reine, pulsierende, intensive Energie (*spanda*) ist." (Bettina Bäumer, *Vijñāna-Bhairava: Das göttliche Bewusstsein. 112 Weisen der mystischen Erfahrung im Śivaismus von Kaschmir*, Grafing: Edition Adyar, 2003, p. 185).

320. Cf. *TĀV*, vol. VII, p. 3385.

321. Cf. *K*, p. 75.

29.134cd-135ab).[322] The powers of the senses, that is, of *anucakra*, stand still (cf. *TĀ* 29.135cd). In regard to the senses, Abhinavagupta only says "seeing (*dṛg*), etc." Unlike him, Silburn makes an interesting differentiation which is important for our topic: by the term "secondary *cakras*," sound, form, smell and taste are indicated, but not touch. For: "The central wheel concerns only touch."[323] This corresponds with her former statement about the special state of "touch" among the five senses, "as it is of a more intimate nature than the other senses, it facilitates contact with the median way, and thus awakens it (. . .)."[324] In a footnote she identifies "the median way" with the term *madhyama cakra*, which is synonymous with the expressions "main centre" (*madhya cakra*), "mouth of the *yoginī*" (*yoginīvaktra*), "heart of the *yoginī*" (*yoginīhṛdaya*) and "superior domain" (*ūrdhvadhāman*).[325] We can conclude that her statement "the central wheel concerns only touch" is to be read in the sexual meaning of "central wheel." She presents the connection between the "central wheel" in the sense of the Centre and the "central wheel" in the sense of female sexual organ like this: by means of the sexual act one can return to the "Centre," the power of universal Consciousness.[326]

---

322. In contrast, Dupuche translates *nirānanda* with "without bliss," which is not plausible from the whole context (cf. Dupuche, *Kula Ritual*, op. cit., p. 274). On *nirānanda* as one of the seven forms of "joy, bliss" (*ānanda*), which Abhinavagupta describes in *TĀ* 5.43-53 in the context of the transformation of breath and the rising of *kuṇḍalinī*, see *K*, p. 75.

323. *K*, p. 193.

324. *K*, p. 138f.

325. Cf. *K*, p. 173.

326. Ibid.

The sexual touch has the effect of calming the powers of the other senses — hearing, smelling, tasting, seeing — and turning them away from the external. The sound, the fragrance, the colours or forms gradually dissolve and collect in the "Centre" (*madhya*).[327] All subjective and objective impressions melt within the Self.[328] Inhalation (*candra*, "moon") and exhalation (*sūrya*, "sun") become equal (cf. *TĀ* 29.146-147) and unite, and the breath enters *suṣumnā* (cf. *ĪPK* III. 2.20 *v*). One reaches the "reality of Bhairava" (*bhairava pada*, cf. *TĀ* 29.145).

Abhinavagupta uses the traditional Tāntric metaphors to indicate the rise of *kuṇḍalinī*, called "fire," within the median way (*suṣumnā*): the "thread" (*mātra*) in the stalk of the lotus (*kamala*), the "root" (*mūla*) of the lotus, the "triangle" (*koṇatraya*) and "fire" (cf. *TĀ* 29.150-153). The reality of *suṣumnā* is symbolized with the extremely fine thread inside the lotus stem. According to Jayaratha (commentary on *Tantrāloka* 3.94-95ab), the triangle (*trikoṇa*) symbolizes, on the one hand, the union of *icchāśakti*, *anuttara* and *ānanda*, and on the other hand, the vagina (the "mouth of the *yoginī*," *yoginīvaktra*, the "base of generation," *janmādhāra* or the "lower opening," *adhovaktra*).[329] Jayaratha says about it: "From there the highest *śakti* [= *kuṇḍalinī*] rises. As it was said: 'She of crooked form (*kuṭilarūpiṇī*) rises from *śṛṅgāṭapīṭha*.'"[330] At this place we meet,

---

327. Cf. *K*, p. 194 (interpretation of *TĀ* 29.136-137).

328. *K*, p. 76.

329. Cf. *K*, p. 27.

330. *TĀV*, vol. II, p. 456. — *Śṛṅgāṭaka* is the fruit of the water-chestnut, symbolic of the triangle. In *Śāktavijñāna* (ed. Jagaddhar Zadoo [KSTS] Srinagar 1947), Somānanda describes it as one part of the bulb (*kanda*). The bulb is located above the lower centre, called *cakrasthāna*, at the root of the *nāḍī*; cf. *K*, p. 106, fn. 3.

so to speak, the "physiological" connection between human sexuality and *kuṇḍalinī*: the subtle dimension of the sexual organ (*kulamūla*) — i.e. the lowest centre, *mūlādhāra*, specifically the "bulb" (*kanda*) — as the place of origin of *kuṇḍalinī*.[331] According to Silburn, the two triangles symbolize man and woman connected by *suṣumnā*; through their "pulsating friction" (*saṁghaṭṭa*), *kuṇḍalinī* starts to rise. Abhinavagupta describes this process in the following way: one attains the "fourth" (*turīya*) state, when ". . . moon, sun and fire unite" (*TĀ* 29.153) — that is, when inhalation and exhalation fuse and rise first as "the vertical breath" (*udāna*) then as *ūrdhvakuṇḍalinī* in *suṣumnā* (cf. *ĪPK* III. 2.20 and *v*). Then one reaches "the state of the eight Bhairavas, [of Bhairava] who is divided into eight energies (*kalā*)." (*TĀ* 29.157ab). Abhinavagupta continues with the verse, which we examine here and whose context is now more evident. I quote it again:

> The highest Bhairava (*bhairava parama*), here residing as sound (*nāda*), with eight aspects (*aṣṭavidha*), of the nature of light (*jyoti*), resonance (*dhvani*) and touch (*samīra*), is known

---

331. Jayaratha expounds *kulamūla* (the sexual organ/the lower centre) as "[. . .] the place of origin of the power of breath (*prāṇa-śakti*)" (*TĀV*, vol. 3, 1020). The *mūlādhāra* is located at the base of the spine, at the junction of the principal energy currents (cf. *K*, p. 27). In the root centre *kuṇḍalinī* lies in her "sleeping," coiled form, prior to her awakening and rising, blocking with her head the access to the "median channel" (*suṣumnā*, cf. ibid.). From this we can deduce: if *kuṇḍalinī* awakens and the access to the median channel opens, the same spiritual power (*prāṇa-śakti*) which is the basis and source of sexual life, breath and semen, is able to enter the median channel and can rise in a transformed form as *kuṇḍalinī*. The tradition (cf. *K*, p. 27) denotes this transformation like this: the same "lower opening" (*adhovaktra*, or *janmādhāra*, "the base of generation") becomes *meḍhrakanda* or *kanda* (bulb), one of the centres of power according to yogic physiology.

> as the supreme pervasion (*vyāptirucyate paramā*) of Māntrī.
> — *TĀ* 29.159cd-160ab

To decode the verse, we have to clarify the meaning of "the eight energies." The term is part of a complex reflection of the Hindu Tantras and its commentators concerning the stages of the rising of *kuṇḍalinī*, which is undertaken under the name "the *uccāra* of *oṁ*." We have dealt with it in connection with Kṣemarāja's commentary on *Svacchandatantra* 4.384, where "the touch of ants" (*pipīlikāsparśa*) is mentioned. This reflection is important to understand the character of *sparśa* in this context of the highest stages of the spiritual rise. I will outline it on the basis of passages in the *Tantrāloka* and *Svacchandatantra*.

"Uccāra of Oṁ"

The word *uccāra* consists of the prefix *ud-*, "up, upwards, upon, on, over, above" (cf. MW 183) and the root *car-*, "to move one's self, go, walk, move, stir" (cf. MW 389); therefore *uccār-* means "to go upwards, ascend, rise" and *uccāra* "rising," "emitting," "uttering" (MW 173). It is used for the ritualistic uttering and recitation of a *mantra*. In the Āgamas and in the manuals of Śaiva-Siddhānta the theme "the *uccāra* of *oṁ*" usually occurs in connection with the rites of initiation (*dīkṣā*).[332] The Tantras use the expression with a different, more esoteric meaning: Here, "*uccāra* of *oṁ*" or "*uccāra* of the *praṇava-mantra*" denotes the subtle rising of the power of breath and of *kuṇḍalinī*, who is the essence of all phonemes, and therefore of all *mantras*.

The general background of these Tāntric views goes back to the earliest documents of Indian thought,[333] the Vedas,

332. Cf. *Vāc*, pp. 404f.

333. See *Vāc*, pp. 1ff (ch. 1: "Early Speculations about the Significance and the Powers of the Word").

beginning with the *Ṛgveda*, with its reflections about the primordial principle "word," "speech," "sound" (*vāc*), the "Goddess Word" (*ṚV* 8.100.11; cf. 19.9.3): about the eternity as well as the creative potency and power (*śakti*) of the "word," "sound," identified with the divine energy (*śakti*) itself, and about the *mantra oṁ* (called *praṇava*) as the main symbol of the Absolute (*Brahman*). In the Tantras, these age-old reflections would be connected with *kuṇḍalinī*: the primordial and eternal sound *oṁ* is revealed itself as *kuṇḍalinī* — possibly based on the concrete experience of the (non-physical) humming sound which occurs during the rise of the power of *kuṇḍalinī* in the human body, which brings the *cakras* into a whirling movement, with its concurrent sound.

This passage where we meet the connection of the *mantra oṁ*, the breath and the rising *kuṇḍalinī* could be related with the doctrine of *oṁ* in the Upaniṣads,[334] where the "High Song" (*udgītha*, cf. *Chāndogya Upaniṣad* 1.1.1) is associated with the breath and with the elevation to the Highest, all of which being identified with *Brahman* (cf. *Kaṭha Upaniṣad* 2.15-16; *Taittirīya Upaniṣad* 1.8). The *Chāndogya Upaniṣad* speaks about *oṁ*: "Now, in regard to the body (*ātman*): It is as breath here in the mouth, which one shall venerate as High Song, because if it moves he makes the sound *oṁ*." (*Chāndogya Upaniṣad* 1.5.3). About the syllable *ud* in *udgītha* — the same like in *uccāra* — it is said in the same Upaniṣad: "The syllable *ud* is just breath (*prāṇa*), because humans rise (*ud-sthā-*) by means of the breath." (*Chāndogya Upaniṣad* 1.3.6). In this way "the High Song" (*udgītha*) is connected with the rising (*udyan*) of the sun (cf. *Chāndogya Upaniṣad* 1.3.1) and of the breath. *Oṁ* is the centre

334. I use following edition: Patrick Olivelle, *The Early Upaniṣads. Annotated Text and Translation*, Oxford: Oxford University Press, 1998.

between inhalation and exhalation — the point at which both breaths meet each other or fall into each other (cf. *Chāndogya Upaniṣad* 1.3.3). The *Kaṭha Upaniṣad* denotes *oṁ* as the "supreme support" (*ālambanaṁ param*) through which one can enjoy the world of *Brahman* (cf. *Kaṭha Upaniṣad* 2.17). *OṀ* (or *praṇava*)[335] is "the bow, the great weapon of the Upaniṣad" (*Muṇḍaka Upaniṣad* 2.3), the aim is *Brahman*, the arrow the Self (*Muṇḍaka Upaniṣad* 2.4). In my view, here we can find a hint to understand *oṁ* in the meaning of *kuṇḍalinī*: the rising of the phonic energy of *oṁ* in the *madhya nāḍī* (*suṣumnā*), if we interpret the "veins" as the main energy conduits (*iḍā nāḍī* and *piṅgalā nāḍī*) or the 72,000 subtle conduits (*nāḍīs*) which unite in the "centre" (*madhya*), in *suṣumnā*: "Where the veins (*nāḍyaḥ*) come together, like spokes on the hub, in it that one moves, taking birth in many ways. 'It is *oṁ*' — meditate thus on this self [. . .]" (*Muṇḍaka Upaniṣad* 2.2.6). The rising to the Highest through *oṁ* is expressed with a striking metaphor in the *Maitrī Upaniṣad*:[336]

> And thus it has been said elsewhere: Two *Brahman*s have to be meditated on, the word and the non-word. By the word alone is the non-word revealed. Now there is the word *oṁ*. Moving upward by it (where all words and all what is meant by them ceases), he arrives at absorption in the non-word (*Brahman*). This is the way, this is the immortal, this is union, and this is bliss. And as the spider, moving upward by the

335. *Praṇava*: from *pra-ṇu*, "to sound, to reverberate, to make a humming sound," derived from the root *nu*, "to praise, command, sound, shout" (cf. *Vāc*, p. 403). Kṣemarāja explains *praṇava* in his commentary (*uddyota*) of *SvT* with: "that by which is eminently praised or expressed the supreme reality" (quoted from ibid.).

336. Translation: Max Müller, *The Upanishads*. Part 2 (Sacred Books of the East; 15) Oxford: Oxford University Press, 1884, p. 321.

> thread, gains free space, thus also he who meditates, moving upward by the syllable *oṁ*, gains independence.
>
> — *Maitrī Upaniṣad* 6.22

In the *Chāndogya Upaniṣad*, the classical document for the doctrine of *oṁ*, we find the connection of breath, word, sexual union and *oṁ* as the essence of all:[337]

> (5) The *Ṛg* is nothing but speech; the *Sāman* is breath; and the High Chant is this syllable *oṁ*. Speech and breath, the *Ṛg* and the *Sāman* — each of these sets, clearly, is a pair in coitus.
>
> (6) This pair in coitus unites in the syllable *oṁ*, and when a pair unites in coitus, they satisfy each other's desire.
>
> (7) So, when someone knows this and venerates the High Chant as this syllable, he will surely become a man who satisfies desires.
>
> — *Chāndogya Upaniṣad* 1.1.5-7

We have to ask: What is the "hidden connection" (*upaniṣad*) of breath, word, sexual union, the *mantra oṁ*, about which the *Chāndogya Upaniṣad* talks afterwards (1.1.10)? What is the "secret doctrine" or the "secret rite" which is denoted by the word *upaniṣad*?[338] I suggest that a connection could exist within the interiorized sexual act (*caryākrama*), the sexual ritual, in which the breath and then the *kuṇḍalinī* accompanied by a subtle sound-pulsation start to rise, which can finally lead to

337. *CU* 1.1.3

338. Cf. H.W. Bodewitz, "The Cosmic, Cyclical Dying (*parimara*): Aitareya Brāhmaṇa 8.28 and Kauṣītaki Upaniṣad 2.11-12," in: W. Morgenroth, *Sanskrit and World Culture* (Schriften zur Geschichte und Kultur des alten Orients; 18) Berlin: Akademie Verlag, 1986, pp. 438-43; here: p. 438, fn. 4 (see Olivelle, *Early Upaniṣads*, op. cit., p. 24, fn. 29).

the highest state. It could be a knowledge which is indicated in an Upaniṣad in an encoded form and which was later unfolded by the Tāntras and its commentators in a more complex and detailed way. Padoux and Silburn underline the prefiguration of Tāntric conceptions in the Vedas, especially in the Upaniṣads,[339] without mentioning these surprising connections to the *Chāndogya Upaniṣad*.

THE PRACTICE OF UCCĀRA ACCORDING TO THE TANTRĀLOKA

In the *Tantrāloka*, Abhinavagupta lists *uccāra* among the means for "immersion" (*samāveśa*), alongside "instruments," "organs" (*karaṇa*), meditation (*dhyāna*), letters (*varṇa*), etc. which all belong to the "way of the limited individual" (*āṇavopāya*, cf. *Tantrāloka* 1.170). In chapter 5 he underlines the connection between *prāṇa* and *uccāra*:

> The intellect (*buddhi*) is meditation (*dhyāna*), the breath is *uccāraṇa*. *Uccāraṇa* is inhalation (*prāṇa*), etc. up to the "pervasive breath" (*vyāna*). The primary form is vitality (*prāṇana*) of the nature of supreme rising (*paroccāra*).
>
> — *TĀ* 5.17cd-18

Later, in the context of the experience of the all-pervasive "universal joy" (*jagadānanda*), the highest of the seven stages of joy (cf. *TĀ* 5.43-53), he says:

> Repose (*viśrānti*) therein can be attained by the union (*yoga*) with the rising of the heart (*hṛdayoccāra*). The perfect (*samyak*) repose therein is nothing other than the place of *anuttara*.
>
> — *TĀ* 5.52cd-53ab

---

339. See *Vāc*, pp. 4ff (the power of the word in the Veda), pp. 15 ff (*oṁ* in the Upaniṣads); *K*, p. 16 (on the Vedic motif of the "snake in the depths," *Ahirbudhnya*), p. 47 (on *Maitrī Upaniṣad* VI), p. 88 (on the offerings for the deities of breath and senses in *CU*).

In the same chapter Abhinavagupta says about *uccāra*:

> The Self (*ātman*), the limited individual (*aṇu*), the root of *kula* (*kulamūla*),[340] śakti, domination (*bhūti*), *citi*, sexual passion (*rati*) and the three energies coloured by subject, object and free from both are denoted as the tenfold void (*kha*) which characterize the gradual rising (*uccāra*).
>
> — *TĀ* 5.93-94ab

Here he lists elements of that practice which is denoted with *uccāra*; its background in the sexual ritual becomes evident. Its connection with the transformation of the breath and the rising (*uccāra*) of *kuṇḍalinī* becomes clearer through the following quotation from *VBh* in Jayaratha's commentary:

> Meditate on the Śakti rising from the root (*mūla*),[341] which is luminous like the rays of the sun and which gets more and more subtle until it dissolves at the end [of the twelve fingers, *dvādaśānta*]. Then the state of Bhairava will awaken.
>
> — *VBh* 28

The sexual context of *uccāra* will become more clear from the next verse which we have already analysed in chapter 2:

> Established in the abode of light (*dhāmasthaṁ*), established in the centre of the abode of light (*dhāmamadhyasthaṁ*), enclosed (*puṭīkṛtam*) from the belly (*udara*) of the abode of light one shall awake (*bodhayet*) in the abode of light through the abode of light. Then one shall contrive (*kuru*) the abode of light to enter into the abode of light. In that (*tad*) abode of light it should be entered (*bhedyaṁ*) by the movement (*gatyā*) of the abode of light, [until one is] at the end (*antam*) within the interior (*antara*) of the abode of light.
>
> — *TĀ* 5.94-95

---

340. The word *kulamūla* denotes the sexual organ and the lowest *cakra*, *mūlādhāra* (cf. *Lumière*, p. 286, fn. 32).

341. I.e. *mūlādhāra cakra*.

The highly encoded language itself gives a hint that the passage refers to the interiorized sexual act, the sexual ritual. Again the commentary is a help to decode these two verses. Jayaratha discusses the correspondences to the ten voids (*kha*) in the preceding verse: one of the meanings of *dhāman* is *kulamūla* or *janmādhāra*, the female sexual organ, another meaning is "power of breath" (*prāṇa-śakti*), another is Self (*ātman*), and *dhāman* in the instrumental case means "by sexual passion (*rati*) and attachment (*āśaktyā*)."[342] Sexual experience and the "direct perception of the highest Reality" (*paratattva-sākṣātkāra*) are directly connected.

In the whole passage in *Tantrāloka* 5, we see resonances between the multi-dimensional terms *anuttara*, *hṛdaya* and *dhāman*. In each of these words, spiritual and sexual connotations overlap each other, and at the same time the words interact with each other, resulting in an iridescence which we only know otherwise within poetic language. It reminds us of the opalescent effect when we see sunlight falling through moving leaves of a tree.

Abhinavagupta again connects the word *hṛdaya* (heart) with *uccāra* when he says: "The highest heart (*hṛdayaṁ param*) of the repose (*viśrānti*) of the rising (*uccāra*) is the non-manifest *liṅga* (*avyaktaliṅga*), not differentiated in Śiva, Śakti or world (*nara*)." (*TĀ* 5.112cd-113ab). As we have seen, he characterizes the non-manifest *liṅga* as "the heart of the *yoginī*" (*yoginīhṛdaya*) — a term in which dimensions of meaning overlie. In the expression "highest heart" we can hear the characterization of the goddess (Śakti) as the "heart," the centre of reality, as the place in which the totality of the 36 *tattva*s reside (cf. *TĀ* 1.82), as the "heart of the highest Lord"

342. Cf. *TĀV*, vol. III, p. 1022.

(*hṛdayaṁ parameṣituḥ*).[343] It denotes the twelfth movement of the *kuṇḍalinī*, called *unmanā-śakti*, the state where thinking has stopped (*nirvikalpa*), one's true nature unfolds and the knowledge of the Self (*ātma-jñāna*) arises. It is that place in which the rising power comes to rest (cf. *TĀ* 5.113). At the same time, the "highest heart" is identified with the "heart of the *yoginī*," the vagina; during the interiorized sexual union (the sexual act in the state of absorption) one enters — by the repose in the "heart of the *yoginī*" — into the repose of the "highest heart."

After the reflection on "the heart of the *yoginī*," including its connection with the sexual ritual (*kulayāga*), Abhinavagupta states: "In this way, the method (*vidhi*) of *uccāra* has been described [. . .]" (*TĀ* 5.128ab). Because of its code language this description of *uccāra* is at the same time both concealing and revealing. However, the sexual dimension of the yogic practice of *uccāra* as described in the *Tantrāloka* is evident. The concrete form of this practice cannot be decoded without oral transmission. With only the text we can merely see that in its centre there is the transformation of the power of breath and the rise of *kuṇḍalinī* within an interiorized form of sexual union. In a general way we can distinguish different stages within this practice:

1. exhalation (*prāṇa*) and inhalation (*apāna*); wakeful state (*jāgrat*); bodily pervasion (*dehavyāpti*); absorption into the joy of sexual union;
2. "equal breath" (*samāna*), then the rising (*uccāra*) of the breath (*udāna*) in *suṣumnā*, rising of *kuṇḍalinī*; experience of the "great joy" (*mahānanda*);

343. *Parāprāveśikā of Kṣemarāja*, ed. with Notes by Paṇḍit Mukunda Rāma Śāstrī (KSTS; 15), Bombay 1918 (benedictory verse).

3. "pervasive breath" (*vyāna*); joy of the experience of *cit* (*cidānanda*); state of the "great pervasion" (*mahāvyāpti*); and
4. experience of "universal joy" (*jagadānanda*).[344]

THE TWELVE MAIN STAGES OF THE POWER

The doctrine of *uccāra* of the *mantra oṁ* is described in different chapters of the *Svacchandatantra*. In this doctrine, twelve main stages of the power of *oṁ* are distinguished. Silburn denotes it as "the twelve movements of *kuṇḍalinī*."[345] They comprise stages of the manifestation of sound, the original phonic energy, stages of a series of transformations and condensations of the phonic energy by which the manifest universe emerges.[346] The cosmic emanation (*sṛṣṭi*) begins from the supreme Śiva (Paramaśiva) in a movement downwards from most subtle dimensions of the power of *oṁ* up to ever-more condensed forms. This process occurs analogously within the individual, with a rising movement from the gross phonic vibration of the phonemes up to more and more subtle, higher energies and finally to its origin, Śiva. It is a movement back to the wellspring of the power of *oṁ* and so of the whole universe, essentially consisting of this vibrating-shining sound-energy, and at the same time the cosmic process of the dissolution (*saṁhāra*) of the manifest universe.

These twelve stages of the power form a basic structure of the Tāntric system, attributing to them cosmic, theological and yogic levels. They are associated with certain *tattvas*, with deities (*devatā*), with the *cakras* of the yogic body, with the 16

---

344. On the stages of "joy, bliss" (*ānanda*) corresponding to the stages of the transformation of the breath, see *K*, pp. 75ff.

345. *K*, p. 49.

346. See Padoux, *Vāc*.

kalās of Śiva,[347] with the twelve phonemes from *A* to *Ḥ* (*visarga*), with the four states and with the seven stages of void (*śūnya*, cf. *Svacchandatantra* 4.288-296).

From the perspective of the individual, these stages represent certain particular stages of the spiritual process experienced during the rise of *kuṇḍalinī* in the state of absorption. According to this kind of *kuṇḍalinī* experience, these stages can be passed over all at once in a flash, or might instead be experienced very slowly, with different stages at different times. This becomes clear from a remark of Abhinavagupta: the practitioner who has crossed the stage of *nāda* has to rise further and attain "the supreme pervasion." "This he should practise daily, until the phonic energy (*rāviṇī*) dissolves in silence (*arāva*)." (*TĀ* 5.100ab). Under the denotation "the *uccāra* of *oṁ*" we find a very refined reflection of the yogic rise to the supreme state. It is not a mere abstract model, but a condensation of the experiences of seasoned practitioners.

I will list the twelve stages in their ascending order:[348]

1. ***A* (*akāra*):** The first phoneme, of which *oṁ* consists; associated with Brahmā, the creator of the gross material existence, with the 24 *tattvas* from *pṛthvī* to *prakṛti*; corresponding *cakra*: heart (*hṛdaya cakra*). State: wakeful state (*jāgrat*).
2. ***U* (*ukāra*):** The second phoneme of *oṁ*; associated with Viṣṇu (who maintains the universe), with the *tattvas* from *puruṣa* to *kāla* (limitation of time); *cakra*: *kaṇṭha* (at

347. *Kalā* denotes the sixteenth part of the moon; from it the idea of 16 *kalās* of Śiva is derived. See *Vāc*, pp. 89ff, 157f, 280ff.

348. See the overview in *Vāc*, p. 408, based on *SvT*, and the brief description in *K*, p. 49.

the back of the throat). Yogic state of *dhyāna*, i.e. *kuṇḍalinī* can rise up to the throat (*kaṇṭha cakra*). To rise higher into the head, it is necessary to remain in a deep and continuous state of absorption (*samāveśa*).[349] State: sleep (*svapna*).

3. ***M* (*makāra*)**: The third phoneme of *oṁ* (when formed as *A-U-Ṁ*); associated with Rudra who presides over the cosmic resorption, and with the level (*tattva*) of *māyā*; transition from the *tattvas* and "worlds" (*bhuvanas*) to the realm of the powers in the form of *kalās*;[350] centre of power: *tālu* or *lambikā* (at the back of the vault of the palate).[351] State: deep sleep (*suṣupti*).

4. ***bindu* (*dot, drop*)**: Concentration of the power (light) at one point; associated with *Īśvara* (cf. *NT* 21.66); *tattvas*: *śuddha vidyā*, *Īśvara*, the first two of the "pure principles" (*śuddha tattvas*); centre of power: *bhrūmadhya*, "between the eyebrows." In the process of the rising of the power of *oṁ* (*prāṇa-kuṇḍalinī*) *bindu* marks the awareness on the point between inhalation and exhalation.[352] State: the "fourth" (*turīya*).

5. ***ardhacandra* (*half-moon*)**: Associated with *lalāṭa* (the point of power in the middle of the forehead);[353] *bindu* turns into the middle of the forehead, into "half-moon."[354] From here starts the state of the "eight

349. Cf. *K*, p. xv.
350. Cf. *Vāc*, p. 334.
351. Cf. *K*, p. 28.
352. Cf. *Vijñāna-Bhairava: The Practice of Centring Awareness*, op. cit., p. 5.
353. Cf. *K*, p. 28.
354. Cf. *Vijñāna-Bhairava: The Practice of Centring Awareness*, op. cit., p. 49.

Bhairavas," divided into eight energies (cf. *TĀ* 29.156f) from *ardhacandra* to *unmanā*. In the process of the rising of the power of *oṁ*, *ardhacandra* marks the state in which the breath stops.[355]

6. ***nirodhikā* or *nirodhinī*: "the hindering (power)":** The practitioner is confronted with opposite forces associated with the three energies Rundhanī, Rodhanī (the obstructing) and Raudrī (cf. *Svacchandatantra* 10.1229);[356] in the spiritual process of the rising of *kuṇḍalinī*, *nirodhikā* marks the state in which the stopping of the breath consolidates.[357]

7. ***nāda, "subtle sound"*:** Beginning of the condensation of the original sound-vibration and therefore of the emergence of the manifest universe; *nāda* remains when all dividing thought constructs (*vikalpas*) vanish (cf. *TĀ* 4.175); associated with Sadāśiva; realm within the yogic physiology: from *lalāṭa* up to *brahmarandhra* ("*Brahman*'s opening" at the crown of the skull);[358] the experience of "the unstruck sound" (*anāhata nāda*) appears at this stage.

8. ***nādānta, "end of the sound"*:** Connected with a subtle inner resonance;[359] *cakra*: *brahmarandhra*; beginning of the state "beyond the fourth" (*turīyātīta*). If the power rises up to this stage, it is connected with the experience

355. Ibid., p. 5.

356. See *Vāc*, p. 104, fn. 52.

357. Cf. *Vijñāna-Bhairava: The Practice of Centring Awareness*, op. cit., p. 5.

358. Cf. *K*, p. 49.

359. Ibid.

of *ghūrṇi*, "vibrant whirling," one of the five major signs of the stages of *yoga* (cf. *TĀ* 5.101ff).[360]

9. ***śakti* (*power, energy, strength, might*):**[361] Associated with Śakti; *tattva*: *śakti*; pure energy, no longer part of the process in the body — *kuṇḍalinī* has left the body through the "opening of *Brahman*" (*brahmarandhra*). Associated with one of the seven voids, i.e. *ūrdhva-śūnya*.[362] At the end of this stage of the rise of *kuṇḍalinī* there is a moment when the three main energies (*icchā, jñāna, kriyā*) merge with each other; this state is called "the wave" (*urmi*). "When one attains *śakti*, one is called "awakened" (*buddha*)." (*Svacchandatantra* 4.239)[363] **At this level the experience of *sparśa* occurs.**

10. ***vyāpinī*, "*the pervading*" (*power*):** Corresponds with the 16th *kalā*, associated with "the great void" (*mahāśūnya*).[364] The bodily limitations disappear, and *kuṇḍalinī* fills the whole universe.[365] "At the level of *vyāpinī* one is said to be 'completely awakened' (*prabuddha*)." (*Svacchandatantra* 4.269).

11. ***samanā*, "*with thoughts*," "*the mental*" (*power*):** Associated with Śiva and the last, 36th *tattva*, *śiva*; connected with the fifth void, the "void of tranquillity,"

---

360. On *ghūrṇi* see *K*, pp. 49, 58, 74.

361. From *śak*, "to be strong or powerful, be able or capable" (cf. MW p. 1044).

362. See Lilian Silburn, "Les sept Vacuités d'après le Çivaisme du Cachemire", *Hermès* 6 (1969), pp. 213-21.

363. *The Svacchandatantram with Commentary 'Udyota' of Kṣemarāja*, ed. Vraj Vallabh Dwivedi, vol. I, Delhi: Parimal Publications, 1985.

364. Cf. *ĪPVV*, vol. II, pp. 63f; see Dyczkowski, *Doctrine of Vibration*, op. cit., p. 119.

365. Cf. *K*, p. 49.

which transcends time and space;[366] state of the "pervasion of the Self" (*ātmavyāpti*),[367] of merging of everything in the Self. "Above it one is called 'perfectly awakened' (*suprabuddha*)." (*Svacchandatantra* 4.269).

12. ***unmanā, the "transmental" (power)*:** The highest form of the sonic energy of *oṁ*; the 17th *kalā*; associated with the supreme Śiva (Paramaśiva) and the sixth void, "void beyond void" (*śūnyāti-śūnya*);[368] state of omnipenetration, the pervasion of Śiva (*śivavyāpti*) or "great pervasion" (*mahāvyāpti*): everything fuses into Paramaśiva.[369] "When the Self, by rising to the realm of *unmanā*, enters the state of the supreme bliss of *cit*, that state is known as *śivavyāpti*."[370] State: "beyond the fourth" (*turīyātīta*).

    Cakra: *sahasrāra* or outer *dvādaśānta*, "the end of the twelve finger's breadth" above the skullcap. Silburn characterizes this state like this: the power is now free from all mental conditions which are reaching up to *samanā*.[371] It transcends the preceding eleven movements and becomes one with the perfectly free

366. *Le Vijñānabhairava: Texte traduit et commenté par Lilian Silburn*, Paris: Ed. de Boccard, 1983, intro.
367. See *ŚSV* 3.7; *TĀ* 5.135 and commentary; *SvT* 4.261 and commentary; *K*, pp. 30, 59, 167.
368. Cf. Kṣemarāja, commentary on *NT* 21.61; *TĀ* 11.20ab; *VBh* 51; *SvT* 4.388).
369. Cf. *K*, p. 167.
370. Kṣemarāja, commentary *SvT* 4; quoted from *ŚS* (ed. J. Singh), p. 149.
371. *Māyā* ". . . is a bond extending up to *samanā*." (Kṣemarāja, *ŚSV* 3.7; ed. J. Singh, p. 148).

power (*svātantryaśakti*).[372] Silburn denotes this dimension of the power as the "supreme heart," based on *Tantrāloka* 5.113: "The supreme heart of repose of the rising (*uccāra*), described in this way, is the non-manifest *liṅga*, not-differentiated in Śiva, Śakti, and world." The *Svacchandatantra* describes *unmanā* in the following way:

> "No time (*kāla*), no division (*kalā*), no movement (*cara*) [commentary: of the breath], and no levels of reality (*tattva*), no cause (*kāraṇa*), the perfect annihilation (*sunirvāṇa*), the supreme (*parā*), pure (*śuddha*), descended from the tradition of the masters (*guruparamparā*). That knowing one is liberated, not born again." (*Svacchandatantra* 4.240-241ab)

For our topic it is important that, with the help of this system of the twelve stages of the rise of *kuṇḍalinī*, we are able to identify the moment in the whole spiritual process where *sparśa* is experienced, and to realize the context of this experience. Striking are the resonances of Buddhist terminology especially in the language of the *Svacchandatantra*, e.g. *śūnya*, *buddha*, and *nirvāṇa*.

From this background of the stages of the rising power, we are able now to classify the statement in *Tantrāloka* 29.159cd-160ab. I will quote the text in its context of the passage:

> (156cd) He who obtains access to the eightfold wheel (*cakrāṣṭaka*) utters the spontaneous (*sahaja*) "recitation" (*japa*) in the supreme abode (*dhāmni*).
>
> (157ab) He attains the level (*padam*) of the eight Bhairavas, himself dividing into eight energies (*kalā*):

372. Cf. *K*, p. 49.

(157cd-158ab) in coming and going [of inhalation and exhalation], in security [typically for the intellect], in hearing, in seeing, in the contact (*samparka*) of both organs,[373] in the sexual union (*saṁmelanayoga*), at the end of the body (= *brahmarandhra*), in the wheel of union (*yāmalacakra*).

(158cd) The undefined sound (= *sītkāra*) arises from the heart, moves through the breasts [of the beloved], reaches the throat and ends on her lips.

(159ab) When the excitation (*kṣobha*) vanishes, he who can hear it, in the centre (*madhya*) between the two *cakra*s attains repose (*nirvānti*).

(159cd) The highest Bhairava (*bhairava parama*), here residing as sound (*nāda*), with eight aspects (*aṣṭavidha*), of the nature of light (*jyoti*), resonance (*dhvani*) and touch (*samīra*), is known as the supreme pervasion (*vyāptirucyate paramā*) of Mantrī.

Now we shall try to decode the passage: "the eightfold wheel" is the union of the two partners, including their movements of breath, their sense-organs, their intellect, and their sexual organs. Abhinavagupta seems to list a hierarchy of means which are used for the rising of the power up to "the end of the body" (*dehānta*), i.e. to the uppermost *cakra*, the "*Brahman*'s opening" (*brahmarandhra*), the open point in the skullcap.

Japa, the recitation of a *mantra*, represents the last part of the worship (*pūjā*) — here in the sense of the "true" (*vāstava*) *pūjā*, in which everything which the senses enjoy is offered to the "deities of the senses," in which the manifold sensations during the sexual act become one, and one melts into "the great void" (*mahāvyoma*, cf. *TĀ* 4.115cd-122ab).

373. Jayaratha comments: "only touch" (*sparśamātram*, *TĀV*, vol. VII, p. 3399), the initial contact of the sexual organs.

The characterization of the "supreme Bhairava" with aspects of "sound," "light" and "touch" reminds us of a verse in the first chapter of the *Tantrāloka*, where Abhinavagupta mentions six aspects of Śiva, based on *Dīkṣottara*:[374]

> Śiva, who consists of *bindu* and *nāda*, is called sixfold: He is of the nature of the world (*bhuvana*), the body (*vigraha*), the light (*jyoti*), the void (*kha*), the sound (*śabda*) and the *mantra*.
>
> — *TĀ* 1.63

In fact, Kṣemarāja quotes this verse in his commentary on *Svacchandatantra* 4.269, in the context of the twelve stages of the rise of *kuṇḍalinī*.[375] Jayaratha explains *kha* with "void" (*śūnya*) and connects it with the stages of *śakti*, *vyāpinī* and *samanā*.[376] It is obvious that "light" and "sound" are mentioned in *Tantrāloka* 1.63, but not "touch," according to the traditional sources used by Abhinavagupta. The more striking is his own addition of "touch" in *Tantrāloka* 29.160.

With "eight Bhairavas" which divide themselves into eight aspects, he denotes the eight highest forms of the power, from *ardhacandra* up to *unmanā* (cf. *TĀ* 29.160cd-161ab), the form of the power beyond thought. It unfolds when *kuṇḍalinī* rises through *brahmarandhra* above the head and exits from the body. In relation to the eight highest energies, Jayaratha attributes

374. *Dīkṣottara* 2.2c-3b: "Inexhaustible Śiva is sixfold, [manifest as] word, ether, light, body and world; [his] *mantra*-form is the supreme." (quoted from Vasudeva, *Yoga of Mālinīvijayottaratantra*, op. cit., p. 257, fn. 27). Cf. *MVT* 12.9: "The category of the aim (*lakṣya*) is considered to be sixfold according to the divisions of void (*vyoman*), body (*vigraha*), drop (*bindu*), phoneme (*arṇa*), world (*bhuvana*) and resonance (*dhvani*). It will be taught how this is." (quoted from ibid., p. 256)

375. Cf. *SvT*, vol. I, p. 210.

376. Cf. *TĀV*, vol. II, p. 100.

"light" to the stage of "the half-moon" (*ardhacandra*), when *kuṇḍalinī* in her rising pierces the centre of power in the middle of the forehead (*lalāṭa*) and "sound" to the stage of sound (*nāda*), when the "energy of *oṁ*" rises above *lalāṭa* through the head up to *brahmarandhra*. About "touch" (*samīra*), Jayaratha says: "Śakti of the nature of touch (*sparśātmā*)." That is to say, "touch" is related to the stage of *śakti*, when *kuṇḍalinī* has left the body and rises above the head. It still represents a lower state of the energy compared to the next stages of *vyāpinī* and *samanā*.[377] Silburn gives us the hint that at the moment when the pure energy (*śakti*) leaves the head, one experiences *ghūrṇi*, a vibrant whirling or reeling, "[. . .] a vibration moving in all directions [. . .]"[378] "[. . .] at the moment one shifts from Self-Consciousness to universal Consciousness [. . .]."[379] This vibration, in its most intensive form, "[. . .] is none other than the fully-unfolded *kuṇḍalinī* in *brahmarandhra*."[380]

From the context of the description of the secret ritual, it is clear that these eight movements of the *kuṇḍalinī* — called "eight Bhairavas," the eight highest stages in the rise of the vibrating and flashing "sonic energy of *oṁ*" — arise at the time of *sāmarasya* of the pair. *Sāmarasya* literally means "same flavour, equal essence (*rasa*),"[381] the state of non-duality and non-difference — in this context of the two partners, their

---

377. Cf. *K*, p. 82.

378. *K*, p. 74.

379. *K*, p. 58.

380. *K*, p. 74.

381. Silburn renders *sāmarasya* as "unique flavour"; she denotes with it the union of "vital energy" (*prāṇa*) and "virile potency" (*vīrya*); the source of both is the conscious energy, *kuṇḍalinī* (cf. *K*, p. 3). She also uses the same term in relation to the highest state (*turīyātīta*) for the "pervasion of Śiva" (*Śivavyāpti*), . . . "where the divine essence is perceived as all-pervading (. . .): at the heart of →

complete "flowing into each other" or absorption, like the mixing of milk with milk. The context of the sexual act is also indicated in the names of the eight Bhairavas given in *Tantrāloka* 29.160-161:[382]

- *Sakala*, "endowed with parts"; Silburn interprets it with the initial stage of union, "a differentiated contact with the sense-organs."[383] This corresponds with the *sakala*-state of the perceiver, the state of conventional, dualistic perception (*sakala pramātṛ*), the lowest level of the "seven perceivers";
- *Niṣkala*, "undivided," "refers to that which has no contact with them [the sense-organs]";[384]
- *Śūnya*, "void";
- *Kalāḍhya*, "rich in *kalā*";
- *Khamala-vikṛta*, "adorned with void (*kha*)";
- *Kṣepaṇaka*, "destroyer";
- *Antaḥstha*, "the one standing within"; and
- *Kaṇṭhyoṣṭhya*, "guttural-labial."

If this order corresponds with the order of the eight energies, then the stage of *śakti* where the experience of *sparśa* occurs would correspond with *khamala-vikṛta*. But here again we meet the limits of a highly encoded language of an esoteric

---

→ this one-savoured unity [= *sāmarasya*], Self and universe merge into the Whole in perfect harmony." (*K*, p. 167) — On *sāmarasya* as an important term in Tāntric Buddhism see Shashi Bhushan Dasgupta, *Introduction to Tāntric Buddhism*, Calcutta: Calcutta University Press, 3rd edn. 1974, pp. 124-28.

382. See *K*, p. 202 and table, 205.

383. *K*, p. 202, fn. 50.

384. *K*, p. 202, fn. 51.

tradition, and without the oral teaching of a master of the tradition it remains unclear what is the exact relation between the "eight Bhairavas," the particular stages of the sexual union and the stages of the rising of *kuṇḍalinī*.

The attribution of *sparśa* to the stage of *śakti* and the three stages of "light," "sound" and "touch" can already be found in the fourth chapter of the *Svacchandatantra*:[385]

> (274) By the meditation on light (*jyoti*) the *yogīs* attain *yogasiddhis*.[386] By the union with it the *yogīs* attain overlordship.
>
> (275) By meditation (*dhyāna*) on sound (*śabda*) he becomes the self (*ātmā*) of sound, and he becomes filled with the nature of the word (*vāṇ*). And by meditation on touch (*sparśa*) he becomes the cause of the universe.
>
> (276) By meditation on the void (*śūnya*) he becomes of the nature of void, all-pervading (*vyāpī*), omnipresent (*sarvagato*). By the practice of meditation on *samanā*, the *yogī* attains omniscience (*sarvajñāna*).
>
> (277) By meditation on *unmanā*, the supreme, most subtle state, one transcends all senses (*indriya*) and thought (*manas*). It is called non-being (*abhāva*),[387] the undenotable (*alakṣya*).[388]
>
> — *Svacchandatantra* 4.274-277

385. *SvT*, vol. I, p. 212.

386. Supernatural powers.

387. See Mark S.G. Dyczkowski, "Abhāvavāda — A Forgotten Śaiva Doctrine," in: *Navonmeṣa: M. M. Gopinath Kaviraj Smriti Granth. Vol. IV: English*, ed. Jaideva Singh, H.N. Chakravarty and G. Mukhopadhyaya, Varanasi 1987, pp. 107-19. — On *abhāva* see *ĪPK* I: *Citi* or *parāvāk*, the "heart" [= Śakti, the goddess], is the "great being" (*mahāsattā*, *ĪPK* I 5.14); in the auto-commentary Utpaladeva clarifies: ". . . it is not to be understood as the counterpart of non-being (*abhāvāpratiyoginī*), [but] it also pervades non-being." (*ĪPK* I 5.14 *v*)

Here we meet again the close connection between the stages of the energy of *oṁ* and the three spiritual phenomena of "light," "sound" and "touch," given in a graded order which reminds us of the three stages of "meditation," "vision" and "touch" in Utpaladeva's *ŚSĀ* 13.6. Kṣemarāja says in his commentary on verse *Svacchandatantra* 4.275: "*śabda* = *nāda*," that is, he identifies the word *śabda* of the verse with the stage of *nāda*, i.e. within the framework of the stages of "the *uccāra* of *oṁ*," as we can infer from the context of the following verses where he mentions *vyāpinī*, *samanā* and *unmanā*. Afterwards he says: "*sparśa* — the attaining of Śakti (*śaktigati*) of the nature of supreme joy (*ānandātmā*)." Grammatically, *ānandātmā* can be related to *sparśa* as well as to *śakti*. This corresponds with a statement in an earlier passage of Kṣemarāja's commentary on the *Svacchandatantra*:

> After having adopted (*gṛhītvā*) the form of "end of sound" (*nādāntarūpatām*) and having come to rest (*layaṁ yāti*) in the reality of *śakti* (*śaktitattve*), he/she — when *nādānta* has ended (*praśamyya*) — takes refuge (*śrayati*) in the "aperture of Brahman" (*brahmavīḷe*) through the touch of joy of the Self (*ānandasparśātmatāṁ*).[389]

In another passage of the *Svacchandatantra* we read:[390]

---

388. Or: the "ungraspable," "that which cannot be aimed at" etc. *Lakṣya* means "denoted, be marked, aim," from the root *lakṣ*, "to perceive, observe, mark, take aim at, to know, understand" (MW p. 891). The "varieties of the goal" (*lakṣyabheda*) designate the destinations of a *yogī*; as we have already seen, for example *MVT* 12.9 lists six aims (*lakṣya*), six aspects of Śiva as "destinations" for the yogic practice: *vyoman* (void), *bindu*, *dhvani*, etc. (see Vasudeva, *Yoga of Mālinīvijayottaratantra*, op. cit., pp. 253ff).

389. *SvT*, vol. I, p. 207 (commentary on 4.260).

390. Ibid., p. 208.

Through knowledge (*vijñāna*) one rises above (*ūrdhvatāṁ vrajet*). One goes to Vyāpinī, Samanā, Unmanā, Śiva.

— *Svacchandatantra* 4.261

It is obvious that *vijñāna* here does not mean discursive knowledge. "Above" means above the stage of *śakti*. In his commentary on this verse, Kṣemarāja again connects this stage with the experience of *sparśa*:

Having experienced touch (*sparśa*) within *śakti*, he/she reaches *vyāpinī* at the root of the hairs (*tvakkeśapade*). At the level of *vyāpinī* she/he attains the pervasion.

In the text of *Svacchandatantra* 4.275 and Kṣemarāja's commentary we can find important hints towards (a) the place of the experience of *sparśa* within the yogic physiology, and (b) the character of *sparśa*.

(a) In the commentary on *Svacchandatantra* 4.260, Kṣemarāja clearly connects the "touch of the bliss of the Self" with the *brahmarandhra*, a tiny opening in the skullcap, through which the rising energy of *kuṇḍalinī* leaves the body after piercing all the *cakra*s.

(b) It is the "touch of joy of the Self" — i.e. the touch of the supreme Reality (*paramārtha*) which is described as "a dense mass of *cit* and *ānanda*" (*cidānanda-ghana*, cf. *Pratyabhijñāhṛdaya*, benedictory verse).[391] *Svacchandatantra* 4.275 says that one realizes oneself "[. . .] as the cause of the universe." This corresponds with the description of the state of *ghūrṇi* as described by Silburn, which is the sign of the piercing of the highest *cakra*, *brahmarandhra*, the full unfoldment of *kuṇḍalinī* at *brahmarandhra*: the shift from Self-consciousness to the

391. Cf. *PHṛ*, p. 45.

universal, primordial *saṁvit*. One recognizes one's own identity with the universe;[392] one realizes that *saṁvit*, the "Heart," is the source of everything, of every manifestation. It is the state of *ātmavyāpti* (Self-pervasion), the melting of everything into the Self, which is related with the fourth state (*turīya*), the stage before the final state of "divine pervasion" (*Śivavyāpti*) or *mahāvyāpti*, "the great pervasion," at the stage of *unmanā*,[393] where the Self dissolves into Śiva and the Divine is experienced as all-pervading.[394]

SPARŚA IN THE PROCESS OF MANIFESTATION: SVACCHANDATANTRA 11

Let us now look to the reversed process, the stages of the energy in descending order. Within the process of the manifestation of the "power of sound," the descent of the power from which the whole emanation of the universe arises, *sparśa* is placed between "void" and "sound" according to the presentation of *Svacchandatantra* 11. The 11th chapter starts with the Goddess asking the Lord how the world — the "ways" (*adhvan*) — had come into being (*Svacchandatantra* 11.1-2ab). Bhairava answers:

> (2cd-3ab) The highest God (*paro devaḥ*), very subtle, the cause (*kāraṇa*) of everything, everywhere present, is Śiva. He is the effective cause (*nimitta-kāraṇa*). I have talked about it, O Goddess.

> (3cd) He creates (*saṁsṛjet*) the whole world (*sarva jagat*), the solid (*sthāvara*) and the mobile (*jaṅgama*).

---

392. Cf. *K*, p. 74.

393. Cf. *K*, p. 59.

394. Cf. *K*, p. 167.

(4ab) out of the play (*līlā*) of the stirring (*kṣobha*) of the void (*vyoma*) by his own heat (*svatejasa*).

(5ab) From this void (*śūnya*) the void has arisen, from it another [void], from it touch (*sparśa*) has arisen (*samudbhava*). I have said it before.

(6) O Goddess, because of the different sounds it [*nāda*] becomes eightfold: *ghoṣa, rāvaḥ, svanaḥ, śabdaḥ, sphoṭa, dhvani, bhāṇkāra, dhvaṇkṛta* — these are the eight sounds (*śabda*).

(7) The ninth is called "the great sound" (*mahāśabda*), which pervades (*vyāpaka*) all.

(8ab) This sound (*nāda*) remains perpetually (*sadā*) in all beings (*bhūta*).

(9ab) From sound (*nāda*), the "point" (*bindu*) emerges with the same radiance (*samaprabha*) of millions of suns (*sūryakoṭi*).[395]

In his commentary on verse five, Kṣemarāja identifies the first void with *samanā-śakti*, from which the void in the form of *anāśrita* arises, in which the whole universe disappears. From this void *vyāpinī-śakti* arises, from which *sparśa* emerges. At this point he makes an important statement about *sparśa*: "Again, *sparśa* is of the nature of *śakti* in the form of a sleeping snake (*prasuptabhujagākāra*), the level of reality (*tattva*) known as *śakti*."[396] The metaphor of the sleeping snake clearly indicates *kuṇḍalinī* in her supreme motionless form, united with Śiva in the phase before the initial sonic vibration through which she takes the form of the three energies, from which the phonemes

395. *SvT*, vol. II, pp. 308ff.

396. Ibid., p. 310.

arise and through them, the whole universe — this according to the presentation in *Tantrasadbhāva*, as well as the *Siddhayogeśvarīmata*, *Jayadrathayāmala* and *Brahmayāmala*, the major texts which build the base of Trika. Jayaratha quotes this important passage in his commentary on *Tantrāloka* 3.67, where Abhinavagupta talks about *kuṇḍalinī*;[397] Kṣemarāja also fully quotes this passage in his commentary on *Śivasūtra* 2.3.[398]

In the process of emanation from "void" (*śūnya*) via "touch" (*sparśa*) as well as "sound" (*nāda*) and "light" (*bindu*), the stages of the highest spiritual experience are reflected in a reversed order — that process when *kuṇḍalinī* ascends through the head of the person through *bhrūmadhya*, the *cakra* between the eyebrows, which is connected with *bindu*, via *lalāṭa*, the point in the middle of the forehead, up to *brahmarandhra*, connected with *nādānta*, the "end of sound." At this point the ascending power leaves the head as the "superior *kuṇḍalinī*" (*ūrdhvakuṇḍalinī*)[399] — the level of *śakti*, where "touch" and the Self-pervasion (*ātmavyāpti*) is experienced. Then one enters the "great void" (*mahāśūnya*), and then into the "void beyond void" (*śūnyāti-śūnya*) of *unmanā-śakti*. In this way, the structure of the highest experience somehow becomes visible, which is described in the Tantras in an encoded form: from the experience of the highest light (= *bindu*) via the experience of a subtle sonic vibration (*nāda*) up to touch (*sparśa*) — the highest experience before one enters into that where the division of

---

397. Cf. *TĀV*, vol. II, p. 429. English translation: *Vāc*, pp. 128-30.

398. *ŚS* (ed. J. Singh), pp. 90ff.

399. "Kuṇḍalinī, lower as she is in *mūlādhāra* (*adhaḥkuṇḍalinī*), converts into intermediate energy at the navel, then into subtle energy in the heart, in the *anāhata* centre, and in the throat (*viśuddhicakra*), and finally into superior energy (*ūrdhvakuṇḍalinī*) when she reaches the *brahmarandhra*." (*K*, p. 131)

experiencer, experience, and experienced vanishes, wherein no "object" can be experienced, but which is rather the supreme "I," the universal subject, the primordial *mantra*: *AHAṀ*. In this process we can incorporate the statements of the *Brahmayāmalatantra* concerning the ten types of subtle (i.e. non-physical) sounds. Abhinavagupta quotes it in the context of *uccāra* (*TĀ* 5.93-95) in 5.97cd-98. Afterwards he says: the great *yogī*, who has crossed the stage of *nāda*, must ascend further to attain the supreme pervasion (cf. *TĀ* 5.99).

"Light," "Sound," "Touch" as Stages of Nearness

How can we understand these notions of "light," "sound" or "touch" in this context? They are graded aspects of the highest spiritual experience. After the moment of *sparśa*, one dives always deeper into the void. This is confirmed when Silburn attributes the experience of "light" (*jyoti*) to the stages of *ardhacandra* and *nirodhikā*, the appearance of the "sonic vibration" (*dhvani*) to the stages of *oṁ nāda* and *nādānta*, and the experience of "touch" (*sparśa*) to the even higher stages of the rising *kuṇḍalinī*, *śakti* and *vyāpinī*.[400]

One should remember the context of these experiences, i.e. the interiorized sexual act as described by Abhinavagupta in *Tantrāloka* 29. This is the reason why, as the title for her chart where she gives the correspondences between the stages of the rising energy and the experiences of light, resonance and touch, Silburn uses "The Rising of Kuṇḍalinī to *Unmanā* during Union."[401]

In another place, Silburn describes this experience like this:

> A la phase suivante de l'energie, *kuṇḍalinī* parvient grâce à l'illumination (*vijñāna*) jusqu'au *brahmarandhra* et on la

400. Cf. *K*, p. 205.

401. Ibid.

> nomme *ūrdhvakuṇḍalinī*. Cette phase révèle selon Kṣemarāja l'omnipénétration propre à la sensation (*sparśavyāpti*) qui se traduit par une jouissance dans l'apaisement.[402]

Silburn identifies the experience of "light" (*jyoti*) — in the words of *Svacchandatantra* 4.274, "the meditation on light (*jyoti*)" — with the state of enlightenment. Also from *Svacchandatantra* 4.274 we know that at this state one attains supernatural powers (*yogasiddhi*s). In this way, *sparśa* in this system denotes an even higher stage in the spiritual ascent, even above "enlightenment," the unfolding of the "supreme knowledge" (*vijñāna*). Here we also meet the expression *sparśavyāpti*, which seems to be synonymous with *ātmavyāpti*, here characterized as "all-pervasion, that of the sensation (*sparśavyāpti*)," in other words, the all-pervasion, characterized by "touch," which will be followed by an even greater pervasion, *Śivavyāpti*.

These stages of nearness to the Supreme can be found also in Bhaṭṭa Nārāyaṇa's[403] hymn *Stavacintāmaṇi* — stages of

---

402. Silburn, *Vijñāna-Bhairava*, op. cit., p. 50. — "In the following phase of the energy, due to enlightenment (*vijñāna*), *kuṇḍalinī* rises up to *brahmarandhra* and it is called *ūrdhvakuṇḍalinī*. According to Kṣemarāja, this phase reveals the all-pervasion, that of the sensation (*sparśavyāpti*), which results in a joy in the resting state." Dupuche's following statement (in the context of *TĀ* 29.160) is based on Silburn's *VBh* (50): "*Sparśa*, "touching" is an alternative name for the term *śakti*." (Dupuche, *Kula Ritual*, op. cit., p. 289, fn. 178). But I cannot find any proof for this statement in page 50.

403. Bhaṭṭa Nārāyaṇa is quoted by Abhinavagupta (10th/11th cent.), therefore has to be put before him (cf. *Stavacintāmaṇi of Bhaṭṭanārāyaṇa: Philosophical Hymnal Verses in Adoration of Lord Śiva*, ed. and transl. Ram Shankar Singh, Delhi: Parimal Publishers, 2002, p. vi, intro.). Singh views him, because of stylistic similarities with the Utpaladeva's *Śivastotrāvalī* (about first half of tenth century), as his contemporary (ibid.). According to Gonda, he →

the nearness to the "beloved," as he says: One embraces him, sees him, touches him, before one "attains him," becomes one with him. "Touch" is here a "fragment of a language of love" (Roland Barthes), which can be related to the human and divine beloved:

> In the embracing (*stutau*), in the remembering (*smṛtau*), in the meditating (*dhyāno*), in the seeing (*darśane*), in the touching (*sparśane*) and in the attaining (*prāptau*) I venerate (*namaḥ*) the beloved (*dayitāya*), who is the accumulation of all kinds of joy (*ānandavṛndāya*). — *Stavacintāmaṇi*, verse 36[404]

Kṣemarāja comments: "*dhyāne* — chime in (*ekatanata*), *darśana* — immediate vision (*sākṣātkāra*), *sparśana* — resting in it, *prāptau* — attaining of oneness (*ekātmatā*)."[405]

As we have already seen, the same graded order of spiritual experiences is described by Utpaladeva:

> Where the supreme Lord (*parameśvara*) Himself (*svayam*) is meditated upon (*dhyāyate*), followed by (*tadanu*) being seen (*dṛśyate*) and thereafter (*tataḥ*) being touched (*spṛśyate*) — there (*yatra*), where You are experienced (*bhavato 'nubhāvataḥ*), may occur to me (*sa me*) always the great festival of Your worship (*pūjanamahotsava*). — *Śivastotrāvalī* 13.6[406]

---

wrote his hymn in the second half of the ninth century (Jan Gonda, *Medieval Religious Literature in Sanskrit*, Wiesbaden: Harassowitz, 1977, p. 32). Accordingly, he could have been the disciple of Vasugupta (ibid.).

404. *The Stava-Chintāmaṇi of Bhaṭṭa Nārāyaṇa with Commentary by Kṣemarāja*, edited with notes by Mahāmahopādhyāya Paṇḍit Mukunda Rāma Śāstrī (KSTS; 10) Srinagar: The Research Department of Jammu & Kashmir, 1918, p. 44.

405. Ibid., p. 45.

406. *ŚSĀ*, p. 127.

These passages prove that Abhinavagupta, in his description of the gradual order of sound, light and touch, refers to a tradition that pre-existed him.

Other evidence of this traditional knowledge — the immediate connection of the "touch" of the Self (*ātmavyāpti*) and thereafter becoming one with the Divine (*śivavyāpti*) — is in a seminal text of the Kashmiri Trika from the ninth century, the *Spanda-Kārikā*:[407]

> The will (*icchā*) of the limited individual alone cannot vitiate the impulse of the will. But by the touch (*sparśa*) with the power (*bala*) of the Self (*ātmā*) man (*puruṣa*) becomes equal (*sama*) with that (*tat*). — *Spanda-Kārikā* 1.8

Kṣemarāja comments on the word *sparśa* in the verse: "nothing (*mātra*) [other] than the immersion (*āveśa*) into that."[408] It denotes the moment of the entering into "that" (*tat*) — an expression of a "negative theology," which refuses to denote that where language comes to a halt. Kṣemarāja interprets the verse in the following manner: The limited individual (*puruṣa*) is not able to observe (*parīkṣā*) reality (*tattva*) as it is because it does not belong to the realm of deterministic thought. Only when he has allowed himself to fulfil the longing for objects of enjoyment and is orientated towards it does he "touch" (*spṛśati*) "the reality of vibration" (*spanda tattva*). "Through it one becomes equal with it (*tadā tatsamo bhavet*)."[409] Through the complete immersion (*samāveśa*) into this reality, one attains freedom (*svatantratā*) everywhere, like that [like this reality itself]. At the end of the commentary, Kṣemarāja states: "The

407. *Spandakārikās of Vasugupta with the Nirṇaya by Kṣemarāja*, ed. Madhusudan Kaul (KSTS; 42), Srinagar 1925, p. 21.

408. Ibid., p. 22.

409. Ibid.

formulation 'by the touch of the power of the Self' has been used because touch (*sparśa*) dominates at the stage of *śakti* (*śaktibhūmeḥ*)."[410]

From his explanation we could come closer to understand: what is touched, or what touches, at this level of the spiritual ascent? He uses the expression *spanda tattva*, and equates it later with "freedom" (*svatantratā*). These are the main characteristics of *citi*, revered as the Goddess (Śakti, Parāvāk), as we have seen, e.g. in *Īśvarapratyabhijñākārikā* I. 5.13-14. The power of freedom (*svātantryaśakti*) is the highest power of Śiva, which includes all other energies (cf. *Tantrāloka* 1.67-168). Utpaladeva defines *svātantrya* with the "absence of duality" (*ĪPK* I. 5.16 *k*) and "perfect fullness" (ibid., *vṛtti*), which are attributes of *citi*.[411] In other words: It is Śakti which touches, and whose nature is "touch," as Jayaratha explains. Or, in another perspective: it is Bhairava who touches in the form of one of his eight supreme aspects, one of his powers, i.e. *śakti*s "of the nature of touch." This corresponds with a fundamental statement of the *Vijñāna-Bhairava* that the divine power is the access to Śiva: "Śakti is called the entrance (literally: *mukha*, "mouth") of Śiva." (*VBh* 20). At the same time, in the integral, non-dualistic vision of Trika, they cannot be separated: the power of touch in the organ of touch, the skin, the sexual touch, the sensation of touch — all these are forms of the Power, though not at the same level of the Power. The sensual and spiritual realms are not divided. It is significant that the supreme

---

410. Ibid.

411. Utpaladeva exclaims in his *ŚSĀ*: "In this threefold world (*jagattraye*), which is not free (*asvatantra*), including gods (*āsura*), *ṛṣi*s, and men — they are only free when they "live towards" (*anujīvinaḥ*) you, the only free one." (*ŚSĀ* 3.2). The "threefold world" or *triloka* means heaven, earth and the world in between.

embrace occurs within the most intimate embrace of two persons, according to *Tantrāloka* 29.

Jaideva Singh underlines in his note to this passage that Kṣemarāja would mention here an important point of Trika: "It believes that while Śakti, the Divine Creative Power, rejects all perceptual qualities like *rūpa, rasa, gandha,* etc., she retains *sparśa* or touch."[412] In this generality, his assertion about Śakti cannot be valid — rather, that touch is experienced as the last sensual quality in its supreme, most subtle form, holds true for the level of *śakti* (*śaktibhūmi*), as Kṣemarāja clarifies.

It seems that we can receive more information from the existential knowledge (Existenzwissen) of the Tantras and its commentators: it could be that the last experiences before one dies are those of light, of sound, and finally the experience of touch in its supreme form, before one becomes one with "that." In Indian thought, the life energy, the *praṇava*[413] — a name for *oṁ* — leaves at the moment of death via this same way: it rises up the "opening of *Brahman*" (*brahmarandhra*) into the empty space. The last experience could be that one falls into the embrace of the Divine. Each practice of *kuṇḍalinī yoga* is, from this perspective, an exercise in the art of dying (*ars moriendi*).

---

412. *Spanda-Kārikās: The Divine Creative Pulsation. The Kārikās and the Spanda-nirṇaya*, trans. Jaideva Singh, Delhi: Motilal Banarsidass, 1980, reprint 1994, p. 60.

413. Cf. *Vāc*, p. 403. — Padoux quotes here *NT* 22.14 ("The *praṇava* is the vital breath of animate beings present in all living creatures") and the commentary of Kṣemarāja: "The *praṇava* is that energy which gives life to creatures; it is the universal vivifying power; it is the generic *spanda*, the synthetic awareness, the "unstruck" sound; it is none other than the initial move (*abhyupagama*) [toward manifestation], the cause of all knowledge, action and objectivity."

4

Conclusion

The Question of the Liberating and Critical Potential of Trika Śaivism

[Contemplation] knows God by seeming to touch Him.
Or rather it knows Him as if it had been invisibly touched
by Him. (. . .)
Touched by Him Who has no hands,
but Who is pure Reality and the source of all that is real!
Hence contemplation is a sudden gift of awareness,
an awakening to the Real within all that is real.
— Thomas Merton

WE have examined the notion of *sparśa* in selected texts of non-dualistic Kashmir Śaivism, especially Utpaladeva's *Śivastotrāvalī* and some passages of Abhinavagupta's monumental *Tantrāloka*. The difference is striking: in the case of Utpaladeva, the experience of *sparśa* is reflected in the context of the philosophy and spirituality of the "recognition" (*pratyabhijñā*) that one's own Self (*ātman*) is identical with Śiva. We find no trace of the practice of the "secret ritual." In the case of Abhinavagupta, we find *sparśa* as one of the last stages of the *uccāra* of the power of *oṁ*, or, in other words, of the rise of *kuṇḍalinī* in the body. This rise occurs within the interiorized sexual union (*caryākrama*), the sexual ritual (*kulayāga*) as described in *Tantrāloka* 29. Here we clearly find the strong influence of the Kaula and Krama traditions within Abhinavagupta's Trika, especially on his texts of the last period of his work, the *Tantrāloka* and *Parātriśikāvivaraṇa*. This influence became especially strong after Abhinavagupta's initiation into Kaula Tantrism by his master Śambhunātha and his partner in the *kulayāga* (*dūtī*), Bhāgavatī (see *TĀ* 1.13). These differences demonstrate the evolution of Trika Śaivism between Utpaladeva in the second half of tenth century and Abhinavagupta's (*c.* 975–1025) last works, in the second generation after Utpaladeva.

Focusing on our topic, "the touch of Śakti," we have found different contexts and meanings in which the word *sparśa* occurs in connection with Śakti, the divine power, revered as the Goddess. An interesting conclusion is how significant is the experience of touch in the context of *kuṇḍalinī yoga*, associated with the experience of "the touch of ants" (*pipīlikasparśa*), which we have explored by the example of *Tantrāloka* 11.29-32. The most important result of our study is that we found that *sparśa* denotes one of the highest stages of the spiritual process, of the rise of *kuṇḍalinī*, even above the experience of enlightenment (*vijñāna*). We have suggested that it is connected with the moment of Self-pervasion (*ātmavyāpti*) before one enters into the highest forms of void (*śūnya*) and finally attains the "pervasion pertaining to Śiva" (*śivavyāpti*), or in other words, the oneness with Śiva, as one's true state. This description of *sparśa* as one of the highest stages in the spiritual ascent — above "light" and "resonance" — in the *Tantrāloka* corresponds with the description of these stages found already in Utpaladeva's *Śivastotrāvalī* (especially 13.6), here without the context of the *kulayāga*. From this we can conclude that this experience is obviously not confined to the sexual ritual, though we can find here a core of Tāntric thought:

the senses are used as the pre-eminent means for the realization of one's own true nature, especially in their most intensive, integral form, in the sexual union, if experienced at the level of non-dual consciousness (*nirvikalpa* or *paśyantī*).[1] The breakthrough to the highest state, the "Bhairava-state" — or to *citi, anuttara, pratibhā* — can occur during orgasm or while sneezing, in the experience of extreme fear or in meditation etc., as the *dhāraṇā*s of the *Vijñāna-Bhairava* demonstrate.

In the experience of the Trika authors, the essential nature of Reality is the divine power itself, Śakti. Their vision, but also their concrete experience, is that the radiating, pulsating, vibrating, brilliant, dynamic, absolute free power, which is essentially pure light and supreme joy, is the core, the "Heart" (*hṛdaya*) of Reality, of everything. In its different forms and stages it is the essential nature of the world — of a blade of grass, a dust particle, humans, rocks, water, trees, animals, a spiral nebula, an atom, a thought, a phoneme, a sensation — and at the same time it *transcends* the world.[2] In this way the Advaita doctrine of Trika Śaivism offers an alternative to the illusionism of Advaita Vedānta, which devaluates and negates the phenomenal world, and also to the idealism of Yogācāra Buddhism.[3] Trika says one can touch everything, because everything consists in the final sense of the supreme light and

1. See Prabha Devi, "The Significance of Tantra Rahasya," in: Das/ Fürlinger (eds.), *Sāmarasya*, op. cit., pp. 63-66.

2. See the beginning of Kṣemarāja's *PP*: "We adore *saṁvit*, which flashes forth/flares (*sphurantīm*) in the form of the original Highest Śakti (*parāśākti*), the heart of the Highest Lord, she who consists of the world and transcends it." (*Parāprāveśikā of Kṣemarāja*, ed. with Notes by Paṇḍit Mukunda Rāma Śāstrī [KSTS; 15] Bombay 1918, p. 1).

3. Cf. Alexis Sanderson, "Abhinavagupta," in: *EncRel* (Eliade, first edition 1987), Vol. 1, pp. 8-9.

joy. And every moment it can happen that one is touched by the rays of the Power, and one's true nature of supreme light and joy (*ānanda*) unfolds, maybe only for a few moments.

At the end, we have to ask: is it not escapism to study an Indian spiritual tradition which had its peak in the tenth and eleventh century, almost 1000 years ago, subtle aspects of spiritual processes in the midst of the present miserable conditions of a disrupted world?

It could be escapism — if one would fail to interpret non-dualistic Trika Śaivism of Kashmir in the context of the social, political, economic and ecological crises of our time. It would be a kind of shirking, if we would not "contextualize" and understand Kashmir Śaivism in the presence of the signs of our time. I would like to suggest a triad of reflections:

1. Non-dualistic Śaivism of Kashmir is sometimes described as a "monism." In fact, non-dualistic Trika Śaivism does not present a monism, but rather a complex ontology: the "triad" (*trika*) of Śiva (the one Absolute), Śakti (the dynamism of the Absolute) and phenomenal, plural world (*nara*), their pervasion (Gr. *perichoresis*). Abhinavagupta denotes it as "supreme non-dualism" (*paramādvayavāda*) — the "Real" or the "Highest" unites in itself both plurality and unity in a paradoxical way, through its Power (*kuṇḍalinī*) which ejects/emits the plurality and manifoldness of the world, unseparated from Her nature, within the One Absolute Light. The abyss of the "Real" is precisely characterized by this coincidence of opposites (Lat. *coincidentia oppositorum*). There is not simply a hierocratic, monarchial *monos* which annihilates the plurality of the universe, but rather the *oikonomia* of the dynamic life within the one Real, without losing

its fullness, perfection, unity. If one considers the enormous, hidden influence of theological paradigms on the development of political paradigms,[4] then the consequences are important: any political theology which founds the transcendence of the sovereign power in the one God, any theory of sovereignty, is deprived of its metaphysical basis by this triadic ontology: the highest value — called "God," "Śiva," "Absolute," "Unsurpassable" (*anuttara*) — is not a *monos*, a single one, but transcends the idea of the "one," and is rather the coincidence of oneness and

---

4. In 1922, the German legal theoretician Carl Schmitt has presented the thesis that all crucial terms of modern state doctrine are secularized theological terms. He argues for the correspondence in each epoch of the form of social authority and the theological world-view, for example monarchy as correlative with monotheism (Carl Schmitt, *Political Theology: Four Chapters on the Concept of Sovereignty*, trans. George Schwab [Studies in Contemporary German Social Thought] Cambridge, MA: MIT Press, 1986). — Schmitt's major respondent was the theologian Erik Peterson. In his brillant treatise (Erik Peterson, *Der Monotheismus als politisches Problem. Ein Beitrag zur Geschichte der politischen Theologie im Imperium Romanum*, Leipzig: Hegner, 1935), Peterson reconstructs the development of "Political Theology," centred on the term of divine monarchy: the divine monarchy as the paradigm of political monarchy on earth (one God, one Roman Empire). He demonstrates that the trinitarian dogma destroys the doctrine of the divine monarchy, a monarchical understanding of theism and liberates Christian faith from its enchainment with the Roman empire; he states the principal impossibility of any political theology (in the sense of the ideology of political religion) in the perspective of Christian trinitarian theology. Thirty-five years later Schmitt responded in detail to Peterson's rejection of political theology (Carl Schmitt, *Politische Theologie II: Die Legende von der Erledigung der Politischen Theologie*, Berlin: Duncker & Humblot, 1970).

manifoldness, of the absolute fullness of the light and absolute dynamism and creativity. In the perspective of Trika (but also from the perspective of Christian Trinitarian theology), any dangerous cult of the absolute monism of power loses its metaphysical base — be it mono-culturalism (one single dominating culture: the modern West and its values), one homogeneous organic national "body," mono-economism (one single economic model: politically unleashed capitalism), mono-lingualism (one single language for the global society: English) and mono-domination (the Empire: USA and the international institutions controlled by it), one paradigm for the social, political and economic structures ("progress" or "development" according to the one model of Western modernity).[5] On the contrary, the vision of Trika means the celebration of life and society in its plurality, diversity and manifoldness. The plurality (Śakti) is in every aspect unseparated from the unity of the Highest (Śiva) which is essentially pure light, beauty and joy. It is a thinking which resists to the fascination of the one. It does not provide any theological and metaphysical basis for totalitarian structures, for totalitarianism, for the process of annexation of the many into the one — into the one body, the one block, the one integral community.

2. According to Trika, the Highest is "the sole free one" (*Śivastotrāvalī* 3.2). Or, from the perspective of its

---

5. In this critique I am inspired by Raimon Panikkar, *Cultural Disarmament: The Way to Peace*, trans. Robert R. Barr, Louisville, Kentucky: Westminster John Knox Press, 1995; "Raimon Panikkar on Colonialism and Interculturality": *Harvard University Center for the Study of World Religions News*, vol. 2, no. 1 (fall 1994), pp. 1-5.

dynamism: the supreme among all powers of the Highest (*anuttara*) is its power of absolute freedom (*svātantrya*): ". . . he has one attribute which includes within itself all the others, that is, the power of freedom (*svātantryaśakti*)." (*TĀ* 1.67). Śakti, the core of reality, "is freedom in the absolute sense, the sovereignty (*aiśvaryam*) of the supreme Self" (*ĪPK* I. 5.13). From a theological perspective, this would explain why contemporary quantum physics does not find "eternal laws of nature," but rather the phenomenon of absolute accident.

Correspondingly, one of the most important self-designations of Trika Śaivism is *svātantryavāda*, "the way of freedom," or, as Kṣemarāja names it, "the way of the non-duality of the absolute free Śiva" (*svātantraśivādvayavāda*).[6] It understands itself not as a "religion,"[7] but as a way which finally leads to the "wayless way" or the "non-way" (*anupāya*), which is not even "liberation" (*mokṣa*), because there is no more duality between the one liberated, the one liberating, or that from which one has to be liberated (cf. *TĀ* 3.272-273), but only the sheer Freedom, the pure sovereignty of the Highest. The highest goal of this way is the complete breaking through of all contractions and the blossoming up or the unfolding (*unmeṣa*) of one's identity with the "Power of Freedom" (*svātantryaśakti*).

---

6. Kṣemarāja, *Spandasaṁdoha* (KSTS; 16) Srinagar 1917, p. 10; quoted by Sanderson: *Doctrine of Mālinīvijayottaratantra*, op. cit.

7. "Kashmir Śaivism is not a religion. It is a philosophy open to those who have the desire to understand it . . .." (Swami Lakshman Joo, "Kashmir Śaivism," *The Malini* [April 1995] pp. 11-13; here: p. 11).

What would be the condition of a society which lives after a God, a highest value, which is not an almighty, all-seeing, all-controlling monarch or single superpower, but rather pure freedom? In the midst of our more and more controlled societies, where the "steely walls" (Max Weber) seem to close more and more, which sacrifice freedom and civil rights for the illusion of perfect security, flanked by a brain science which denies the free will of humans, it is important to keep awake the rumour of the Highest, the absolute freedom, the playful wisdom: "She is joy in everything which is joyful. She is beauty in everything which is beautiful. She is the desiring in everything desirable." (Nicholas de Cusa, *Idiota de sapientia*)

3. At the core of this Tāntric Advaita tradition is the conviction or the experience of the interconnectedness of reality as a whole (not simply the "unity" of reality as a whole). The Divine (Śiva), its dynamism (Śakti) pervade the world (*nara*), and at the same time transcend it. Śakti, the power of the "Highest" (*anuttara*), is the vibrating and shining dynamic "heart" of reality, of everything. Every thought, sense experience, acting, movement, the life and life-force of every human being is essentially a form of the one brilliantly pulsating Power of the Absolute Reality itself, called Śakti, the "Heart," *citi*, the "primordial Word."[8]

Within the framework of this Tāntric experience of the world and its philosophical unfolding, any discrimination according

---

8. Similarly, Nicholas de Cusa says about the touching of God: "We touch the ground of all things as the indivisible ground of everything." (*De beryllo* n. 3, 5)

to race, gender, caste, culture, colour, religion, poverty, wealth, sexual orientation or age loses its base. The same Un-nameable is present with its unimaginable light, might and pulsation in the leaders and the lost, in the rich and the lowliest, in men and women, in children, in Dalits, tribals, in the most successful and in outsiders, in plants, animals, rocks, a drop of water, a star . . ..

Advaita, "non-duality" means that God is not something absolutely separated and distant from me. The whole phenomenal reality — from a dust particle up to a spiral nebula — exists within God. Is it not also the Christian vision that there is a creative, dynamic, energising Presence in the world which pervades and enlivens and maintains everything, and which Christians understand as God's dynamism, the "Holy Spirit"?[9] If the Divine, its power, is the true, "real reality" of everything — then we can touch nothing without coming in touch with the Divine. Then there is nothing "untouchable."

Precisely in this way Gandhi understands one of his eleven Ashram-vows, "the removal of untouchability" (*aspṛśyatā-nivāraṇa*), besides of "truth" (*satya*), "non-violence" (*ahiṁsā*), "chastity" (*brahmacarya*), etc.:

> None can be born untouchable, as all are sparks of one and the same fire . . .. This observance is not fulfilled, merely by making friends with "untouchables" but by loving all life as one's own self. Removal of untouchability means love

9. See Michael Morwood, "A New Pentecost," in: *Rainbows on a Crying Planet. Essays in Honour of Tissa Balasuriya*, ed. Lieve Troch, Tiruvalla: Christava Sahitya Samithi, 2004, pp. 205-13.

> for, and service of the whole world, and it thus merges into *ahiṁsā*.[10]

Tāntric Advaita Śaivism represents (in principle) a spirituality, a being-in-the-world, which realizes God in the dust and in joy, in a drop of water and in the rhythm of the ocean, in fear and pain, in aesthetic experience and sexuality — and in the "invisible men" (Ralph Ellison): the kids, who work and sleep on the streets of the Indian megapolises, the garbage collectors, the handicapped, the landless, the poorest in rural India, and the children of the poorest, the victims of a politically unleashed economic dynamism . . .

As Tagore has put it:

> When I try to bow to thee, my obeisance cannot reach down to the depths where the feet rest among the poorest, the lowliest and the lost.
>
> Pride can never approach to where thou walkest in the clothes of the humble among the poorest, and lowliest, and lost.
>
> My heart can never find its way to where thou keepest company with the companionless among the poorest, the

---

10. The eleven Ashram vows are for the first time contained in weekly letters (July till October 1930) written by Mahatma Gandhi from his imprisonment at Yeravda Central Prison to the Satyagraha Ashram (founded in 1915 in Kochrab, then shifted to Ahmedabad), later published under the title "From Yeravda Mandir: Ashram Observances." Gandhi was under arrest after his historical salt march, which he started on 12 March 1930. He was arrested on 4 May 1930 and released on 26 January 1931. — I am grateful to Professor Ramachandra Gandhi (New Delhi), the grandson of Mahatma Gandhi, to make me aware about this connection between Advaita and Gandhiji's fight against untouchability (personal communication, fall 2005).

> lowliest and lost. (No. X)[11]
>
> Leave this chanting and singing and telling of beads!
>
> Whom dost thou worship in this lonely dark corner of a temple with doors all shut?
>
> Open thine eyes and see thy God is not before thee!
>
> He is there where the tiller is tilling the hard ground and where the path-maker is breaking stones. He is with them in sun and in shower, and his garment is covered with dust. Put off thy holy mantle and even like him come down on the dusty soil! Deliverance? Where is this deliverance to be found? Our master himself has joyfully taken upon him the bonds of creation; he is bound with us all for ever.
>
> Come out of thy meditations and leave aside thy flowers and incense! What harm is there if thy clothes become tattered and stained? Meet him and stand with him in toil and in sweat of thy brow. (No. XI)[12]

Tagore precisely formulates the criticism of every form of a world-neglecting, individualized and merely interiorized religiosity which "does not leave the temple" or the meditation room — be it within Śaivism, Christianity, Islam, or any religion. During our analysis of Utpaladeva's *Śivastotrāvalī* we have met many times the motive of "the touching of the feet of the Lord." We shall keep in mind Tagore's important interpretation: the feet of the Highest (*anuttara*) rest among the poorest, the lowliest and the lost . . .. We could say that we pay obeisance to the Highest when we touch the most

11. Rabindranath Tagore, *Gitanjali: Song Offerings* (1913), Delhi: Full Circle, 2002, reprint 2005, p. 26.

12. Ibid., p. 27.

marginalized, forgotten and invisible, and participate in their lives and struggles. And more than that: we will find the Highest and its "feet" there.

These are some aspects in which way one could raise the liberating and critical potential of this spiritual tradition of non-dualistic Śaivism of Kashmir in our contemporary context. As far as I can see it has not yet unfolded, indeed not even by my study. These few musings can only be the framework for future reflections.

Bibliography

A. Non-dualistic Kashmir Śaivism/Indian Philosophy

I. PRIMARY TEXTS AND TRANSLATIONS

Utpaladeva: *Ajaḍapramātṛsiddhiḥ*, in: *The Siddhitrayī and the Pratyabhijñā-Kārikā-Vṛtti of Rājānaka Utpaladeva*, ed. with notes by Pt. Madhusudan Kaul Shastri (KSTS; 34), Srinagar, 1921.

The Dhvanyāloka of Ānandavardhana with the Locana of Abhinavagupta, trans. Daniel H.H. Ingalls, Jeffrey Moussaieff Masson and M.V. Patwardhan, ed. with an introduction by Daniel H.H. Ingalls, Cambridge, Mass./London: Harvard University Press, 1990.

The Īśvarapratyabhijñākārikā of Utpaladeva with the Author's Vṛtti. Critical edition and annotated translation by Raffaele Torella, corrected edition Delhi: Motilal Banarsidass, 2002.

Bhāskarī. A Commentary on the Īśvarapratyabhijñāvimarśinī of Ācārya Abhinavagupta, ed. K.A. Subramania Iyer/K.C. Pandey, vol. I: Varanasi (1938), 2nd edn. 1998; vol. II (1950): Delhi: Motilal Banarsidass, 2nd edn. 1986; vol. III: An English Translation by K.C. Pandey, Varanasi (1954), 2nd edn. 1998.

Bhaṭṭa Rāmakaṇṭha's Commentary on the Kiraṇatantra. Vol. 1: chapters 1-6. Critical edition and annotated translation by Dominic Goodall (Publications du Département d'Indologie; 86.1) Pondichéry: Institut Français de Pondichéry/École Française d'Extrême-Orient, 1998.

The Mahānaya-Prakāśa of Rājānaka Śītikaṇṭha, ed. Mukunda Rāma Śāstrī (KSTS; 21) Bombay: Research Department Jammu & Kashmir State, 1918.

Arṇasiṁha: *Mahāyānaprakāśa*, National Archives Nepal, Mss. 5-5183/151 (A 150/6); edited and translated by Mark S.G. Dyczkowski (unpublished).

Mālinīvijayottaratantram, ed. Madhusudan Kaul (KSTS; 37) Bombay 1922.

Hanneder, Jürgen, *Abhinavagupta's Philosophy of Revelation. An edition and annotated translation of Mālinīślokavārttika I*, 1-399 (Groningen Oriental Studies; 14), Groningen: Egbert Forsten, 1998.

Netratantra with the commentary Uddyota by Kṣemarāja, 2 vols. (KSTS; 46 and 61), Bombay 1926-39.

Nityāṣoḍaśikārṇava with two commentaries, ed. V.V. Dvivedi (Yoga-Tantra-Granthamālā; 1) Varanasi 1968.

The Kulacūḍāmaṇi Tantra and the Vāmakeśvara Tantra with the Jayaratha Commentary. Introduced, translated and annotated by Louise M. Finn, Wiesbaden: Harrassowitz, 1986.

The Paramārthasāra of Ādiśeṣa, ed. S. S. Suryanarayana, Bombay: Karnatak Publishing House, 1941.

The Paramārthasāra by Abhinavagupta with the Commentary of Yogarāja, ed. Jagadisha Chandra Chatterji (KSTS; 7), Srinagar: Research Department of the Kashmir State, 1916.

Essence of the Reality or Paramārthasāra of Abhinavagupta. With English translation and notes by B.N. Pandit, Delhi: Munshiram Manoharlal, 1991.

Silburn, Lilian, *Le Paramārthasāra de Abhinavagupta* (Publications de L'Institut de Civilisation Indienne, Fasc. 5) Paris, 1979.

Parāprāveśikā of Kṣemarāja, ed. with Notes by Paṇḍit Mukunda Rāma Śāstrī (KSTS; 15), Bombay 1918.

Abhinavagupta, *Parātrīśikā-Vivaraṇa: The Secret of Tāntric Mysticism*. English translation with notes and running exposition by Jaideva Singh. Ed. Bettina Bäumer, Delhi: Motilal Banarsidass, 1988. Reprint 2000.

Patañjali, *Die Wurzeln des Yoga. Die Yoga-Sūtren des Patañjali mit einem Kommentar von P. Y. Deshpande*. Mit einer neuen Übertragung der Sūtren aus dem Sanskrit herausgegeben von Bettina Bäumer, München/Wien: Barth, 1976, 5. Aufl. 1985.

Yoga Philosophy of Patañjali with Bhāsvatī by Swāmi Hariharānanda Āraṇya, trans. P.N. Mukerji (1963), University of Calcutta, 2000.

Pratyabhijñāhṛdayam: The Secret of Self-recognition, trans. Jaideva Singh (1963), Delhi: Motilal Banarsidass, 4th rev. edn. 1982. Reprint 1998.

Śivadṛṣṭi of Somānanda, with Utpaladeva's Vṛtti (KSTS; 54) Srinagar 1934.

Gnoli, Raniero, "Śivadṛṣṭi by Somānanda," *East and West* 8, no. 1 (1957), pp. 16-22.

The Śivastotrāvalī of Utpaladevācārya, with the Sanskrit commentary of Kṣemarāja, ed. with Hindi commentary by Rājānaka Lakṣmaṇa (Chowkhamba Sanskrit Series; 15) Varanasi: Chowkhamba Sanskrit Series Office, 1964.

Shaiva Devotional Songs of Kashmir: A Translation and Study of Utpaladeva's Shivastotravali by Constantina Rhodes Bailly, Albanay: State University of New York Press, 1987; Delhi: Sri Satguru Publications, 1990.

The Śivasūtravimarśinī of Kṣemarāja: Being a Commentary on The Śivasūtra of Vasugupta, ed. Jagadisha Chandra Chatterji (KSTS; 1), Srinagar 1911. Reprint, New Delhi: Bibliotheca Orientalia, 1990.

Śiva Sūtras: The Yoga of Supreme Identity — Text of the Sūtras and the Commentary Vimarśinī of Kṣemarāja, trans. Jaideva Singh, Delhi: Motilal Banarsidass, 1979. Reprint 2000.

The Aphorisms of Śiva: The Śiva Sūtra with Bhāskara's Commentary, the Vārttika, trans. with Expositions and Notes by Mark S.G. Dyczkowski, Albany: State University of New York Press, 1992; Varanasi: Indica, 1998.

Spanda-Kārikās of Vasugupta with the Nirṇaya by Kṣemarāja, ed. Madhusudan Kaul (KSTS; 42), Srinagar, 1925.

Spanda-Kārikās: The Divine Creative Pulsation — The Kārikās and the Spanda-nirṇaya, trans. Jaideva Singh, Delhi: Motilal Banarsidass, 1980, reprint 1994.

Stanzas on Vibration: The Spandakārikā with four Commentaries, trans. with an Introduction and Exposition by Mark S.G. Dyczkowski, Varanasi: Dilip Kumar Publishers, 1994.

The Stava-Cintāmaṇi of Bhaṭṭa Nārāyaṇa with Commentary by Kṣemarāja, ed. with notes by Mahāmahopādhyāya Paṇḍit Mukunda Rāma Śāstrī (KSTS; 10) Srinagar: The Research Department of Jammu & Kashmir, 1918.

The Svacchandatantram with Commentary "Udyota" of Kṣemarāja, ed. Vraj Vallabh Dwivedi, 2 vols., Delhi: Parimal Publications, 1985.

The Tantrāloka of Abhinavagupta with the Commentary of Jayaratha (KSTS), Srinagar, 1918-1938. Reprint, ed. R.C. Dwivedi/Navjivan Rastogi, 8 vols., Delhi: Motilal Banarsidass, 1987.

Abhinavagupta, *La Lumière sur les Tantras. Chapitres 1 à 5 du Tantrāloka.* Traduits et commentés par Lilian Silburn et André Padoux (Collège de France. Publications de l'Institute de Civilisation Indienne, Série in-8, fasc. 66) Paris: Édition-Diffusion de Boccard, 1998.

Gnoli, Ranier, *Luce delle Sacre Scritture di Abhinavagupta* (Classici delle Religioni: Le religioni orientali), Torino: Unione Tipografico-Editrice Torinese, 1972.

Tantrasāra of Abhinavagupta (KSTS; 17), Bombay 1918.

Sferra, Francesco, "The Tantroccaya by Abhinavagupta. An English Translation": *AION* 59 (1999), pp. 109-33.

Olivelle, Patrick, *The Early Upaniṣads: Annotated Text and Translation*, Oxford: Oxford University Press, 1998.

Bäumer, Bettina, *Befreiung zum Sein. Auswahl aus den Upanishaden* (Klassiker der östlichen Meditation. Spiritualität Indiens) Zürich/Einsiedeln/Köln, 1986.

Vātūlanāthasūtra with Anantaśaktipādas Vṛtti (KSTS; 29), Bombay, 1923.

The Vijñāna-Bhairava with Commentary partly by Kṣemarāja and partly by Śivopādhyāya, ed. with notes by Pt. Mukunda Rāma Śāstrī (KSTS; 8) Bombay, 1918.

Bäumer, Bettina, *Vijñāna Bhairava. Das göttliche Bewusstsein. 112 Weisen der mystischen Erfahrung im Śivaismus von Kaschmir*, Grafing: Edition Adyar, 2003

Vijñāna-Bhairava: The Practice of Centring Awareness. Commentary by Swami Lakshman Joo, Varanasi: Indica, 2002.

II. LEXICA UND ENCYCLOPEDIAS

Amarakośa of Amarasimha. With the Commentary of Ācārya Kṛṣṇamitra, ed. Satyadeva Mishra, Kuala Lumpur: University of Malaya, 1972.

Encyclopedia of Indian Philosophies. Vol. IV: Sāṁkhya: A Dualist Tradition in Indian Philosophy, ed. Gerald James Larson/Ram Shankar Bhattacharya, Delhi: Motilal Banarsidass, 1987.

Halāyudhakośaḥ, Lucknow, 1957, 2. Aufl. 1967.

Monier-Williams, Monier, *Sanskrit-English Dictionary: Etymologically and Philologically arranged with Special Reference to Cognate Indo-*

European Languages (1872). New enlarged edn., 1899. Reprint: Delhi: Munshiram Manoharlal Publishers, 2002.

Tāntrikābhidhānakośa. Dictionnaire des termes techniques de la littérature hindoue tantrique/A Dictionary of Technical Terms from Hindu Tantric Literature, ed. Hélène Brunner, Gerhard Oberhammer, André Padoux. Vol. I (Beiträge zur Kultur- und Geistesgeschichte Asiens; 35), Vol. II (Beiträge zur Kultur- und Geistesgeschichte Asiens; 44), Wien: Verlag der österreichischen Akademie der Wissenschaften, 2003ff.

III. STUDIES

Alper, Harvey P., "Śiva and the Ubiquity of Consciousness. The Spaciousness of an Artful Yogi": *Journal of Indian Philosophy* 7 (1979), pp. 345-407.

Bäumer, Bettina, *Abhinavagupta. Wege ins Licht. Texte des tantrischen Śivaismus aus Kaschmir* (Klassiker der östlichen Meditation. Spiritualität Indiens) , Zürich: Benziger, 1992.

———, "Vāyu," in: *Kalātattvakośa. Vol. III: Primal Elements — Mahābhūta*, ed. Bettina Baumer, Delhi: Indira Gandhi National Centre for the Arts/Motilal Banarsidass, 1996, pp. 143-187.

———, "Brahman," in: *Kalātattvakośa. Vol. I: Pervasive Terms — Vyāpti*, ed. Bettina Bäumer, Delhi: Indira Gandhi National Centre for the Arts/Motilal Banarsidass, 1988 revised edition 2001, pp. 1-28.

———, "The Four Spiritual Ways *(upāya)* in the Kashmir Shaiva Tradition," in: *Hindu Spirituality: Postclassical and modern*, ed. K. R. Sundararajan/ Bithika Mukerji (World Spirituality; 7) New York: Crossroad, 1997, pp. 1-22.

——— *Trika: Grundthemen des kaschmirischen Śivaismus.* Herausgegeben von Ernst Fürlinger (Salzburger Theologische Studien 21; interkulturell 1) Wien/ Innsbruck: Tyrolia, 2003, zweite Aufl. 2004.

Brooks, Douglas R., "The Canons of Siddha Yoga. The Body of Scripture and the Form of the Guru," in: *Meditation Revolution: A History and Theology of the Siddha Yoga Lineage*, Delhi: Muktabodha Indological Research Institute/Motilal Banarsidass, 2000, pp. 277-346.

Arindam Chakrabarti, "Logic, Morals and Meditation: Tarka, Dharma, Yoga": *Evam* (New Delhi) 3: nos. 1 & 2 (2004), pp. 190-200.

———, "The Heart of Repose, The Repose of the Heart. A Phenomenological Analysis of the Concept of Viśrānti," in: Sadananda Das/Ernst Fürlinger (eds.), *Sāmarasya: Studies in Indian Arts, Philosophy and Interreligious Dialogue in Honour of Bettina Bäumer*, New Delhi: D.K. Printworld, 2005, pp. 27-36

Chakravarty, Hemendra Nath, "Prāṇa," in: *Kalātattvakośa. Vol. I: Pervasive Terms — Vyāpti*, ed. Bettina Bäumer, Delhi: Indira Gandhi National Centre for the Arts/Motilal Banarsidass, 1988, rev. edn. 2001, pp. 123-153.

Chatterji, J. C., *Kashmir Shaivism* (1914) Srinagar: Research and Publication Department 2. Aufl. 1962. Reprint, Delhi: Parimal Publications, 1987.

Davidson, Ronald M., *Indian Esoteric Buddhism: A Social History of the Tantric Movement*, New York: Columbia University Press, 2002.

Devi, Prabha, "The Significance of Tantra Rahasya," in: Sadananda Das/Ernst Fürlinger (eds.), *Sāmarasya: Studies in Indian Arts, Philosophy and Interreligious Dialogue in Honour of Bettina Bäumer*, New Delhi: D.K. Printworld, 2005, pp. 63-66.

Dupuche, John R., *Abhinavagupta. The Kula Ritual As Elaborated in Chapter 29 of the Tantrāloka*, Delhi: Motilal Banarsidass, 2003.

Dyczkowski, Mark S.G., *The Doctrine of Vibration. An Analysis of the Doctrines and Practices of Kashmir Shaivism*, Albany: State University of New York Press, 1987; Delhi: Motilal Banarsidass, 1989.

———, "Abhāvavāda — A forgotten Śaiva Doctrine," in: *Navonmeṣa: M. M. Gopinath Kaviraj Smriti Granth. Vol. IV: English*, ed. Jaideva Singh, Hemendra Nath Chakravarty, and G. Mukhopadhyaya, Varanasi 1987, pp. 107-119.

———, *The Canon of the Śaivāgama and the Kubjikā Tantras of the Western Kaula Tradition* (SUNY Series in the Shaiva Traditions of Kashmir) Albany: State University of New York Press, 1988; Delhi: Motilal Banarsidass, 1989.

Flood, Gavin D., *Body and Cosmology in Kashmir Śaivism*, San Francisco: Mellen Research University Press, 1993.

———, "Shared Realities and Symbolic forms in Kashmir Śaivism": *Numen* 36, no. 2 (1989), pp. 225-247.

Gonda, Jan, *Medieval Religious Literature in Sanskrit* (A History of Indian Literature; Vol. II, Fasc. 1), Wiesbaden: Harrassowitz, 1977.

Goudriaan, Teun (ed.), *Ritual and Speculation in Early Tantrism: Studies in Honor of André Padoux*, Albany: State University of New York Press, 1992; Delhi: Sri Satguru Publications, 1993.

Goudriaan, Teun/Gupta, Sanjukta (ed.), *Hindu Tantrism* (Handbuch der Orientalistik; II 7) Leiden.: Brill, 1979.

———, *Hindu Tāntric and Śākta Literature* (A History of Indian Literature; II, Fasc. 2) Wiesbaden: Harrasowitz, 1981.

Jürgen Hanneder, "Sāhib Kaul's Presentation of Pratyabhijñā Philosophy in his *Devīnāmavilāsa*," in: *Le Parole E I Marmi. Studi in onore di Raniero Gnoli nel suo 70° compleanno.* A cura di Raffaele Torella (Serie Orientale Roma; XCII, 2), Roma 2001, pp. 399-418.

Hariharānanda Āraṇya, Swāmi, *Yoga Philosophy of Patañjali with Bhāsvatī* (1963), Calcutta: University of Calcutta, 3. rev. Aufl. 1981, 3. erw. Aufl. 2000.

Kaul, Jankinath, "Kamal" (ed.), *The Awakening of Supreme Consciousness: Lectures of Swami Lakshman Joo*, Srinagar/Jammu/Delhi: Ishwara Ashrama Trust/Utpal Publications, 1998.

Kaviraj, Gopinath, "The Doctrine of Pratibhā in Indian Philosophy" (1923/24), in: id.: *Aspects of Indian Thought*, University of Burdwan, 2. Aufl. 1984, pp. 1-42.

———, *Notes on Religion and Philosophy by Gopinath Kaviraj*, ed. Gaurinath Sastri, Varanasi: Sarasvati Bhavana Library, 1987.

———, *Selected Writings of M. M. Gopinath Kaviraj*, ed. M. M. Gopinath Kaviraj Centenary Celebrations Committee, Varanasi 1990.

King, Richard, "Asparśa-Yoga: Meditation and Epistemology in the Gauḍapādīya-Kārikā": *Journal of Indian Philosophy* 20 (1992) pp. 89-131.

———, *Early Advaita Vedānta and Buddhism*, Albany: State University of New York Press, 1995.

———, *Indian Philosophy: An Introduction to Hindu and Buddhist Thought*, Edinburgh: Edinburgh University Press, 1999.

Lakshmana, Rājānaka [= Swami Lakshman Joo], *Śrīkramanayapradīpikā*, ed. Prabha Devi, Srinagar: Guptaganga, Isvara Ashram, 1959.

Lakshman Joo, Swami, *Kashmir Śaivism: The Secret Supreme*. Audio Study Set, Culver City, CA: Universal Shaiva Fellowship, 2002.

———, "Kashmir Śaivism": *The Mālinī* (April 1995), pp. 11-13.

———, "Kuṇḍalinī Vijñāna Rahasyam". Part I: *The Mālinī* (April 1996), 5-10. Part II: July 1996, 6-11. Part III: September 1996; Part IV: January 1997, 6-11. Part V: April 1997, pp. 7-13.

———, *Shiva Sutras: The Supreme Awakening — With the Commentary of Kshemaraja, revealed by Swami Lakshmanjoo*, Audio Study Set, Universal Shaiva Fellowship, USA, 2002.

Larson, Gerald James, *Classical Sāmkhya: An Interpretation of its History and Meaning*, Delhi: Motilal Banarsidass, 1969, 2. rev. Aufl. 1979. Reprint 2001.

———, "The Aesthetic (rasāsvadā) and the Religious (brahmāsvāda) in Abhinavagupta's Kashmir Śaivism": *Philosophy East and West* 26, no. 4 (1976), pp. 371-87.

———, "The Sources for Śakti in Abhinavagupta's Kāśmīr Śaivism: A Linguistic and Aesthetic Category": *Philosophy East and West* 24, no. 1 (1974), pp. 41-56.

Matilal, Bimal Krishna, *Perception: An Essay on Classical Indian Theories of Knowledge,* Oxford: Oxford University Press 1986; Reprint, Delhi: OUP, 2002.

Mishra, Kamalakar, *Kashmir Śaivism: The Central Philosophy of Tantrism*, Delhi: Sri Satguru Publications, 1999.

Mohanty, J. N., *Classical Indian Philosophy*, Oxford/New York: Oxford University Press, 2002.

Muller-Ortega, Paul Eduardo, *The Triadic Heart of Śiva: Kaula Tantricism of Abhinavagupta in the non-dual Shaivism of Kashmir* (SUNY Series in the Shaiva traditions of Kashmir) Albany: State University of New York Press, 1989; Delhi: Sri Satguru Publications, 1997.

———, "Shaktipat. The Initiatory Descent of Power," in: Douglas Renfrew Brooks et al., *Meditation Revolution: A History and Theology of the Siddha Yoga Lineage*, Delhi: Motilal Banarsidass, 2000, pp. 407-44.

Padoux, André, "A survey of Tantric Hinduism for the historian of religions" [Review of S. Gupta/ T. Goudriaan/ D.J. Hoens: Hindu Tantrism, Leiden 1979]: *History of Religions* 20, no. 4 (1981), pp. 345-60.

———, "Tantrism: An Overview/Hindu Tantrism," in: *The Encyclopedia of Religion*, ed. Mircea Eliade, vol. 14, New York/London: Macmillan, 1987, pp. 272-80.

———, "Yoga and Ritual," in: *Studies in Indology. Prof. Rasik Vihari Joshi Felicitation Volume*, ed. A. Kumar/J. L. Mée/M.M. Agrawal, New Delhi: Shree Publishing House, 1988/89, pp. 85-92.

———, "The body in Tantric Ritual: The Case of the Mudrās," in: Teun Goudriaan (ed.), *The Sanskrit Tradition and Tantrism. Panels of the 7th World Sanskrit Conference*, vol. 1, Leiden: Brill, 1990, pp. 66-75.

———, *Vāc. The Concept of the Word In Selected Hindu Tantras*, trans. Jacques Gontier, Albany: State University of New York Press, 1990; Delhi: Sri Satguru Publications 1992.

———, "Maṇḍalas in Abhinavagupta's Tantrāloka," in: Gudrun Bühnemann, *Maṇḍalas and Yantras in the Hindu Traditions* (Brill's Indological Library; 18) Leiden/Boston: Brill, 2003, pp. 225-38.

———, "On the Pārvaṇa Rites According to Abhinavagupta's Tantrāloka," in: Sadananda Das/Ernst Fürlinger (eds.), *Sāmarasya: Studies in Indian Arts, Philosophy, and Interreligious Dialogue in Honour of Bettina Bäumer*, New Delhi: D.K. Printworld, 2005, pp. 49-55.

Pandey, Kanti Chandra, *Abhinavagupta: A Historical and Philosophical Study* (1936) (The Chaukamba Sanskrit Studies; 1) Varanasi: Chaukamba Amarabharati Prakashan, 1963, 3. Auflage 2000.

Raghavan, V., *Abhinavagupta and His Works* (Chaukhambha Oriental Research Studies; 20) Varanasi/Delhi: Chaukhambha Orientalia, 1981.

Rastogi, Navjivan, *The Krama Tantricism of Kashmir: Historical and General Sources*, vol. 1, Delhi: Motilal Banarsidass, 1979. Reprint 1996.

———, "Abhinavagupta's Notion of Tantra in the Tantrāloka": *The Indian Theosophist* 82, nos. 10 and 11 (October–November 1985). Thakur Jaideva Singh Felicitation Number, pp. 110-20.

———, *Introduction to the Tantrāloka: A Study in Structure*, Delhi: Motilal Banarsidass, 1987.

Sanderson, Alexis, "Purity and power among the Brahmans of Kashmir," in: Michael Carrithers/Steven Collins/Steven Lukes (eds.), *The Category of the Person: Anthropology, Philosophy, History*, Cambridge: Cambridge University Press, 1985, pp. 190-216.

———, "Maṇḍala and Āgamic Identity in the Trika of Kashmir," in: André Padoux (ed.), *Mantras et Diagrammes Rituelles dans l'Hinduisme*, Paris: CNRS, 1986, pp. 169-207.

———, "Krama Śaivism," "Trika Śaivism," "Śaivism in Kashmir," in: *The Encyclopedia of Religion*, ed. Mircea Elidae. Vol. 13, New York/ London: Macmillan, 1987, pp. 14-17.

———, "Śaivism and the Tantric Traditions," in: Stewart Sutherland/Leslie Houlden et al. (eds.), *The World's Religions*, London: Routledge, 1988, pp. 660-704.

———, "Review of Muller-Ortega, Paul Eduardo: The Triadic Heart of Śiva": *Bulletin of the School of Oriental and African Studies* 53, part 1 (1990), pp. 354-57.

———, "The Visualization of the Deities of the Trika," in: André Padoux (ed.), *L'image divine, culte et meditation dans l'hindouisme*, Paris: CNRS, 1990, pp. 31-88.

———, "The Doctrine of Mālinīvijayottaratantra," in: Teun Goudriaan (ed.), *Ritual and Speculation in Early Tantrism. Studies in Honor of André Padoux*, Albany: State University of New York Press, 1992; Delhi: Sri Satguru Publications, 1993, pp. 281-312.

———, "Vajrayāna: Origin and Function," in: *Buddhism into the Year 2000. International Conference Proceedings*, Bangkok/Los Angeles: Dhammakaya Foundation, 1994, pp. 87-102.

———, "Meaning in Tantric Ritual," in: Ann-Marie Blondeau (ed.), *Le Rituel*, vol. 3, Paris: Ecole Pratique des Hautes Etudes, 5è section, 1996, pp. 15-95.

———, "History Through Textual Criticism in the Study of Śaivism, the Pañcarātra and the Buddhist Yoginītantras," in: François Grimal (ed.), *Les Sources et le Temps. Sources and Time* (Publications du Département d'Indologie; 91) Pondicherry: Institut français de Pondichéry, 2001, pp. 1-47.

———, "The Śaiva Religion among the Khmers: Part 1": *Bulletin de l'École Française d'Extrême-Orient*, Tome 90-91 (2003-2004), pp. 349-462.

———, "A Commentary on the Opening Verses of the *Tantrasāra* of Abhinavagupta," in: Sadananda Das/Ernst Fürlinger (eds.), *Sāmarasya: Studies in Indian Arts, Philosophy and Interreligious Dialogue in Honour of Bettina Bäumer*, New Delhi: D.K. Printworld, 2005, pp. 89-148.

Sharma, Prem Lata, "Śarīra," in: *Kalātattvakośa. vol. I: Pervasive Terms — Vyāpti*, ed. Bettina Bäumer, Delhi: Indira Gandhi National Centre for the Arts/Motilal Banarsidass, 1988, rev. edn. 2001, pp. 89-121.

Silburn, Lilian, *Kuṇḍalinī: The Energy of the Depths. A Comprehensive Study Based on the Scriptures of Non-dualistic Kaśmir Śaivism*, trans. Jacques Gontier (SUNY Series in the Shaiva Traditions of Kashmir), Albany: State University of New York Press, 1988.

———, *La Kuṇḍalinī ou L'énergie des profondeurs*, Paris: Les Deux Océans, 1983.

Singh, Jaideva, *Vedānta and Advaita Śaivāgama of Kashmir: A Comparative Study*, Calcutta: Ramakrishna Mission Institute of Culture, 1985, reprint 2000, 18 (= *Banka Bihari Hemangini Pal Lecture*, 21.12.1984).

———, *Mahamahopadhyaya Gopinath Kaviraj Memorial Lectures 1979*, University of Calcutta, Estates and Trust Office, 1981.

———, "The Non-Dualistic Śaiva Philosophy of Kashmir," in: *In Honour of Dr. Annie Besant. Lectures by Eminent Persons 1952-88*, Varanasi: The Theosophical Society, 1990, pp. 137-47.

Snellgrove, David, *Indo-Tibetan Buddhism: Indian Buddhists and Their Tibetan Successors*, vol. 1, Boston: Shambala, 1987.

Takashima, Jun, "Dīkṣa in the Tantrāloka": *The Memoirs of the Institute* of *Oriental Culture* (The University of Tokyo) 119 (1992), pp. 45-84.

Tola, Fernando/Dragonetti, Carmen, "Some Remarks on Bhartṛhari's Concept of Pratibhā": *Journal of Indian Philosophy* 18 (1990), pp. 95-112.

Torella, Raffaele, "A Fragment of Utpaladeva's Īśvarapratyabhijñāvivṛti": *East and West* 38 (1988), pp. 137-44.

———, "The Word in Abhinavagupta's Bṛhad-Vimarśinī," in: N.B. Patil/ Mrinal Kaul "Martand" (eds.), *The Variegated Plumage: Encounters with Indian Philosophy. A Commemoration Volume in Honour of Pandit Jankinath Kaul 'Kamal'*, Jammu and Kashmir: Sant Samagam Research Institute/Delhi: Motilal Banarsidass, 2003, pp. 80-104.

———, "On Vāmanadatta," in: S.P. Narang/C.P. Bhatta (eds.), *Pandit N.R. Bhatt Felicitation Volume*, Delhi: Motilal Banarsidass, 1994, pp. 481-98.

Vasudeva, Somadeva, *The Yoga of the Mālinīvijayottaratantra.* Chapters 1-4, 7, 11-17. Critical Edition, translation and notes (Collection

Indologie Pondichéry; 97) Pondichéry: Institut Français de Pondichéry/École française d'Extrême-Orient, 2005.

Vatsyayan, Kapila, "Indriya," in: *Kalātattvakośa, Vol. IV: Manifestation of Nature — Sṛṣṭi Vistāra*, ed. Advaitavadini Kaul/Sukumar Chattopadhyay, Delhi: Indira Gandhi National Centre for the Arts/Motilal Banarsidass, 1999, pp. 1-68.

Wayman, Alexis, "An Historical Review of Buddhist Tantras," in: *International Symposium on Indo-Tibetan Tantric Buddhism*. Central Institute of Higher Tibetan Studies, Rare Buddhist Texts Research Project, Sarnath, 27-29 March, 1995, papers.

White, David Gordon, *The Alchemical Body: Siddha Traditions in Medieval India*, Chicago/London: The University of Chicago Press, 1996.

———, (ed.), *Tantra in Practice* (Princeton Readings in Religions; 8), Delhi: Motilal Banarsidass, 2001.

———, "Transformations in the Art of Love: Kāmakalā Practices in Hindu Tāntric and Kaula Traditions": *History of Religions* 38, no. 2 (1998), pp. 172-98.

———, *Kiss of the Yoginī: "Tantric Sex" in its South Asian Contexts*, Chicago/London: The University of Chicago Press, 2003.

Woodroffe, John, *The World as Power: Power as Mind*, Madras: Ganesh & Co., 1922.

———, *Power as Reality (Tattva-śakti)* (1921) Madras: Ganesh & Co., Reprint 2001.

———, *The Serpent Power: Being the Ṣaṭ-cakra-nirūpaṇa and Pādukā-pañcaka. Two works on Laya-Yoga* (1918), Madras: Ganesh & Co. Reprint der 3. Aufl., 2001.

B. Tibetan Buddhism

Dalai Lama, *The Gelug/ Kagyü Tradition of Mahamudra*, Ithaca, New York: Snow Lion Publications, 1997.

Dzogchen. The Heart Essence of the Great Perfection. Dzogchen Teachings given in the West by His Holiness the Dalai Lama. Trans. Geshe Thupten Jinpa and Richard Barron, ed. Patrick Gaffney, Ithaca, New York: Snow Lion Publications, 2000.

The Life and Teaching of Naropa. Translated from the original Tibetan with a philosophical commentary based on the oral transmission by

Herbert V. Guenther, Oxford: Clarendon Press 1963. Reprint, Boston: Shambhala South Asian Editions, 1999.

Tsongkhapa's Six Yogas of Naropa by Tsongkhapa Lobzang Drakpa. Translated, edited and introduced by Glenn H. Mullin, Ithaca, New York: Snow Lion Publications, 1996.

C. Hermeneutical Reflection

Brück, Michael von, "Interreligious Encounter. A Reconception Process of Religion's Identity in the 21st Century: Buddhism and Christianity," in: Anthony Kalliath (ed.), *Pilgrims in Dialogue: A New Configuration of Religions for Millenium Community*, Bangalore 2000, pp. 69-92.

Dallmayr, Fred, "Heidegger, Bhakti, and Vedanta. A Tribute to J. L. Mehta," in: id., *Beyond Orientalism. Essays on Cross-Cultural Encounter*, Albany: State University of New York Press, 1996; Delhi: Rawat Publications Reprint, 2001, pp. 89-114.

Garfield, Jay L., "Western Idealism through Indian Eyes. A Cittamatra Reading of Berkeley, Kant, and Schopenhauer," in: id., *Empty Words: Buddhist Philosophy and Cross-Cultural Interpretation*, New York: Oxford University Press, 2002, pp. 152-69.

———, "Philosophy, Religion, and the Hermeneutic Imperative," in: Jeff Malpas/ Ulrich Arnswald, Ulrich/Jens Kertscher (eds.), *Gadamer's Century: Essays in Honor of Hans-Georg Gadamer* (Studies in Contemporary German Social Thought) Cambridge, Mass./ London: MIT Press, 2002, pp. 97-110.

Inden, Ronald, "Orientalist Constructions of India": *Modern Asian Studies* 29 (1986), pp. 401-46.

King, Richard, *Orientalism and Religion. Postcolonial Theory, India and the 'Mystic East'*, London/New York: Routledge, 1999.

Lopez, Donald S. Jr. (ed.), *Buddhist Hermeneutics*, Delhi: Motilal Banarsidass, 1993.

Metha, J. L., "Problems of understanding": *Philosophy East and West* 39, no. 1 (1989), pp. 3-12.

———, *India and the West: The Problem of Understanding — Selected Essays of J.L. Mehta*. With an Introduction by Wilfred Cantwell Smith (Studies in World Religion; 4) Chico, California 1985.

Michaels, Axel, "Between Similarity and Contrast: The Function of Comparison in Interreligious Debates," in: Sadananda Das/Ernst Fürlinger (eds.), *Sāmarasya: Studies in Indian Arts, Philosophy and Interreligious Dialogue*, New Delhi: D.K. Printworld, 2005, pp. 541-55.

Mignolo, Walter D./Freya Schiwy, "Double Translation. Transculturation and the Colonial Difference," in: Tullio Maranhao/Bernhard Streck (eds.), *Translation and Ethnography: The Anthropological Challenge of Intercultural Understanding*, Tucson: University of Arizona Press, 2003, pp. 3-29.

Nicholson, Hugh, "A Correlational Model of Comparative Theology": *The Journal of Religion* 85, no. 2 (April 2005), pp. 191-213.

Panikkar, Raimon, *The Intra-Religious Dialogue*, New York: Paulist Press, 1978, rev. ed. 1999.

———, *Myth, Faith, and Hermeneutics*, New York: Paulist Press, 1979.

———, "What is Comparative Philosophy Comparing?" in: Gerald James Larson/Deutsch, Eliot (eds.), *Interpreting Across Boundaries. New Essays in Comparative Philosophy*, Princeton: Princeton University Press, 1988, pp. 122-28.

Pohl, Karl-Heinz, "Translating the Untranslatable. Approaches to Chinese Culture," in: Rolf Elberfeld/Johann Kreuzer/John Minford/Günter Wohlfahrt (Hg.), *Translation und Interpretation* (Schriften der Akadémie du Midi; 5) München: Fink, 1999, pp. 179-88.

Prabhu, Joseph (ed.), *The Intercultural Challenge of Raimon Panikkar* (Faith Meets Faith), Maryknoll, New York: Orbis Books, 1996.

Said, Edward W., *Orientalism: Western Conceptions of the Orient*, New York: Routledge/Kegan Paul, 1978. Reprint 1995.

Steinkellner, Ernst, "Remarks on Tantristic Hermeneutics," in: Louis Ligeti (ed.), *Proceedings of the Csoma de Körös Memorial Symposium held at Màtrafüred, Hungary, 24-30 September 1976* (Bibliotheca Orientalis Hungarica; 23), Budapest: Akadémiai Kiadó, 1978, pp. 445-58.

Sweetman, Will, "Unity and plurality. Hinduism and the religions of India in early European scholarship": *Religion* 31, no. 3 (2001), pp. 209-24.

Taylor, Charles, "Understanding the Other: A Gadamerian View on Conceptual Schemes," in: Jeff Malpas/Ulrich Arnswald/Jens

Kertscher (eds.), *Gadamer's Century*, Cambridge, Mass. 2002, pp. 279-98.

Urban, Hugh B., "The Extreme Orient: The Construction of "Tantrism" as a Category in the Orientalist Imagination": *Religion* 29 (1999), pp. 123-46.

——— "The Cult of Ecstasy: Tantrism, the New Age, and the Spiritual Logic of Late Capitalism": *History of Religions* 39, no. 3 (2000), pp. 268-304.

Waldenfels, Bernhard, "Levinas and the Face of the Other," in: Simon Critchley/R. Bernasconi (eds.), *Cambridge Companion to Levinas*, Cambridge: Cambridge University Press, 2002, pp. 63-81.

General Index

Abhinavagupta, vii, 2, 5ff, 9ff, 13ff, 22f, 24, 28f, 40, 47, 57ff, 72, 93, 102, 115, 120ff, 126, 132, 133ff, 150, 152, 194, 203ff, 206ff, 212, 229f, passim

Abhishiktananda, Swami, 53

advaita, 96, 129, 150
- Trika as "supreme non-dualism" (*paramādvaya-vāda*), 12, cf. 145, 157, 250
- non-difference of the universe and the "highest Śiva", 105
- and social, political consequences, 255

Advaita Vedānta, 40, 45, 133, 153

akula / kula, 144f, 200

anākhya, 160, 200, 202, 255

ānanda, 49, 89, 92, 97f, 161, 163, 191f, 198, 205, 242, 250
- and rising of *cit-kuṇḍalinī*, 189
- as a lower state of the unfolding Kuṇḍalinī, 196
- *cidānanda*, 146, 223
- "condensed mass of *cit* and *ā*.", 56, 184, 236
- "juice of *ā*." (sexual fluids), 208
- realization of one's nature as pure *cit* and *ā*., 189
- *see* Kuṇḍalinī, "five signs" of the rise of K.
- seven stages of *ā*., 219, 222f
- the deity is characterized by *cit* and *ā*., 49

Ānanda-Bhairava, 132

Ānandaśakti, 144f, 159, 201

Anāśritaśiva, 176f

anuttara, 6, 25, 27, 40, 55, 78, 80, 97, 102, 106, 131f, 143, 148, 156ff, 192ff, 207, 219
- identified with "the heart of the *yoginī*" (*yoginī-hṛdaya*), 162
- of the essence of universal bliss, 207
- translation of *a*., 165

Anuttara-Trika-system, 136, 158

ārdra, 110

Arṇasiṁha, 31

ars moriendi, 245
asparśa, 133
ātman, 127, 172, 221
see cit
ātmavyāpti, 196, 228, 237, 239, 241, 243, 248
see turīya
Augustine, 126

Barthes, Roland, 242
Bäumer, Bettina, 164, 211
Bailly, Constantina Rhodes, 75, 77f, 95, 99, 116
Beauty, 130f, 143, 148
"All things have alone the purpose of beauty" (Kṣemarāja), 131
and the "highest power", 142
Bhagavad-Gītā, 29
Bhairava, 4, 132f, 213
"the state of B.", 193f, 198, 220, 249
"Bhairavī, the self of B.", 199
"eight aspects" (energies) of B., 203ff, 214, 225f, 229, 231ff, 244
"of the nature of light, resonance and touch" (Abhinavagupta), 203ff
names of the eight B., 233
bhairavī-mudrā, 171
bhakti, 74, 94, 96, 110f, 130
Bhaṭṭa Nārāyaṇa, 241f
bimba / pratibimba, ix, 126, 149, 151, 200
bindu, 29, 225, 238f
bodha / abodha, 151f
Body, 149
dimensions of the b., 86, 98, 126f
melting of the body in nothingness, 48, 171
subtle form, *see vapus*
Tantric theology of the b., 207f
as a sacred space, 209
as one the six aspects of Śiva (Abhinavagupta), 231
Breath, 100, 103, 168
dimensions of b., *see udāna, vyāna*
empirical b. denoted as "wind", "air" *(vāyu)*, 104
process of the transformation of b., 113, 170, 185f, 187, 198, 213f, 222
and "High Song", 216
and its connection with word, sexual union, *oṁ*, 218
end of the movement of b., 229
see prāṇa, madhya, Centre
Buddhism, 5, 8, 96, 134
Tantric traditions, 163
Buddhist terminology in the

Svacchandatantra, 229

cakra, 171, 190f, 194f, 230, 239
five main *cakra*s in Trika Śaivism, 205
as a code word for the male sexual organ, 209f
and subtle, non-physiological sound, 216
and the twelve stages of the rising, expanding Kuṇḍalinī, 223ff, 231f, 236
see tālu

camatkāra, 55, 94, 130, 173, 193, 195

Caraka, 20

caryākrama, 115, 155, 161, 173f, 218, 222, 240, 247
see Sexual ritual

Centre
between inhalation and exhalation, 188, 216f, 225
see madhya

Chakravarty, Pt. Hemendra Nath, 63, 102

cit, 23, 41, 48, 86, 132, 142, 149f, 166f, 193, 228
translation, x, 39ff, 51
"Goddess *cit*" (Kṣemarāja), 105
"the beautiful body" (*vapus*) consisting of pure *cit*, 123f
Bhairava of the nature of *c.*, 132
"the Self, one's own nature", 172
cit-kuṇḍalinī, 189
citśakti, 201

citi, 220, 244, 249
"the heart of the supreme Lord" (Utpaladeva), 147

"clear light", 46f

Code language, 136

coincidentia oppositorum, 250

Cusa, Nicholas of, xv, 26, 254

Daoism, 165

Diderot, Denis, 39

dīkṣā, xi, 138, 175, 215

Discrimination, 254f

Dissolution, Cosmic (*pralaya*), 99

Dyczkowski, Mark, 41, 45, 54, 173f

Eckhart, Meister, 26

Ellison, Ralph, 256

Experience, Religious, 27

Finn, Louise M., 65

"Five signs" of the rise of Kuṇḍalinī, 79, 92f, 191f, 196, 227

Five states, 197f

see suṣupti, turīya, turīyātīta, Kuṇḍalinī

Forman-Katz-debate on the character of religious experience, 27

Frauwallner, Erich, 54

Fullness (*pūrṇa*), 145, 170, 172, 192ff, 244

entering of the breath into the state of f., 187

"the touch of f.", 191ff

the characteristics of *anuttara*, 192

Gadamer, Hans-Georg, 56, 58

Gandhi, Mahatma, 255f

Garfield, Jay, 50

Geertz, Clifford, 165

ghūrṇi, 93f, 191, 196, 236

see Kuṇḍalinī, "five signs" of the rise of K.

as a sign of the "great pervasion" (*mahāvyāpti*), 93

and the process of the unfolding Kuṇḍalinī, 227, 232

Gnoli, Raniero, 137, 156

Gorakṣa, 195

Goudriaan, Teun, 137

Grace (*anugraha*), 79, 88, 91, 95

and spiritual process, 119

see śaktipāta

guru, 77f

to find an authentic *g.* (*sadguru*) as the fruit of grace, 88f

the tradition of the *g.*, 229

Hermeneutics, 39ff

principle of "hermeneutic equity", 59

homo interior ("inner man"), 126

hṛdaya, 41f, 44, 46, 97, 103, 105f, 145, 153, 160, 221

aesthetic-spiritual experience of the person "with heart" (*sahṛdaya*), 144

Citi (Śakti) as "the heart of the supreme Lord", 147, 221f

"heart of the *yoginī*" (*yoginīhṛdaya*), 161, 206, 212, 221f

"rising of the heart", 219

multidimensionality of the term, 221

and *uccāra*, 221

svātantryaśakti as the "supreme heart", 229

Ingall, Daniel H.H., 134

Interconnectedness of reality, 254

japa, 230

Jayadrathayāmalatantra, 3, 5, 7, 28,

31, 37, 239
Jayaratha, 13, 16f, 24f, 64f, 66, 69, 80, 84, 133ff, 146f, 159f, 169, 172f, 196, 202, 206, 220f, 231, passim
jīvanmukta, 2
jñāna, viii, 2, 6

kalādhvan, 174f, 179
Kālasaṁkarṣiṇī, 5, 153
Kālī, 3ff, 7, 46, 152f
Kallaṭa, 101
kāma, 65
kampa, 92, 191, 196
see Kuṇḍalinī, "five signs" of the rise of K.
kanda, 24, 214
Kaula tradition, 6, 18, 25, 134f, 165, 248
kaulikī, 144, 200
Kaviraj, M.M. Gopinath, 50
Krama, vii, ix, 1, 6, 11, 13, 28, 31ff, 152
krama-mudrā, 115
Kṣemarāja, xiii, 15f, 33, 36, 40, 53, 73, 79, 81, 85, 87, 91f, 94, 108f, 113, 115, 120, 123f, 127, 141, 170, 201, 231, 235, 238, 242, 253, passim
kula, 144f
kuṇḍagolaka, 167, 207
Kuṇḍalinī, xi, 28f, 30, 44, 69, 79, 92, 118, 128, 131, 155, 169, 171, 185f, 189f, 194f, 200, 213, 217, 224ff, 232, 236f
microcosmic and macrocosmic dimension, xv, 44
synonym *nāsikā*, 29ff
"the crooked", 30f, 69, 213
rise of K. in twelve stages (*see* "*uccāra* of *oṁ*"), 36, 118, 180f, 215ff, 222ff, 231f
supreme K. (*para-k.,*), 40, 181, 201
"five signs" of the rise of K., 79, 92f, 191f
awakened by the touch or by the sight of an authentic *guru* (*sadguru*), 89
different names and synonyms, 106
and love, 111
prāṇa-K., 112, 185, 190
"lower" and "ascending " K., 113, 171, 187, 239
process of the transformation of the power of breath, 112f, 214
and "spiritual ways" (*upāya*), 118f
denoted as *kaulikī*, 144f
dimensions of K. (*śakti*-K., *prāṇa*-K., *parā*-K.), 148, 187
śakti-K., 155
cit-kuṇḍalinī, 189f
and five states, 197f
"physiological" connection

with human sexuality, 214
and *udāna*, 214
and *oṁ*, 216
and the process of emanation, 238f
see prāṇaśakti, prāṇakuṇḍalika, suṣumnā

Lakshman Joo, Swami, ix, 47, 71, 83, 85, 110f, 113f, 115, 117ff, 123, 130f, 152, 154f, 168, 180, 183, 185f, 189f, 197f, 201
lotus, 91, 95
Love, Transcendental, 123
and Kuṇḍalinī, 111
See bhakti

"M", Three, 205
Madhusudhan Kaul, Pandit, 137
madhya, 30, 92, 95, 168f, 185, 205f, 212f, 217, 230
see suṣumnā, mukhya cakra
unfolding of the "centre", 185
mahāvyāpti, 93f, 95f, 97, 113, 169, 174, 191, 197f
as the final expansion of the rising Kuṇḍalinī, 113, 171, 223, 228, 237
as the attaining of one's own true nature, 191
see śivavyāpti
mahotsava (spiritual meaning), 127f
maṇḍala,
and sexual ritual, 208ff
mantra, xi, 124, 215
mantra SAUḤ, 166
as one of the six aspects of Śiva, 231
see oṁ
mātṛkā cakra, 199f, 201
Merton, Thomas, 247
Mirror, Simile of the, 149ff
Monism, 250
mudrā, viii, ix, 32
mukhya cakra (or *madhya cakra*), 205, 212
and female sexual organ (*yoni*), 210
see suṣumnā
Mukund Ram, Pandit, 137
Muller-Ortega, Paul Eduardo, 156, 164f
Multidimensionality of reality, 44, 58
mūrti, 76
Music
and spiritual experience, 143ff
Mysticism, Western, xii, 26
and "Spiritual Senses", 125

nāda, 182, 226, 232, 235, 238, 240
nāsikā, 29

Negative theology, 160, 243
New, the, 27
nidrā, 93, 191, 196
  see Kuṇḍalinī, "five signs" of the rise of K.
nirnāma, 26, 103 (fn. 61), 160
  see anākhya
nirvikalpa, 6, 26, 168ff, 185, 204, 222, 249

oṁ, 216
  see uccāra of *oṁ*
orgasm, 169, 211, 249
  beginning of o., 189ff
  see caryākrama, Sexual and spiritual experience

Padoux, André, 18, 63, 124, 138, 156f, 164, 219
Pandey, K.C., 134f
Panikkar, Raimon, 44, 252 (fn. 5)
paramārtha, 43, 236
Patañjali, 183f
Perception, 96f
Plotinus, 26
Political theology, 251
Possession, xi, 79
Prabha Devi, Sushri, 113, 128
prakāśa, 40, 43, 54f, 102, 167
  the Highest is of the nature of light, 40, 105ff, 120f, 178, 200
  "the light between being and not-being, 48, 185
  Śakti flashes and bursts forth from its groundless ground, that is p., 104
  the 17th energy (*kalā*) as "the light of all things", 148
  and phenomenal world, 148
  and *vimarśa*, 151
  "resting in the great light", 193
prāṇa, 23, 99, 101, 219
  and *saṁvit*, 101f
  and the "highest power", 141
  and *kalādhvan*, 175, 179
  five forms of *p.*, 186
  and "secret ritual", 204
prāṇaśakti, 34, 67, 69, 112f, 117, 180, 185, 187, 221
  names of p., 103
  identified as *ūrdhva kuṇḍalinī* (rising or higher *kuṇḍalinī*) by Silburn, 187
  see udāna, vyāna
prāṇa-kuṇḍalika, 148
prāṇa-kuṇḍalinī, 185, 190
pratibhā, 103, 169, 183, 249
Pratt, Mary L., 52
Pratyabhijñā school, 5f, 8, 11, 13, 71, 135

Quantum physics, 253

rasa, 110, 112, 114, 232
Ritual, viii, xi, 138, 164f
  see Sexual ritual
Rudra, 88, 225
  rudraśakti, xi, 87ff

Sāhib Kaula, 17
Śaiva-Siddhānta, viii, 1ff, 5, 215
sākṣāt (direct perception), 67, 94, 96f, 166
Śakti, 34, 40, 46, 49, 56, 68, 76f, 80, 193, 198, 221, 249
  the Highest Ś. (*paraśakti*) or Highest Kuṇḍalinī, 24, 40, 81f, 91, 97, 103ff, 144, 198
  different names, 44
  as *svātantrya*, 91
  denoted as *citi*, 107
  as the integration of the Divine and the World, 129, 133, 254
  immanent and transcendent dimensions, 146
  the world is the nature of Ś., 153f
  and sound, word, 216
  as the "entrance to Śiva", 244
  as the "heart" of reality, 249
  see citi, Kuṇḍalinī, *hṛdaya*, *spanda*, *urmi*, *vimarśa*, *svātantrya*, *nirnāma*, *vāc*,
śaktipāta, 78, 89, 91
  stages of intensity of *ś*., 89
  see Grace
samādhi, 10, 170f, 184, 197
  with closed and with open eyes, 94, 113, 170f
  see samāveśa
sāmarasya, 68, 200, 232
samāśleṣa, 122f
samāveśa, xi, 6, 23, 79, 87, 95, 99, 110, 115, 122, 219, 225, 243
  a key-word of Tāntric Śaivism, 80ff
  "inner absorption" (*antaḥ s.*), 111f
  "seeing of the supreme Lord", 117, 120
  sexual ritual in the state of *s*., 155
  the means for *s*., 219
saṁghaṭṭa, 146, 154f, 170, 194, 200, 214
saṁkoca / *vikāsa*, 112f, 170
Sāṁkhya, 20, 139f
saṁvit, 32, 39, 41, 48f, 93, 102f, 131, 145, 152, 161, 167, 184, 206f, 237
  supreme *s*. is the Goddess (*devī*), 40
  and *prāṇa*, 101
  "of the highest reality of light" (Abhinavagupta), 102

"of the form of voidness", 102, 178, 181
revered as the goddess Kālī, 152f
entering into s. by the sexual act in the state of absorption, 161
"direct perception of the supreme s.", 166
"pure, of the nature of the firmament" (Abhinavagupta), 178
"the inner organ of s." (Abhinavagupta), 205
the awakening of "the wheel of s.", 208

Sanderson, Alexis, vii, 4, 13, 83, 156, 165

Scholasticism, 135f

Subtle sensations, 183

Senses, xi, 18ff, 92, 96, 98, 100, 130ff, 142f, 202, 233, 249
and contact with the "Highest", 125
as means to realize the Self, 142
as the secondary centres of the energy (*anucakra*) in relation to the "main wheel", 205f
"*cit*-dimension" of the s., xiii, 125
calming of the outflow of the power of the s. at the beginning of meditation, 185
"deities of the s. (*aṇucakra-devya*)" (Abhinavagupta), 132, 206, cf. 208f, 210ff, 230
hierarchy of s. in the Western traditions, 174
onepointedness of the powers of the s., 170
refinement of the senses, 146
sexual character of sensual experiences (Swami Lakshman Joo), 154
"Spiritual Senses", 125f
Tantric "theology of the s.", 132, 204, 207
the inner power of the s. as the veiled form of Śakti (*dikcarīśakti*), 142

Sexual act, 18, 25f, 80
as the "supreme *cakra*", 209

Sexual and spiritual experience, 58, 62, 80, 164, 194, 221

Sexual fluids, 207ff
see kuṇḍagolaka

Sexual practices to attain the "Highest" (*anuttara*), 161

Sexual ritual (*kulayāga*) or "secret ritual", 6f, 11, 62, 68, 122, 162, 164, 167, 204ff, 247
denoted as *mahāmelāpa*, 154f
ritual with sexual fluids, 207ff
and Upaniṣads, 218

and the process of the rising of Kuṇḍalinī, 232
see caryākrama, kuṇḍagolaka
siddhi, 182, 234, 241
Silburn, Lilian, 63, 79f, 93, 107, 124, 138, 146, 156, 164, 170, 183, 187, 190, 195f, 198, 205, 212, 214, 219, 223, 228, 232f, 236, 240f
Singh, Jaideva, 48f, 150, 156f, 245
Śiva
to become one with Ś., 18
"the state of Ś." (*śivatālābha*), 96
the "highest reality, of the nature of light", 120
and Śakti, 200
six aspects of Ś., 231
śivavyāpti, 196, 228, 237, 243, 248
see mahāvyāpti
Śivastotrāvalī, 9, 13, 71ff
Somānanda, 7, 71f, 82
Sound, 143, 232, 234, 237f
as one of the six aspects of Śiva, 231
as one of the stages of nearness, 240ff
spanda, 7, 15, 41, 44, 103, 211, 243f
the state of the void, nondual self, 102
"s. in the heart" during the experience of music and other sensations, 144, 146
as a name of Śakti, 160
Spanda-school, 6
sparśa (touch),
different meanings of, 19ff
in Āyurveda, 21ff
sexual meaning of, 23ff
"inner touch" (*āntara sparśa*), 23
in early texts of non-dualistic Kashmir Śaivism, 28ff
touch of *kuṇḍalinī*, 28, 34
"touch of *saṁvit*", 32, cf. 131
"touch of power of the Self", 33f
touch of ants (*pipilikāsparśa*), xii, 34ff, 174ff, 179f, 184, 186, 188ff, 248
touch of Śakti (*śaktisparśa*), 71ff, 88f, 97f, 101, 114
in the *Śivastotrāvalī*, 74ff
the "touch of the feet" of the "Highest Lord", 76
the "touch with the plenitude" (*pūrṇatā-sparśa*), 79, 191ff, 194, 196
mutuality of touching, 84
and *samāveśa*, 87f
synonym *sambandha*, 88
experience of s. at the level of the *tattva* "Śakti", 90
"touch of *śakti*" and grace, 91
"touch of *śakti*" and yogic process, 92

synonym *samira*, "the touch of realization (*bhāvana*), 121
"being touched by the Supreme" within the "beautiful body" (*vapus*), 124
as the highest stage of spiritual experience, 122, 128ff, 239, 248
"the touch of *anuttara-saṁvit*", 131, 154ff, 173
as one of the *tanmātra*s, 139, 177f
as consonant, 199ff
the touch of the sexual fluids, 207ff
and "central wheel" (*mukhya cakra*), 212
"Śakti of the nature of touch" (Jayaratha), 232
"the touch of joy of the Self" (Kṣemarāja), 235f
in the process of manifestation according to *Svacchandatantra*, 237ff
and the stage "śakti" within the twelve stages of the rising Kuṇḍalinī, 244

sparśa-liṅga, 65
sparśavyāpti, 241
sphurati, 104, 112
sphurattā, 106f
citi (Śakti) characterised by *s.* (Utpaladeva), 147

śṛṅgāṭapīṭha, 213
Śrīvidyā, ix, 16ff, 64
Sufis, xii, 96
suṣumnā, xi, 30, 100, 113, 161, 170, 185, 188, 213, 214
moving of *kuṇḍalinī* in the *s.*, 187, 190, 198, 217, 222
symbolized with thread inside the lotus stem, 213

suṣupti, 99f, 197, 225
Svacchanda Tantra, 16, 36, 141, 179, 215, 223ff, 227f, 229, 234ff, 241
svātantrya, 41, 66, 91, 108, 151, 243, 253
svātantryaśakti, 27, 159, 229, 244, 253

Synaesthetic experience, 152

Tagore, Rabindranath, 1, 256f
tālu, 112, 225
tanmātra, 21, 35, 139f, 177f, 182, 185, 201, 245
Tantrāloka, 133ff
Tantrasadbhāva, 3, 32, 37, 239
Tāntric language, x, 57ff
use of metaphor, 57f

tattva, 90, 140f, 175f, 199f, 201f, 221, 223
37th *t.*, 177

Threefoldness or cosmo-theandric unity of Śiva, Śakti, Nara, 104, cf. 250f, 254

Tibetan Buddhism,
  understanding of consciousness, 46
Torella, Raffaele, 9, 41, 43, 54, 56, 81, 83
Transcendence
  and immanence of Śiva, 105, 112, cf. 133, 200
  and non-dualism, 157
Transgression
  and sexual ritual, 210f
  and extreme situations of fear, surprise or joy, 211, 249
Triadic ontology, 251
Trika Śaivism of Kashmir, 1ff
  Scriptural authority 2ff
  Historical development, 4ff
  Trika as "supreme non-dualism" (*paramādvaya-vāda*), 12, 250
  and Śrīvidyā, 17
  multi-dimensionality of its worldview, 44
  (mis-)interpreted within Christian categories, 52
  philosophical foundation by Utpaladeva, 71ff
    a "new, easy path" (Utpaladeva), 73
    Kuṇḍalinī as the core of T., 104
    Yoga of T., 117, 129
    Tantrāloka as the main work of T., 133ff
    denoted as "*Anuttara-Trika*-system" by Abhinavagupta, 136, 158
    three goddesses of T., 4, 159
    contextualization of T., 250ff
    denoted as *svātantrya-vāda*, 253
Tripurasundarī, 16f, 18
turīya ("fourth" state), 100f, 186, 195, 197, 214, 225
  corresponds with *udāna*, 186
turīyātīta ("beyond the fourth"), 115, 197
  corresponds with *vyāna*, 187
  difference between *turīya* and *t.*, 195f
  in the process of the unfolding Kuṇḍalinī, 226, 228

uccāra of *oṁ*, 118, 180f, 204, 215ff, 223ff
  see Kuṇḍalinī
udāna, 100, 106, 113, 185f, 187, 198, 214, 222
  defined as the "elevated energy of *prāṇaśakti*" (Lakshman Joo), 185
  see prāṇaśakti, turīya
udbhava, 92, 191, 196
  see Kuṇḍalinī, "five signs" of

the rise of K.
ullāsa, 193
unmanā-śakti, 222, 226, 228, 234ff, 237, 239
Upaniṣads, 149, 216ff
upāya, viii, 18, 80, 82, 113, 118ff, 124, 129, 152, 159, 253
Untouchability, 255f
Untranslatibility, 51
urmi, 103 (fn. 61), 160, 227
Utpaladeva, x, 8f, 13, 19, 23, 34, 41f, 55, 71ff, 107, 116, 122, 147, 186, 198, 242, passim

vāc, 216
vapus, xii, 104, 123ff, 126, 130
Venuti, Lawrence, 51
Vijñāna-Bhairava Tantra, 34f, 47f, 50, 119, 123, 129, 143, 168, 170f, 184, 190, 192f, 194, 199, 211, 220, 244
vimarśa, 40f, 51, 67, 105f, 202
  translation, x, 53ff
  yogis attain the nondual, void state of *saṁvit* through v., 102
  identified with *śakti*, 105
viṣa, 168ff
visarga, 145, 162
visio Dei, 114, 174
viśrānti, 103, 161, 173, 219
Void (*śūnya*, *kha*), 23, 48, 85f, 99, 102, 148, 178, 181, 208, 211, 237ff
  Five spheres of voidness, 31f
  in Tibetan Buddhism and Trika Śaivism, 46f
  supreme voidness, 48, 248
  and *khecarī* (who moves in the void), 142
  "*Śivatattva* is the void beyond void, Anāśrita", 176
  V. between exhalation and inhalation, 187
  voidness of *madhya*, 206
  and female sexual organ, 209
  the tenfold void (*kha*), 220f
  seven stages of v., 224ff, 227, 230
  as one of the six aspects of Śiva, 231
  as one name of the eight Bhairavas, 233
  meditation on the void, 234
vyāna, 187, 188, 219, 223
Vyāpinī, 179f, 227, 231, 235f, 238, 240
Vyāsa, 184

Weber, Max, 254
White, David Gordon, 61f
Wittgenstein, Ludwig, 26, 52
Woodroffe, John, 45, 48, 60, 157

Yoga,
    see Trika Śaivism of Kashmir
    criticism of Haṭha-Y., 129
Yogasūtras, 183f
yoginīhṛdaya
    see hṛdaya
yoni, 65, 68f, 161, 210